TEXTS, CONTEXTS AND CULTURES

VERITAS

TEXTS, CONTEXTS AND CULTURES: ESSAYS ON BIBLICAL TOPICS

SEAN FREYNE

VERITAS

Dedication

For family and friends, colleagues and students past and present, all of
whom have inspired my work.

Published 2002 by
Veritas Publications
7/8 Lower Abbey Street
Dublin 1
Email publications@veritas.ie
Website www.veritas.ie

ISBN 1 85390 626 3

Maps on pp 7 and 8 first published in *Galilee from Alexander the Great to Hadrian 323 BCE to
135 CE* by Sean Freyne (T&T Clark, Edinburgh, 1998).

Quotations from Josephus throughout from Josephus' *Jewish Antiquities*, *Jewish Wars* and
Life (Loeb Classical Library).

A catalogue record for this book is available from the British Library.

Cover design by Pierce Design
Book design by Colette Dower
Printed in the Republic of Ireland by Betaprint Ltd, Dublin

*Veritas books are printed on paper made from the wood pulp of managed forests. For every tree felled,
at least one tree is planted, thereby renewing natural resources.*

CONTENTS

Theological Themes

MAPS

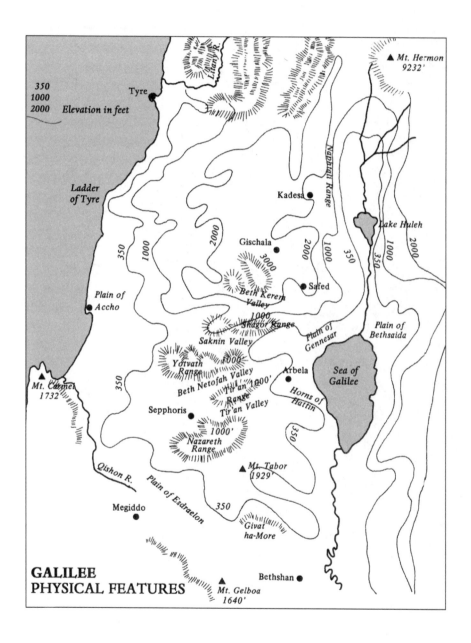

Mt. Hermon
9232'

350
1000
2000   Elevation in feet

Tyre

Litani R.

Ladder
of Tyre

Kadesa ●

Naphtali Range

Lake Huleh

350

1000

2000

Gischala ●

3000

2000

1000

350

1000

2000

Plain of
Accho ●

*Beth Kerem
Valley*

Safed ●

1000

Shagor Range

*Plain of
Gennesar*

Plain of
Bethsaida

Saknin Valley

▲ Mt. Carmel
1732'

350

*Yotvath
Range*

1000

Beth Netofah Valley

Arbela ●

Sea of
Galilee

*Tir'an
Range*

1000'

*Horns of
Hattin*

Sepphoris ●

Tir'an Valley

1000'
*Nazareth
Range*

350

Qishon R.

Plain of Esdraelon

▲ Mt. Tabor
1929'

Megiddo
●

350

*Givat
ha-More*

GALILEE
PHYSICAL FEATURES

Bethshan ●

▲ Mt. Gelboa
1640'

PALESTINE in HELLENISTIC and ROMAN TIMES

Chief routes
Territorial, Boundaries
▲ Hellenistic Cities
■ Roman (Herodian) Towns

ABILENE

Sidon

Damascus

PHOENICIA

Tyre

Paneas (Caesarea Phillippi)

Antiochia

TRACHONITIS

Seleucia

Ptolemais (Accho)

Bethsaida (Julias)

GALILEE

GAULANITIS

BATANAEA

Tiberias

Sepphoris

Hippos

Dion

Taricheia

Arbila

AURANITIS

N

Dora

Gaba

Itapyrion (Tabor)

Gadara

Scythopolis

DECAPOLIS

Straton's Tower (Caesarea)

Pella

Samaria (Sebaste)

Gerasa

Shechem

SAMARIA

PERAEA

Joppa

Philadelphia

Lydda

JUDEA

Jamnia

Azotus

Jerusalem

Marisa

Gaza

Adora

IDUMAEA

INTRODUCTION

The title I have chosen for this collection of essays – *Texts, Contexts and Cultures* – describes the stages of my own development as a student of the Bible, over the past thirty-five years. My early training at the Biblical Institute in Rome was heavily focused on the various books of the Bible, their structure, style and syntax, as a way of accessing their meaning. Later, as an Alexander von Humboldt Fellow at the Institute for Jewish and Hellenistic Studies in Tübingen, the concentration was on the varied contexts of both Judaism and early Christianity within the larger setting of Greco-Roman society. More recently, I have developed an interest in the archaeological data from the region, which, when interpreted in the light of social scientific models, provides a very different view to that provided by the literary evidence in isolation. Now one is often seeing the world 'from below', the everyday world of interactions between peoples of different cultural affiliations. The literary evidence usually reflects the elite view of the world and represents it in a highly selective manner. Attention to the artefactual, architectural and other data which archaeology can provide, often suggests a much more complex network of relationships, in which cultures mingle, borrow from each other and adapt, in order to cope with the realities of life that the inhabitants of a particular region experience in different historical circumstances. Inevitably, religion and religious texts play a crucial role in that process. After such a detour into context and culture, a return to the texts, which previously had been studied in isolation, can be a chastening, but challenging experience.

There is, however, another context, namely, one's actual situation, that is just as important in shaping the ways in which ancient texts are approached and interpreted. My first, formal training in biblical studies happened to coincide with the Second Vatican Council in Rome (1961-65). In order to symbolise its call that the Bible should become 'the soul of Theology' an open copy of the Gospels was placed in a prominent position in the assembly hall of St Peter's throughout the daily meetings of the Council. As a student in Rome, I had the privilege of attending a session of the Council, thanks to my Ordinary, Archbishop Joseph Walsh, who delighted in showing me around and introducing me to various Church dignitaries of the day. The image of the Book of the Gospels has remained more vividly in my mind than many of the other sights of that, for me, momentous occasion, even when it has seemed over the years as though the post-conciliar Church was honouring its symbolism more in the breach than in the observance. Formal study at the Biblical Institute was enlivened greatly by the discussions that went on all over Rome in those years – at dinner tables, in coffee shops, in formal lectures by experts at various colleges, and in the news media and daily press conferences. For a young Irish person, they were indeed heady days, when the insularity of my own theological formation in Maynooth was being subjected to a rapid revision through questioning, disputes and the scheming of the various parties to get their point of view included in the final documents of the Council. If I had previously believed, with St Peter, that the Holy Spirit decided conciliar decrees (Acts 15, 28), I soon came to realise that the same Spirit had several different and competing opinions!

Despite the disappointments and frustrations of the post-conciliar experiences, I could never subsequently forget the impact that that initiation had on my personal and academic life. In all my research and teaching, the theological significance of the Bible has continued to be at the heart of my concerns, even when experience has taught me that the Bible too is not wholly innocent, and that the Holy Spirit has indeed spoken in many and different voices and with very different emphases and perspectives. My original undergraduate degree was in Ancient Classics, consisting largely of language competency in Greek and Latin and the reading of a considerable number of ancient authors from Homer to Augustine in the original. This training was ideally suited for the Catholic approach to biblical studies as these were pursued at the Biblical Institute in those days. The influence was largely that of French Catholic scholarship, which was more concerned with texts and their structures than with history and its context. Later, when I had the opportunity to study in Germany, I became acutely aware that historical issues about Christian origins were central to the discussion, because of the previous two hundred years of critical scholarship of the Bible. This was exemplified in the towering influence of Rudolph Bultmann in the first half of the twentieth century, whose study of the Gospels seemed to remove the very foundations of Christian belief.

Noise of these battles had reached Rome also. Just as I began my studies two eminent professors at the Biblical Institute, Maximilian Zerwick, SJ and Stanislaus Lyonnet, SJ, were suspended by the Holy Office for their views on the Matthean account of the promise to Peter (Mt 16, 16-19) and Paul's ideas about the 'sin of Adam' (Rom 5, 11-12), respectively. The fact that both men – highly respected as excellent scholars by their peers, both Catholic and Protestant – were restored to their posts within a year showed that the whole thing was a storm in a tea-cup, largely due to the highly conservative Head of the Holy Office at the time, Cardinal Ottaviani. He also sought to impose his views on the Council in the original draft of the document dealing with Divine Revelation. An ahistorical and uncritical approach to the Bible had been proposed, ignoring both the views of Pope Pius XII in his rightly acclaimed encyclical on the interpretation of the Bible, *Divino Afflante Spiritu* (1943), as well as the previous two hundred years of critical scholarship, in favour of a view of the Bible as a collection of timeless proof-texts that was at the service of the post-Tridentine, scholastic synthesis.

Pope John XXIII withdrew the proposed document from the first session of the Council, and an official instruction on the *Formation of the Gospels* was published by the Biblical Commision in 1964, under the signature of the new pope, Paul VI. For Catholic scholars this changed the whole climate of fear and suspicion that surrounded the historical study of, in particular, the New Testament. The document endorsed the methods of Form and Redaction Criticism, which recognised the creative role of both the community and the evangelists in transmitting and editing the received traditions about Jesus, in order to address different situations of the early Church. Redaction Criticism was to provide me with a new and exciting approach to investigate a Gospel theme, and my doctoral dissertation, published subsequently by Sheed and Ward (London 1968), was entitled *The Twelve: Disciples and Apostles. A Study of the Theology of the First Three Gospels*. The ingenuity and creativity of the evangelists in their different accounts continue to fascinate and excite me. It was chastening to discover many years later that we did not have to await the findings of Redaction Criticism to uncover this insight. As I suggest in Chapter 4, the artists who designed the famous 'Window of the Evangelists' at Chartres Cathedral in France had already perceived the diversity of the early Christian perceptions of Jesus and given it a most evocative expression in stained-glass.

I began my teaching career at St Columban's missionary seminary in Dalgan Park, Navan, as the sole Professor of Scripture, a daunting, but in retrospect richly rewarding, experience. I had always a deep admiration for the Columban spirit of mission, and during my four years in Rome had come to know it more intimately by living at *Collegio San Colombano*, where our evening discussions with Columban bishops from various continents were lively encounters, dealing with reports of topics being debated in that day's meeting by the world's bishops. One got a clear sense of how differently these discussions were likely to reverberate in Burma, Korea or Japan on the one hand, where they would encounter Asian religious beliefs, and in the Philippines and Latin America on the other, where the task of Christian mission was to shed the trappings of a colonial Church in favour of the 'option for the poor'.

The students at Dalgan Park were preparing to minister in these far-flung, foreign fields also, and a growing awareness of the challenges that lay ahead for them made me conscious that the diversity of the Bible and its cultures, which I was discovering through my studies, would be more than matched by the diversity of my students' experiences. It was a humbling acknowledgment that life's truths are not contained within the covers of books, and I have continued to learn from these now seasoned veterans of 'life on the margins' whenever I encounter them or hear of their exploits. I was not surprised, but deeply edified, by the martyrdom of Father Rufus Hally in the Philippines, this past year. As we explored the Scriptures together in Dalgan many years ago, he had the pioneering vision and courage that was to inspire his work for ecumenical peace and justice in the Philippines, leading ultimately to his death. With these students I learned my first lessons in the demands that enculturation of the Gospel made, and this sharpened my focus on similar processes at work in both early Israel and early Christianity. Cultures and contexts were not just concepts, but conditions of life that had to be negotiated by real people. As several essays in this volume will show, this focus has continued to be one of the guiding principles of my approach to biblical studies, especially in dealing with the question of the historical Jesus.

My appointment in 1969 as lecturer, and later Professor of New Testament at St. Patrick's College, Maynooth, my old *alma mater*, was a very different experience. The *Furrow* magazine, under the editorship of the inspirational Canon J.G. McGarry, reflected the open spirit of Vatican II faithfully, and sought, as it still does today, to inform its readership of that alternative vision of Church. I contributed regularly to it under various headings, including a 'Questions and Answers' section in which the editor felt free to pose the questions when no suitable ones arrived in the mail! Likewise, the annual Maynooth Union Summer Schools were stimulating occasions when scholars from at home and abroad (Raymond Brown and the early Joseph Ratzinger are two names that come to mind from those days) addressed large and diverse audiences in what was now a Vatican II mode of theology, one that included biblical reflections on all the topics being addressed. These occasions and the pages of the *Irish Theological Quarterly*, provided a forum for expressing some new ideas, but already the feeling was that it was always under the (mostly) benign but critical eyes of the Irish Hierarchy, who were themselves unsure of how the Council's insights should be interpreted for the Irish Church.

The emphasis was very much on different models of Church, and hence the community experiences of the first Christians were highly significant, if controversial issues. I recall in particular the rather dismissive reaction several years later of the late Cardinal O' Fiaich to reports of the first meeting of *Pobal*, a movement for disseminating the Council's notion of the Church as 'the people of God,' which had been organised by his great friend and admirer, Sean MacReamonn, at which I and others spoke. Yet, ironically, there have been few prelates in Ireland who by disposition have been more in tune with the people's aspirations than Tomás O'Fiaich. Unfortunately, temperament and theology did not match, and conservative voices in the hierarchy insured that 'no change' would continue to be the motto of the official Catholic Church in Ireland towards the real spirit of Vatican II.

It was while I was still a Professor in Maynooth that I successfully applied to the Alexander von Humboldt Foundation for a post-doctoral fellowship, which was eventually to take me to Tübingen, there to study under the direction of Professor Martin Hengel, an expert on the impact of Hellenistic culture on Jewish life and religion. This was, and continues to be, a central issue in determining the cultural and religious influences at work in early Christianity, both in terms of Jesus' own ministry and that of Paul. For me this was a very different way of approaching the New Testament from the one to which I had been introduced at the Biblical Institute. I became acquainted with a considerable amount of literature, Jewish and Greek, that helped to place the New Testament writings in a larger literary context. I also came to appreciate that one could approach these texts as windows on the world of the movements that had produced them and to which they were addressed. The emphasis was on context and culture in order to understand the texts properly. Every avenue that could contribute to an understanding of that context had to be explored, and Professor Hengel's thoroughness in mastering the literary, inscriptional, numismatic and archaeological evidence from the eastern Mediterranean set a very high standard indeed. At his suggestion and under his guidance I began what was to turn out to be a life-long preoccupation with the social and religious world of Galilee. At the time that I produced my first study, *Galilee from Alexander the Great to Hadrian* (1980). I did not, I believe now, fully appreciate the real importance of the project on which I had embarked. It was only with the rise of interest in the historical Jesus in the 1990s that the full significance of Professor Hengel's suggestion became clear to me: in order to do full justice to Jesus in historical terms, it was important to situate his ministry in its proper cultural and social settings, a topic which is addressed in more than one of the articles in this collection.

After my formal laicisation from the priesthood, and subsequent marriage, I had to resign from my Maynooth post and seek employment elsewhere, thus opening up a whole different chapter in my wrestling with the Bible. Unlike many confreres in the priesthood who took the same route, I was fortunate in having already the foundations of a career, one that did not mean having to abandon my love of academic study of the Bible. Finding a suitable context to pursue that love was not so easy, however, since one of the conditions of laicisation imposed by the Roman authorities was that one could not again teach in a Catholic school. However, it became clear – at least in the heady 1960s – that 'Catholic' meant one thing in Rome and another in the United States, and it was there that I sought a teaching position, eventually spending four very happy years as Professor at Loyola University in New Orleans. I had had the experience of teaching Summer School at Notre Dame University, Indiana and in New Orleans in the years while I was still on the staff of Dalgan Park and Maynooth, and had made many helpful contacts in the process. I had also become familiar with the study of the Bible in the United States. Both the Catholic Biblical Association and the Society of Biblical Literature were extremely active and innovative in the ways in which they fostered the academic study of the Bible. Catholic scholarship in particular was now recognised as being on a par with its counterpart in other Christian Churches in terms of methodology, thoroughness and scholarly approach. Denominational differences began to disappear in the genuinely ecumenical spirit of the times and the works of Catholic scholars such as Raymond Brown, Roland Murphy, Joseph Fitzmyer and John L. McKenzie were just as significant as those of other scholars who had a much longer history of scholarly freedom on which to draw. In many respects the American scene was more diverse, less ideologically driven and certainly as well-resourced as that in Germany. The experimentation with different approaches to the Bible in the U.S. was explained to me by one colleague as the result of the move of Biblical Studies from Divinity Schools to Departments of Religious Studies or Near Eastern Studies, and the impact that such a move had in terms of the 'secularisation' of the discipline. Certainly, this academic climate was for me a very new context to which I had to adapt if I wanted to continue to teach biblical studies engagingly.

As a result of my teaching at various Institutes and Summer Schools in New Orleans I was familiar with the situation of renewal in the city and the prominent role that the local church was playing at every level. The role of the Bible in this enterprise was quite significant, partly due to the Catholic ethos of New Orleans with its French connections, but also because of the influence of Afro-American culture there. The Bible had played such a prominent role in the history of the black people of the South and their deep spirituality. Themes such as slavery, exodus, freedom and the like contributed to the emergence of a new self-confidence, especially in the biblically charged rhetoric of such evangelists of freedom as Martin Luther King. The biblical apostolate certainly found a fertile soil in this context, and New Orleans provided me with the opportunity to work with various groups in different parochial contexts, as well as in renewal conferences for clergy and religious orders. It was a time of great optimism in the American Church, and the energy and excitement of renewal was still very palpable.

However, it was the challenge of having to teach the Bible to young American students in the Arts and Humanities that proved to be the most challenging experience. It was this setting that caused me to experiment with new ways of reading the Bible. One approach was to treat the Bible as literature, by reading biblical narratives, such as the parables of Jesus, or the Book of Job in conjunction with contemporary writings like the short stories of Flannery O'Connor or JB by Archibald McLeish. Character, plot, situation and irony were just some of the aspects of the biblical stories that were highlighted in a fresh and personally challenging way by this type of intertextual reading. The social scientific approach to understanding the origins of early Christianity appealed greatly to those students also, since from their background they could more easily relate to political, economic and social questions than to the more theological and philosophical issues raised by the texts. Indeed, a course devised for that audience, dealing with 'Christian Origins,' eventually resulted in my book *The World of the New Testament* (Veritas, 1980), which, while not ignoring the theological dimensions of Jesus and his movement, sought to provide a broader context in which to understand its distinctive perspective both with regard to its Jewish and Greco-Roman competitors.

After a brief stint at the Department for the Study of Religions at the University of Queensland in Brisbane, I returned to Ireland in 1980 as Professor of Theology at Trinity College, Dublin, charged with responsibility for overseeing a new degree course within the Faculty of Arts (Humanities). My American experience was certainly of crucial significance for this task. It seemed to me that the methodology which I had evolved for teaching the Bible, namely understanding the biblical texts within the larger context of the cultural, social and political worlds in which they were produced, could be equally applied to the study of Christian theology. Without in any way prejudicing the strictly theological enterprise, the great theologians could also be studies in their historical and cultural contexts, or to borrow the approach of Hans Küng, within the different paradigms through which western thought had evolved – Hellenistic, Byzantine, Medieval, Renaissance, Enlightenment, Modern and Post-Modern. This approach immediately avoided the pitfalls of a purely confessional theology and allowed the different strands of the Christian tradition – Catholic, Orthodox and Protestant – a hearing, both in terms of their adequacy with respect to their particular situations and their re-interpretation of the biblical message.

The establishment of a modern School of Hebrew, Biblical and Theological Studies at Trinity came at a critical juncture in Irish life. The optimism of the 1970s that Vatican II had generated with regard to the renewal in the Irish Church had already begun to wane by the 1980s, and this disillusionment with institutional religion continued even more rapidly in the 1990s. This did not mean that there was a decline of interest in religious questions, however. As a centre-city university, Trinity College was uniquely placed to provide a forum for discussion and dialogue. Over the years series of evening lectures were offered and availed of by large and enthusiastic audiences, delivered both by members of 'the home team' and by distinguished theologians from abroad, notably, Hans Küng, Jürgen Moltmann, Martin Hengel, Gustavo Gutierrez, Rosemary Reuther, David Tracy, Elizabeth Schüssler-Fiorenza, Sandra Schneiders, John Collins, Hans Frei, Stephen Sykes and John Domnick Crossan, among others. The topics varied from year to year, sometimes concentrating on contemporary theological issues and sometimes on aspects of the biblical world. Several of the essays in this volume were delivered in that context and are here published for the first time. Re-reading and revising them for this publication has enabled me to evaluate what, if any, new directions my own thinking has taken as a result of these experiences, especially with regard to the Bible and its role in contemporary theological discussions within the context of modern Ireland. The themes in the final section of the collection emerged within the context of these series of lectures and reflect the issues which we considered timely and important for enthusiastic Irish audiences of the 1980s and 90s.

My thinking of the role of the Bible in modern theology has been greatly influenced also by membership from 1986 to 2002 of the Board of Direction of the international journal for theology, *Concilium*, with special responsibility for the New Testament. The journal had been established by the great Vatican II theologians – Yves Congar, Karl Rahner, Edward Schillebeeckx and Hans Küng – in order to communicate and explore the insights of the Council for as wide an audience as possible. When I joined the board, Küng and Schillebeeckx were still actively engaged, and a new generation of post-conciliar theologians was drawn from all continents. It was a privilege to be associated with such an enterprise and to work closely with those who had greatly influenced my own theological formation. The annual meetings of the editorial board, held each year in Pentecost week, were intense, but rewarding, workshops in which contemporary issues were debated and different approaches discussed, before selecting the themes to be treated in the following year. One got a sense of how global and local theologies maintained an uneasy tension as *Concilium* gradually shed its Eurocentric concerns and began to listen to the voices of Liberation, Feminist and Asian Theologies.

The task of proposing themes in the biblical area and subsequently co-editing numbers of the journal (six in all) was a real challenge. Several of the numbers for which I have been responsible dealt in one way or another with the reception of the Bible: *The Bible and its Readers* (1991); *Messianism through History* (1993); *The Bible as Cultural Heritage* (1995); *The Many Voices of the Bible* (2002). Editing of these numbers sharpened my awareness of the need to read the Bible contextually, that is, with an awareness of the different contexts in which the different texts were produced and the different circumstances of their reception in our world. In particular it was difficult to be part of those editorial discussions without being alerted to the ways in which feminist and liberationist theologies appropriated the Bible, as the one sought to deal with the gender bias of the texts, and the other found in them the message of hope that the biblical God was a God of justice for the poor. I have tried to make both perspectives central to my own reading of the Bible and its contexts, but they were lessons that had to be learned anew despite all the academic study of my earlier years. Other issues too came to the fore with a new urgency from those discussions – care for the earth and the dangers of globalisation; the significance of dialogue with other world religions and the deep anti-Jewish biases of so much of the Christian tradition.

Trinity College continues to offer a most stimulating environment in which to pursue one's explorations of the Bible and our indebtedness to its insights, despite the ambivalences just mentioned. Two current developments in particular excite me as being highly significant. The establishment, in 2000, of an endowed Chair of Jewish Studies within our School is the natural development of the College's long tradition of teaching Hebrew. Jewish Studies are highly popular in Arts programmes today, and for very good reason. Jewish civilisation, contrary to some ill-informed Christian opinions, continued to foster a vibrant intellectual environment, despite its marginalisation within European culture over the centuries. Since the eighteenth-century Enlightenment in particular, Jewish thinkers, writers and historians have been at the forefront of Western intellectual life. Yet their history and experiences have been largely ignored or grossly distorted in our accounts of Western history. When Johan Baptist Metz declared that 'Christian Theology should never again do its work with its back turned to Auschwitz,' he was, by implication at least, calling for ongoing dialogue with the whole Jewish tradition, as this had developed in the shadow of Christianity, and not just reminding Christian theologians of Europe's collective responsibility for the Holocaust.

For me, a greater familiarity with post-biblical Judaism has been highly instructive in terms of understanding how a shared biblical heritage developed in such different directions after 'the parting of the ways' occurred between parent and sibling in the late first and early second centuries c.e. When one examines the paths chosen and not chosen by both emerging Judaism and Christianity, the possibilities and emphases of the shared biblical tradition stand out in a much clearer relief. One can grasp how quite different religious systems can be supported by the same roots, to borrow and adapt Paul's horticultural metaphor for the relationships in his day (Rm 11, 17-22). One shared symbol, that of messianic hopes, is the subject of an essay in this collection, and the subject offers an intriguing new perspective for many Christians on how various strands of Judaism developed their own version of how that dream might be realised, despite Christians claims as to its final realisation in the career of Jesus of Nazareth.

A research grant from the National Programme for Research in Third Level Institutions (PRTLI) has made possible another exciting development that brings together two dimensions of my own training and background, namely Classical and Biblical Studies. This funding, which includes for the first time the areas of Arts and Humanities as well as Science, is one of the more felicitous achievements of the recent economic boom. It has allowed the Schools of Classics and Jewish, Biblical and Theological Studies at Trinity to develop a Joint Programme for Mediterranean and Near Eastern Studies, which will hopefully blossom into undergraduate degree courses as well as graduate research. For me, it provides a framework within which to continue to pursue long developed interests in seeing the world of the Classics (Greece and Rome) and the world of the Bible as a single, if complex, world. The fact that over the past two hundred and fifty years academic disciplines in both areas have developed in ways that either ignored each other or treated the other with suspicion, was more a product of European Enlightenment prejudices than a true reflection of the complex relationships which existed from the dawn of civilisation.

A deeper exploration of these complex relationships between East and West will, I believe, uncover commonalities, borrowings and adaptations that provide the proper context for understanding not just the biblical texts, but the classics of Greece and Rome as well. Our access to that world today is largely through collections of texts that have become Canonical for the three world religions of Judaism, Christianity and Islam, all of which have contributed to the preservation of the ancient texts of Greece and Rome as well. It is to be hoped that a better understanding of the origins of these religions might help towards better relations between them today. As Hans Küng so trenchantly reminds us: 'There will be no world peace without peace among the world's religions.' Thus, the introduction of Islamic studies in conjunction with Christian and Jewish studies at Trinity College is a development which, I believe, can contribute to very different relations even here in Ireland. When one considers their origins and early histories, the legacy of religious hatred that is part of the history of these religions is one that need not continue, despite the situation that currently exists, especially in the Middle East.

This brief account of my own development in terms of research and teaching of the Bible will, hopefully, not be seen as either self-serving or self-congratulatory. It is intended to provide a thread on which to hang this collection of essays, garnered from different times and places, which, I hope, may be of help to others in their search for a fuller understanding of the Bible and its message. As will be clear from this account of my academic interests, I am a firm believer in the part that context plays in the creation and decipherment of meaning. This applies as much to us who seek to find in this collection of ancient texts an understanding of life's complexities, as it does to those who first produced them, and felt so convinced by them as to commit them to writing. This was a highly significant enterprise in the ancient world, where writing had a very different function to what it has today. If we are no longer in a position to understand fully their motivation and commitment, we must at least show them the respect of paying attention to their world and its questions. The texts which they have produced and preserved have offered, and continue to offer, nourishment for the journey of life for countless millions of people, even when at different periods of history different strategies for reading and interpreting these texts have been employed. It is this 'surplus of meaning' that defines the Bible as a classic in its own right, and calls forth new ways of reading and new interpretative approaches. The essays in this collection reflect some of the explorations that constitute present efforts to tap into these riches from the past.

1

EAST MEETS WEST: EARLY JUDAISM AND EARLY CHRISTIANITY AS PLACES OF ENCOUNTER

This paper was delivered as one of a series dealing with the United Nations proposal for 'Civilisations in Dialogue'. It is indeed a sad fact, as true for the modern as for the ancient world, that when civilisations or cultural realms do encounter each other, it is generally not for dialogue, but for destruction. This perception of conflict is reflected even in the manner in which academic disciplines have traditionally been organised into Departments of Classics on the one hand, and Departments of Biblical Studies or Near Eastern Studies on the other, simply mirroring the perceived endemic conflict between East and West. However, as the title of Jonathan Z. Smith's book, *Map is not Territory*, (1978), pithily suggests, when it comes to cultural allegiances and cultural borrowings, our politically motivated divisions do not always hold good. It is all the more important, therefore, to identify those moments in human history where things appear to have been different, and where genuine reciprocity and receptivity were achieved.

The Hellenistic Age, that is, the period initiated by the extraordinary achievements of Alexander the Great in the decade from 333-323 b.c.e up to and including the period of the early Roman empire (first century c.e.), has often been seen as one such epochal moment in human history. While this period was certainly not without its wars of aggression and military conquest, it is more often judged as having laid the foundations of what we today describe loosely as 'western civilisation'. It gave rise not only to the spread of Greek culture and technical skills over a vast territory, but also to the development of Roman legal and political institutions and the stability that they achieved. Furthermore, this period saw the emergence of two world religions from the region, Judaism and its young offshoot, Christianity, as well as providing the underpinning for a third, Islam, each in their different ways living examples of the east/west exchanges that our series is addressing.

Alexander the Great has captured the imagination of scholars, schoolboys and other starry-eyed savants as the initiator of a 'Golden Age' in which dreams of a one-world culture were set in motion by the power and indefatigable nature of one man and his vision.[1] This picture is, to some extent at least, a myth of modern consciousness, one that expresses the enduring dreams of humankind and is increasingly in vogue in some versions of our modern, global culture. The very fact that Hellenism and Hellenisation have been appealed to for purposes of supporting various modern, and often conflicting ideologies is a clear indication of the significance of this legacy from the past for the modern period. It should also put us on our guard against any simplistic descriptions of the process of Hellenisation itself, either positive or negative, especially in an age when notions of a global culture are rampant.

At the outset it is good to be reminded that the Hellenistic Age was not the first cultural encounter between east and west. Indeed, the more one explores the issue, the more the question arises when is east, east and west, west? Where are we to draw the imaginary line between the two cultural realms? In our current state of knowledge it is not possible to trace all the details of the evolution of the system of writing from the hieroglyphics of the Egyptians and the cuneiform pattern of the Mesopotamians, through the cuneiform-syllabic script of Ugarith, to the development of the North West Semitic alphabets, of which the Phoenician one is the best known. Herodotus, the father of Greek history, writing in the fifth century, spoke of the Greek alphabet as *grammata phoinikeia* 'Phoenician letters' (*Hist.* 5, 58), thus acknowledging their indebtedness to the Phoenician alphabet. Nevertheless, in adopting, the Greeks also adapted the Phoenician system. This latter, like all Semitic systems of writing, had no signs for the vowel sounds, but only for consonants, twenty-two in all. To this the Greeks added separate notations for the vowels, and in addition added several consonants not found in the Phoenician system. This development meant that a more complete description of a word according to Greek pronunciation and phonetics was possible, since the absence of notations for vowel sounds made the reading and understanding of the Semitic languages more problematic.

It was scribes, not military conquerors, who were responsible for these developments, thereby leaving a legacy of great significance for future generations. As long as writing was essentially pictographic, as in cuneiform and hieroglyphics, writing (and reading) remained confined to a very small elite, since mastery of over six hundred signs made huge demands on memory. Abstract thought was impossible and communication difficult and cumbersome with so many signs to be learned. The reduction of this number to twenty-two characters in Phoenician and twenty-nine in Greek meant that far more people could master writing and reading, even though illiteracy was to remain high in all ancient cultures for a very long time. Thus the development of the shorter alphabet by the Phoenicians and the Greeks has rightly been hailed as a democratisation of learning, and this in turn lead to a greater democratisation of political life.

From the possibilities for expression that this development offered, the great Homeric epics, *The Iliad* and *The Odyssey* emerged, usually dated to the eight century b.c.e. Much has been written about these works as the product of an oral culture. While there may be some element of truth in these claims, anyone who is vaguely familiar with the imaginative power of the similes and descriptions, the subtlety of the characterisations and the narrative skill of the various episodes can scarcely doubt that there is a creative authorial genius, probably the same person, behind both works. In this regard, certain sections of the Hebrew Bible, such as the narratives about the Patriarchs, the accounts of the exploits of various Judges and the Court Succession Story make for highly interesting comparisons in terms of narrative techniques, characterisation and plot development. Yet both are heirs to a much older mythological and epic tradition from the Ancient Near East, which provides the context within which this literature should be judged, even when one must allow for the creative geniuses lying behind both the Homeric and the Biblical traditions also. Such epics as *Enuma Elish* and *Gilgamesh* have long been studied as backgrounds for the creation and flood stories in Genesis, but their possible relationship with Hesiod and Homer has not got the recognition it deserves.[2] Just as some Biblical scholars, had, for theological reasons, felt uneasy with regard to any 'external' comparisons with their texts, Classical scholars, too, considered that comparisons with Semitic antecedents might impugn the originality and creativity of the Greek authors. Once this modern bias of racial superiority is ignored, however, many detailed points of comparison between the two traditions emerge.

A well-known account by the Jewish historian, Josephus, claims that Alexander marched on Jerusalem on his way to Egypt, but was met outside the city by the Jewish high-priest and the populace wearing white robes. On seeing them Alexander reputedly recalled a dream he had had that he should invade Asia, and now declared himself to be under the protection of the God of the Jews, entering the city in triumph. He offered sacrifice under the direction of the priests at the temple and gave permission for the Jews to continue to practise their laws, promising the same treatment for the Jews of Babylon and Media (*Jewish Antiquities* 11, 329-40). Versions of this story circulated in other Jewish writings also, indicating that in all probability it was a piece of later Jewish propaganda, based on the fact that unlike the coastal cities of Tyre and Gaza that resisted Alexander's advance to Egypt, Jerusalem remained untouched. Even so, it is of considerable interest for our discussion, since it suggests that from a Jewish perspective there was nothing essentially incompatible between Judaism and Hellenism, and that indeed each could be mutually beneficial to the other.

Alexander's main objective was to pursue the Persian king, Darius, whom he had previously defeated at the Issus river in Asia Minor, to the very heart of his empire. He traveled first by the coast to Egypt, where he visited the shrine of the Egyptian god, Ammon, at Siwa, and was crowned as Pharoah and given the title 'Son of Ammon'. He then established the city of Alexandria in the Nile Delta, a city that was to become the outstanding statement of the wedding of Greek and Oriental cultures. From Egypt he travelled through modern day Jordan and Syria. Having routed Darius for a second time at the river Tigris, he marched on to the important Persian cities of Babylon, Susa, Persepolis and Ecbatana. Eventually, he caught up with the retreating Persian forces, and the deposed Darius surrendered to him. Alexander was now the undisputed king of the vast Persian territories. Imperceptibly, he had also become 'orientalised' in terms of dress and manner, much to the disgust of the closest of his Macedonian troops. His eventual marriage to Roxana, the daughter of Darius, was a symbolic statement of his desire to join east and west together in one empire.

Given the vast scale of Alexander's journeys that brought him to the borders of India, as well as his daring character, it is easy to see how the so-called Alexander legend developed. The various extant *Lives of Alexander* are, in part at least, based on contemporary records, some of which had been compiled by members of his travelling retinue. In time, however, there arose an idealised picture of the philosopher-king who had a vision of creating a one-world culture, an account that may well have begun already in his own life-time. The reality, however, was in all probability much less high-minded. One of his ancient biographers speaks of his *pothos* or desire constantly to go further, but this was undoubtedly a combination of military pragmatism and a sense of adventure in exploring the (to the Greeks) very strange world of the Orient. It is difficult to separate fact from legend in the various accounts, but it must be remembered that even if the idea of a one-world culture did not originate with Alexander, his younger contemporary, the Stoic philosopher, Zeno, could speak about the 'whole inhabited world' (*oikumene*) as being 'like a city state where law reigns supreme.' In other words, the idea of the ideal human society as described by Plato and Aristotle, the *polis* or city state with its constitution encompassing the *demos* or body of free-born citizens, now became the symbol for the total human family, all sharing in the same law of nature, thereby nullifying local laws and customs, which must have struck the Greeks as very strange as they heard reports from the troops on the eastern front.

It is against this larger backdrop that we can best assess the encounter between Greek and Jewish culture in the centuries after Alexander. Apart from one brief period in the mid-second century b.c.e., it must be said that the Jewish encounter, though distinctive when compared with their near neighbours – the Phoenicians, the Itureans and the Nabateans, for example – was not at all as hostile as modern scholarship has tended to portray the situation.[3] The brief interlude, in the reign of one of the successors of Alexander, Antiochus IV, Epiphanes, the king of Syria, was a short-lived attempt to outlaw distinctive Jewish practices altogether, identifying the cult of Yahweh with that of Zeus and Dionysus. It is debatable to what extent this episode was instigated by some Jewish aristocrats who had wanted to assimilate totally to Greek culture (1 Macc 1, 11), or whether it was due to Antiochus' ambitions to emulate Alexander's one-world culture. At any rate, the Jerusalem temple was profaned by the erection of an altar to Zeus in the temple area – 'the abomination of desolation' of which the Book of Daniel (9, 27) speaks – and the active persecution of those observing Jewish practises throughout the country. This gave rise to the Maccabean resistance movement and the rededication of the temple after three and a half years, a moment of Jewish history that has ever since been seen as the paradigm of Jewish refusal to succumb to political pressures, no matter

I0188664X

how severe. As Jewish historian Tessa Rajak notes: 'What has happened is that the militant Judaism depicted in the Books of Maccabees has, by extension, been attached to the entire history of the dynasty ... And the view of Palestine as deeply polarised between Greek and Jew is only a step away.'[4]

Archaeological evidence from this very period of emerging Jewish nationalism, points to commercial contacts even in Jerusalem with the Greek world – imported fine ware, Greek coins, jar handles for import of wine, mostly officially stamped from the island of Rhodes. This evidence suggests not just passing contacts, but more permanent associations that were part of an ongoing process over centuries. Thus a much more complex situation than that of simple polarity has to be envisaged, one that points both to changing attitudes on the Jewish side and the changing nature of Hellenism itself, as it encountered various near eastern cultures, including Judaism. The acid test will always be changes in the religious realm, especially in the ancient world. Just to take one pertinent example, one of the most sacred realities of Jewish belief was, and is, attachment to the ancestral land as God-given. The Maccabean wars of conquest are portrayed in 1 Macc as the re-acquisition of this national territory that had been unjustly taken from them. Yet, despite this deep attachment to the land one finds that in the very same period the Jewish population of Egypt, of all places, given the Exodus story, increased dramatically. This emigration did not mean any diminution of loyalty to the homeland and its religious attachment, since we hear from Josephus of disputes as to which of the native sanctuaries – that of Jerusalem and the Samaritan one on Gerazim – should receive the offerings from the Egyptian Jewish community.

There had been a long history of Jews in Egypt since the time of the Babylonian captivity, and it was natural that other Jews might gravitate there with the increased opportunities and contacts of the Hellenistic Age in terms of travel and commerce. In the century immediately following Alexander, for example, the Bible was translated into Greek in Egypt (the LXX) c. 250 b.c.e., presumably to deal with the needs of pious Jews there who could not deal with the Hebrew original, despite the status of that language as the 'holy tongue'. Increasingly, a body of literature from Alexandrian Jewry in particular begins to emerge, as well as the ongoing process of translation of books written in the homeland in Hebrew such as 2 Macc and the *Wisdom of Ben Sirach*. However, it is with the first-century Greco-Jewish philosopher, Philo, that one finds the most complete synthesis of the two worlds of Greece and the east. Much has been written about his Jewish identity and his philosophy, as though it were necessary to choose between them. Philo himself had no difficulty in achieving a thoroughly Platonic reading of his own tradition in a number of commentaries, based on Moses' insights as the true philosopher-ruler. Thus, in the *Life of Moses* he puts flesh on the standard Jewish apologetic claim that Moses was the first philosopher. In Philo's hands, as distinct from the Pentateuchal account, Moses was the wise ruler whose insights were based on his intimate knowledge of the divine, 'sharing in the very darkness where God is.' One can detect here a conscious contrast with some of the current *Lives of Alexander* in which he was treated in similar terms as the son of Ammon-Zeus. A narrative pattern of a Life or 'Bios' was thus at hand for the early Christians to adapt in writing their Gospel Lives of Jesus of Nazareth.

The intellectual achievements of Philo and other Jewish apologists had the effect of winning many adherents to Judaism from the various pagan mystery religions then flooding the empire. We hear of an increasing numbers of 'god-fearers' attached to Jewish diaspora synagogues, attracted by Jewish ethical as well as religious claims, it would seem.[5] In the homeland also the encounter of Jewish faith with the Hellenistic *zeitgeist* took on many different expressions, so that the image of a monolithic and monochromic Jewish identity, implacably opposed to the 'evil' of Hellenism is a modern stereotype. It is based on the much later image of the European Jewish ghetto, which refused to assimilate, that is, abandon the Jewish faith and practises for the Enlightenment culture of reason, which was supposed to bring about the brotherhood of all. Many nineteenth-century German-Jews were rightly suspicious of such claims, since behind them lay the doctrine of the super-race, which eventually gave rise to the policy of Jewish genocide in Nazi Germany.

The reality of the Hellenistic age was different and more complex. Greek had gradually replaced Aramaic as the *lingua franca* of trade, commerce and administration with the demise of the Persian Empire. This meant that Jews who participated in the administrative life of the various kingdoms that emerged after Alexander's untimely death, and were, therefore, city-dwellers, were likely to be more Hellenised. Yet this did not necessarily mean abandoning their Jewish belief system. We know from Egypt and elsewhere that the native elites were able to maintain their positions side by side with the Greek administrative officials, and indeed after a few generations the two classes were likely to be merged, as we see with the Jewish priestly aristocracy, for example, in the first century c.e. It is no surprise that we hear of a Greek school in

Jerusalem and a Greek-style education that cultivated the body as well as the mind. It is a moot point whether this school should be regarded as an outright attack on Jewish life and belief, as portrayed in the Books of Maccabees, or whether it should not rather be seen as a development similar to that of the Jews in Alexandria taking place also in the 'mother city' of all Jews.[6]

Two writers from the third and second centuries b.c.e. can illustrate the battle for Jewish identity that was being waged in the encounter with Hellenism. The author of the *Book of Qoheleth* (Ecclesiastes) would appear to have been attracted to the Greek, Epicurean philosophy eat drink and make merry – since life is an unfathomable mystery that makes the future uncertain. There is nothing in this book to enliven the picture with a hope for the future according to Jewish messianic expectations. The author of this work and the circles of Jewish aristocrats that he represents has thoroughly assimilated to the extent that it is difficult to see how his book came to be included in the Hebrew canon, were it not for the fiction that it is the work of Solomon, and a few more orthodox aphorisms became attached to it in time. *The Wisdom of Ben Sirach* (Ecclesiasticus) represents another voice from the literature. He is the self-confessed member of the Jerusalem leisured classes, who has therefore, time to study. He contrasts his own life as a professional scribe with that of others whose work makes up the fabric of the city life – the potter, the smith, the glass-blower, the seal maker, the farmer (Sir 38, 24 – 39, 11). The picture is that of the typical Greek city and the social stratification within it. Sirach sees himself as belonging in the company of kings and rulers, and hence a member of the elite rather than the retainer class, and yet, theologically, he is far removed from Qoheleth's scepticism. While there are echoes of Greek philosophical and moral teaching in the work, he sees the law as a special gift to Israel that marks it off from other nations (ch 24). He delights in the temple and its worship (ch 50) and he prays for the restoration of Israel to its former glory (ch 36). While both of these writers pre-date the attack of Antiochus Epiphanes on Jewish religion, they do represent two contrasting strands that can be documented into the later period also, when a more normal situation was restored again. Thus the encounter of Hellenism and Judaism should be seen more in terms of shades of assimilation and resistance rather than a downright polarity.

It is this plurality that was to continue into the early Roman period (first century b.c.e. - first century c.e.), manifesting itself in the phenomenon of Jewish sectarianism, as the different groups known as

Pharisees, Sadducees, Essenes and Zealots, have been labelled in modern scholarship, thus perpetuating the stereotype of an isolated and isolationist Jewish identity. Undoubtedly, there were real tensions between various elements in regard to the administration of the temple and the interpretation of Torah, and these can be attributed, in part at least to different responses to the reality of Jewish life within a thoroughly Hellenised environment for all Jews. In identifying these differences it is useful to examine them in the context of various trends in the Hellenistic world more generally, as Jewish historian, Josephus, suggests.

At one end of the continuum are the Essenes, who had opted for life away from the cities, including Jerusalem, with their thoroughly Greek ethos. They are best known to us from the Dead Sea Scrolls found in the region of Qumran in the Judean desert. Yet even there it was impossible to escape all aspects of the new cultural matrix within which Judaism of all hues was refashioning its identity. In fact, all the distinctive aspects of the group's philosophy and lifestyle – dualistic determinism, the solar calendar, communal property, belief in a spirit world, celibacy, utopian ideas and communal structures – are not to be found in earlier Jewish tradition, but can be matched from various parts of the Greco-Roman and eastern worlds. Little wonder that of all the Jewish groups this one proved to be of great interest to Roman writers such as Pliny.

The zealots, or extreme nationalists, of the Roman period may also be judged as outright rejectionists, but from another perspective. Their roots were not in the Jerusalem clergy but in the country peasant class and the urban poor. As mentioned already, in addition to generating the idea of a one-world culture, Alexander's conquests also gave rise to a lively interest in ethnography, or the study of other peoples, their characteristics and their territories, since peoplehood and territory went together. Jewish ethnography was based on the account of the emerging peoples from the sons of Noah (Shem, Japheth and Ham) to each of whom and their descendants were attributed different territories within the *oikumene* or inhabited world. It is within this understanding of the 'ideal' world of new beginnings after the flood, that Jewish nationalism and territorial claims are to be understood. The Jews were not the only people to have resisted Rome's imperialistic ambitions, but it was the zealots' combination of religious fervour and ethnic identity that made them such doughty opponents. It is necessary to take account of both aspects of their make-up if one is to avoid the stereotypes of the recalcitrant and xenophobic Jew in discussing what Josephus describes as the Fourth Philosophy.[7]

The Pharisees, despite their name, which suggests separatism, were in many respects the most attuned of all the Jewish groups to the spirit of the Hellenistic world.[8] For them, as for Zeno's Stoics, 'law reigned supreme,' except that in their case it was the Jewish Torah, not the law of nature that was paramount. Thus the Pharisees developed a philosophy of law as the maintenance of an order, which had been established at the beginning. The human task was to bring one's life into conformity with that pattern, and by formulating as comprehensive a system as possible the Pharisees guaranteed their adherents divine blessings wherever they went. For their Greek neighbours, familiar with the idea of different charters sanctioned by the patron gods of different cities, there was nothing strange or hypocritical about the Pharisees or their attitudes, provided they did not seek to propagate them among non-Jews. They were merely different, as the Athenians, the Spartans or the Thebans had different customs, while all were also Greeks. Only if the Jewish law was declared to be the universal law, thereby sanctioning rejection of Rome's universal rule, would Pharisaic Judaism run into difficulties, since the right to follow 'one's ancestral customs' was enshrined in Hellenistic and Roman legal practice. Thus, the Pharisees were the only ones of the various Jewish groups to survive the calamities of two defeats at the hands of the Romans in the revolts of 66-70 and 132-5 c.e., passing over eventually into what we today call Rabbinic Judaism.

On the other hand the Sadducees were the priestly aristocratic class, whom Josephus likens to the Epicureans. He also characterises them as boorish and unpopular with the common people. Qoheleth, it has already been suggested, represented an early Jewish example of the aristocratic lifestyle of the Hellenistic age. While the later Sadducees may not have been as assimilated as this third-century b.c.e. character, they nevertheless represented that class of Jewish aristocrats who had emerged around the native ruling Hasmonean house following the success of the Maccabean revolt and the collapse of Greek rule in Palestine. While less is known about them than the other groups, in all probability they were mainly represented by the Jerusalem priestly elite, espousing a theologically conservative position on such issues as the after-life, while maintaining a luxurious lifestyle in comparison with the peasants whose offerings supported them.

Christianity and the Reception of Hellenism
Writing towards the end of the second century c.e. the Christian apologist Tertullian defiantly asks: 'What indeed has Athens to do with Jerusalem?'

implying that Christian faith had no need to engage with Greek philosophy, since its certainty came from elsewhere. 'Away with all attempts to produce a Stoic, Platonic and dialectic Christianity,' he declares, with a splendid sense of the uniqueness of Christian claims *(De Praescriptione Haereticorum* 7). In the light of the discussion thus far, a Jewish apologist such as Philo or Josephus would have given a very different answer to the same question. An answer from a Christian perspective would call for a paper in its own right. Suffice to say that despite his confident assertions, other Christian apologists saw the need for, but also the opportunities of, dialogue with Greek culture.[9] Indeed, so well did the early Christians adapt to the Greek culture as preserved by the Romans, that some one hundred and fifty years after Tertullian it behoved the empire to embrace it as its official religion. Overnight it had been transformed from outlawed to legitimate, providing the new emperor, Constantine, with the best available option for reuniting a divided empire. Thus, according to the standard account, the triumph of Christianity was the result of its ability to shed its Jewish past and embrace wholeheartedly the universalist, Hellenistic spirit of the age. Such a portrayal requires a critical evaluation, since it operates with stereotypes of both Judaism and Hellenism that ignore the complexity of the relationship.

Any account of the origins of Christianity that seeks to drive a wedge between Jesus and Paul, seeing the latter as the real or 'second' founder of Christianity, because of his alleged openness to the Hellenistic spirit, is deeply flawed. Equally, depictions of Jesus as a Galilean Hellenist breaking with the narrow confines of Jerusalem, are also grossly distorted. Yet both versions – the Hellenist Paul as the true founder of Christianity and the Galilean Jesus abandoning his own tradition – are still frequently advanced for the success of the early Christian movement, in order to free that movement from its mooring within Judaism. The evidence will not support either contention: first-century Galilee was Jewish, and Jesus did not, nor could not bypass Jerusalem as the spiritual centre of that religion. Likewise, Paul was, and remained, deeply rooted in his own Jewish identity, despite his acceptance of the claims of Jesus to messianic status.[10] It is all too easily forgotten that the Hellenists mentioned in Acts of the Apostles (ch 6) as the first Christian missionaries, and Paul likewise, were *Jewish* Hellenists from various parts of the Diaspora, but for whom Jerusalem, not Athens, was their cultural and spiritual home. Jewish prophets such as Isaiah and Ezechiel had articulated a Jewish version of the one-world culture long before Alexander in terms of the coming messianic age. The second century b.c.e. *Book of Jubilees*, drawing on Jewish universalist ideas and in order to counteract the claims of extreme Hellenists, had developed a picture of the seventy nations of the earth being descended from the three surviving sons of Noah in the aftermath of the flood. Thus, Shem had inherited Asia, Japheth Asia Minor and Europe and Ham Africa. Jerusalem stood at the centre of this map, a veritable garden of Eden around which the nations of the earth were located. The universalism of Isaiah, which envisaged the nations coming on pilgrimage to receive wisdom from a restored Zion, received a new and nuanced treatment in line with Hellenistic ethnographic ideas. It was these actualisations of their own ancient texts in the light of the new context of the Hellenistic world, rather than one-world ideas attributed to Alexander or his successors, that in my opinion prompted the universalism of the early Christian missionaries.[11]

As those Christian missionaries moved out from Jerusalem and beyond the confines of Palestine they were indeed able to communicate with a range of diverse audiences, east and west, because of the wide diffusion of Greek as the *lingua franca*, as already mentioned. The Roman provincial structures provided some protection, and the increased commercial activity of the eastern Mediterranean made for the relative ease of travel. These aspects of the Hellenistic world and its benefits were not lost on Luke as he depicts the movement of Christianity from Jerusalem to Rome in Acts of the Apostles. Yet despite all the benefits it had to offer, Hellenism as adopted and adapted by the Romans had not succeeded in obliterating ethnic differences among the peoples of the east. In a brilliant study entitled *The Roman Near East 31 BC- AD 337* (1993) the Oxford Ancient Historian, Fergus Millar, has shown that despite the veneer of Greek culture everywhere, the older cultures of the east have all left various traces of their past in terms of bilingual inscriptions, Semitic customs and religious practises that continued on into the Byzantine period in some instances. Religious practises have a capacity to endure and survive changes in other areas of life. Very often what has taken place is an *interpretatio Graeca* by which an old Semitic deity or custom is retained, but in a Greek dress. However, many examples show that the Greek equivalents were not randomly taken over, but were chosen with special reference to the god or goddess in question and his or her perceived characteristics, as, for example, when the god of Tyre, Melqart is named Heracles, since both were know as travellers and founders of cities, and Eshmun, the god of Sidon, was identified as Asclepios, since both were venerated as healing deities.[12]

This was the world that Christian missionaries encountered as they moved in the direction of the four points of the compass – north to Syria, east to Arabia and Mesopotamia, south to Egypt and North Africa and west to Asia Minor and Europe. Luke's highly graphic account of Paul's movements to the west can give the impression that that was the totality of Christian missionary activity. Even Paul himself was active for some time in Arabia, Damascus and Syria before joining forces with Barnabas in the journey to the west. But we know virtually nothing about that earlier activity, not to mention that of the many other wandering evangelists and preachers that felt impelled to share their good news. Paul declares his own missionary strategy as being Greek to the Greeks and Jew to the Jews, viewing the world from a Jewish perspective as being constituted by Jews and others (Greeks), just as the Greeks divided the world into those who spoke Greek (Hellenes) and Barbarians. Paul presumably meant that he tried to show an awareness of the cultural diversity of his different audiences, a policy that is graphically illustrated by Luke in his account of Paul's *Areopagus* speech in Athens where he is made to quote one of the Greek poets in making his point (Acts 17, 22-31). In this he and others were merely following the pattern set by Jewish Diaspora missionaries and apologists who had 'translated' Moses into categories that were accessible to those of Greek background. We know nothing about the earliest decades of either Syriac or Egyptian Christianity, even though both Churches have left a sizeable body of Christian literature from later centuries, and the Gospels were translated into both languages. It is only from this later perspective that we can begin to fill in the gaps left by Luke for the earlier period, and acknowledge the great diversity of early Christian self-expression in different cultural contexts from the beginning, both Greek and oriental. It would go well beyond the bounds of this talk to pursue the issue of Christianity and Hellenism further. Suffice to say that many of the great Christian Patristic theologians of later centuries as well as the earlier apologists were deeply imbued with Greek philosophical ideas and used these to articulate an understanding of the new religion in their efforts to portray it to interested pagan intellectuals as a philosophy and not a superstition.[13]

At the same time Rabbinic Judaism was developing its strategy of adaptation and survival within imperial structures that had become increasingly Christianised, from the early fourth century onwards in the wake of Constantine's conversion. When the intricacies of Rabbinic *midrash* and commentary are studied today within the larger Greco-

Roman context, we can see how the dialogue between Judaism and Hellenism continued into the Byzantine period. It can be argued that the more Jews had to come to terms with the loss of political autonomy and temple, the more Hellenistic influences in the religious sphere seem to have been acceptable. Nowhere is this more graphically demonstrated than in the acceptance of figurative art in synagogue decoration, something that was earlier strictly prohibited. Pagan motifs such as Helios, the Sun god with his four-horse chariot, as well as the signs of the zodiac on the floors of many synagogues represent a Judaisation of pagan symbols that matches Christian appropriation and re-interpretation of the same symbols.[14] Could this phenomenon be interpreted as a case of religious competition between the parent and the sibling for possession of the soul of the pagan world whose externals were crumbling all around? It would be two centuries later before a third light from the east was to emerge, namely Islam, and in that case also the classical tradition of Greece, especially in science and philosophy, was taken over and was to play an important role in the spread of the new religion in the world previously inhabited by Jews and Christians. The rapid spread of Islam in the east was as sudden as it was surprising, and the contribution of Hellenism to that success is a story that needs to be explored in detail. But that is for another day.

Conclusion

The Roman poet Horace, writing about Rome's fascination with classical Greek culture wrote: 'captured Greek conquered the arms of its capturers.' By this he meant that Greek culture in terms of philosophy, literature, drama and sculpture – to name the most obvious examples – had a capacity to attract the admiration of people long after the political and military power of Greece had waned. It has been one of the arguments of this paper that Greek culture itself owed much to older, eastern cultures, which it appropriated and developed in its own distinctive idiom and style. It has also been suggested that it is not through military conquests or control that true, creative cultural interchange occurs. The everyday contacts of peoples leave very little trace in the official records, then as now. We must be grateful therefore to modern socio- and ethno-archaeologists for giving us a 'text' from below that opens some tiny windows on those processes of genuine cultural interchange and their more lasting effects, which do not always respect the boundaries drawn on a map for political purposes. In these everyday contexts the true nature of the interchange is neither assimilation nor purely formal borrowings from one culture by another, but rather the tension between acceptance and resistance. This process may be seen as the testing by each culture of the other, that eventually gives rise to new configurations where respect for both is maintained, because the best of each can be represented.

Both Judaism and Christianity (but also Islam) are the bearers of these cultures into the modern world as lived realities still. The received wisdom has been that Judaism belonged to an oriental world that, in the eyes of western explorers from the time of Napoleon onwards, was deemed decadent and backward, however exotic it may have appeared in other respects. This also played into the anti-Semitic attitudes of the times generally. The account of Christianity that emerged as a result of these biases was that it represented the new, enlightened world of the Greeks with their universalist outlook. My contention has been that this picture is wrong in both respects. Judaism, cautiously perhaps, and with certain clear identity markers, accepted Hellenism as a positive influence, and Christianity moved east as well as west and was able to adapt itself to both cultural traditions. We who are heirs to western (or Latin) Christianity have largely ignored our eastern inheritance, following the break-up of the Roman empire with the dominance of Islam, and more especially following the great schism between eastern and western Christianity, usually dated to 1054 c.e. Perhaps the time has come for us to begin to dismantle the barrier our intellectual arrogance has erected!

Notes

1. For a brief but useful biography which discusses the man and the myth, see Richard Stoneman, *Alexander the Great*, (London: Routledge, 1997); also Ian Worthington ed. *Alexander the Great: A Reader*, (London: Routledge, 2002).

2. Walter Burkert, *The Orientalising Revolution, Near Eastern Influences on Greek Culture in the Early Archaic Period* (Cambridge, Mass: Harvard University Press, 1992).

3. Lee Levine, *Judaism and Hellenism in Antiquity: Conflict or Confluence?* (Seattle and London: University of Washington Press, 1998) 3-32.

4. Tessa Rajak, 'The Hasmoneans and the Uses of Hellenism,' in Philip Davies and Richard White eds. *A Tribute to Geza Vermes. Essays in Jewish and Christian Literature and History*, (Sheffield: JSOT Press, 1990) 261-280. See also John J. Collins, 'Cult and Culture: the Limits of Hellenisation in Judea,' in John J. Collins and G. Sterling eds. *Hellenism in the Land of Israel*, (Notre Dame, Ind: University of Notre Dame Press, 2001) 38-61.

5. See John R. Bartlett, ed. *Jews in the Hellenistic and Roman Cities*, 94-115 (London: Routledge, 2002).

6. Robert Doran, 'The High Cost of a Good Education,' in Collins and Sterling eds. *Hellenism in the Land of Israel*.

7. See Doron Mendels, *The Rise and Fall of Jewish Nationalism. Jewish and Christian Ethnicity in Ancient Palestine*, (New York and London: Doubleday, 1992).

8. See Anthony J. Saldarini, *Pharisees, Scribes and Sadducees in Palestinian Society*, (Edinburgh: T. and T. Clark, 1989); Jacob Neusner From *Politics to Piety. The Emergence of Pharisaic Judaism*, (Englewood Cliffs: Prentice Hall, 1973).

9. See William R. Schoedel and Robert L. Wilkin eds. *Early Christian Literature and the Classical Intellectual Tradition*, In Honorem Robert M. Grant (Paris: Editions Beauschene, 1979; Henry Chadwick, *The Early Church*, (London: Penguin, 1978)

10. See Sean Freyne, 'The Geography of Restoration: Galilee-Jerusalem Relations in Early Jewish and Christian Experience.' *New Testament Studies* 47 (2001) 289-311; and 'The Jesus-Paul Debate Re-visited and Re-Imaging Christian Origins,' in K. O'Mahoney ed, *Christian Origins*, (Sheffield: Sheffield Academic Press, 2003) (forthcoming).

11. James M. Scott, *Paul and the Nations. The Old Testament and Jewish Background of Paul's Mission to the Nations*, WUNT 84 (Tübingen: J.C. B. Mohr, 1995).

12. Sean Freyne, 'Galileans, Itureans, Phoenicians: A Study of Regional Contrasts in the Hellenistic Age,' in Collins and Sterling eds. *Hellenism in the Land of Israel*, 182-217, especially 184-188.

13. Robert Wilkin, *The Christians as the Romans Saw Them*, (New Haven: Yale University Press, 1984).

14. Lee Levine ed., *Ancient Synagogues Revealed* (Jerusalem: The Israel Exploration Society, 1981); and *Judaism and Hellenism in Antiquity*, 149-60.

2

'AND SO WE CAME TO ROME' (ACTS 28,16)

With a sense of relief, Luke describes the end of Paul's long journey 'by sea and land' from Herod's port of Caesarea in Palestine to the capital of the world, Rome. Little did he know then that Christianity had arrived to stay. Even a century and half later, according to Peter Brown, a superb historian of the Late Antique Period, the future of the new movement within the empire was wholly unpredictable.[1] And yet when we look back from our vantage point it seems as though the Roman Empire was designed for Christian use. Certainly that was the way the first Christian historian, Eusebius of Caesarea, saw things early in the fourth century with his apologetic work *Praeparatio Evangelica*. For him the arrival of a Christian emperor, Constantine, was the confirmation of his reading of history. He described him in Christ-like terms as 'a friend of God', 'interpreter of his word', who aims 'at recalling the whole human race to the knowledge of God, proclaiming the laws of truth and godliness to all who dwell upon the earth'. On the emperor's death a coin was struck that on one side bore the Emperor's head veiled, and on the other he is seated (like the Sun-God, Helios) as a charioteer drawn by four horses, with a hand stretching downwards from above to take him up to heaven'. Thus is the apotheosis of the first Christian emperor achieved – a theme to which we shall return later.[2]

This idyllic picture of peace and harmony, corresponding to the order of the universe established by divine decree, was not, however, new. One has only to read the literature of the Augustan age to recognise that

Eusebius is merely re-echoing 'the rhetoric of empire' that went back to the dawn of the Common Era. After a century and a half of civil strife, Rome had opted for a sole ruler (*Princeps*) when Octavian defeated Antony at the battle of Actium in 31 b.c.e. Gradually and shrewdly he 'allowed' the senate to confer on him various honours, previously to be shared with others, so that the passage of supreme power (*majestas*) from Republic to Empire went quite smoothly. The titles *Princeps, Imperator, Pontifex Maximus, Augustus, Pater Patriae* were all voted on him by the senate at various stages of his long reign. Part of his strategy was to disguise his burning ambition for power under a cloak of modesty, whereby he first declined the honours, only to make the senators more anxious to grant them, wearied as they were from civil strife. Thus he silenced his enemies and even used them to his advantage, as in the case of Herod the Great of Judea who had supported Antony before Actium, but who hastened to Rhodes to make his peace and swear allegiance to Rome, once Octavian had emerged as the sole ruler.

There was need for an appropriate ideology to contextualise and explain this concentration of power and honorific titles in one person, and this was provided by the poets and writers. Virgil's *Aeneid*, based on Homer's *Iliad* and *Odyssey*, traced the origins of Rome to the fall of Troy, when a Trojan settlement was established in Latium, thus providing the origins of the Roman race. Roman history was presented by Livy as a single progression from that glorious origin to the present fulfilment. Virgil's *Fourth Eclogue* is a celebration of the present, 'golden age' in imagery reminiscent of the prophet Isaiah describing Israel's expected messianic age. Horace too joined the inner sanctum of the Augustan poets. His *Carmen Saeculare* was written for the Secular (New Age) festival that Augustus had celebrated in 17 b.c.e .This event was intended as both a renewal of old Roman values and a proclamation of the new morality and the new state. Sacrifices and elaborate rituals were conducted, with the emperor himself carrying out some of the priestly functions. The theme was that of fertility as a reward for *virtus* and respect for the *mos maiorum*, the ancient customs, which had in the past served Rome and ensured her greatness, but which had been eroded in the previous hundred years of civil turmoil. As Horace writes in the *Carmen Saeculare*:

Trust and Peace and Honor and ancient manners
Venture back among us, and long-neglected
Upright conduct. Plenty comes too and brings her
Horn of abundance.

Augustus himself also got in on the act. In his *Res Gestae*, allegedly written towards the end of his life, the restoration is described as a bringing of long-awaited peace to the empire, restoring the worship of the Roman gods and establishing the foundations of prosperity to territories long ravished by war and strife.[3]

1. The Roman Political and Social System

A major factor in Rome's success was the fact that the name stands for both a city and an empire. Unlike the rapid expansion of the Greek empire under Alexander, Rome's progress was slow and piecemeal, taking over two centuries to achieve its maximum expansion in the east. Citizenship of Rome was granted to local elites and others who earned it through service to the state as judged by provincial governors or the emperor himself, or in the case of the establishment of Roman *coloniae* such as Corinth and Philippi. Italy and North Africa were the first territories to be taken over, before the expansion to the east began in the second century b.c.e. – first Macedonia (146), followed by Asia (130), Cilicia (100), Bithynia (74), Cyrene (74), Syria (64). While Gaul and Spain had been conquered by Caesar, Augustus reorganised these into a number of separate provinces and added new ones: Egypt (30), Achaia (27) Galatia (25), Raetia and Noricum (15), Moesia (6) and Panonia (10 c.e.). Later emperors added Britain and Lycia (43 c.e, Tiberius), Thrace (46 c.e., Claudius), Arabia (105 c.e., Trajan), Dacia (107 c.e., Trajan) and Mesopotamia (198 c.e., Septimus Severus). What is significant about this provincial system is that it imposed a uniform bureaucratic structure on far-flung territories that were culturally and ethnically very diverse.

The system of taxation, administration of justice, policing and military presence, all helped to impose and maintain Roman *ordo*. However, this system was not experienced uniformly at all levels of a highly structured society. Roman society was based on the patron-client relationship whereby a network of dependency operated at every level and gave rise to an honour-shame culture in which the ability to grant favours to others was seen as the hallmark of success. The pattern was established at Rome itself with the emperor in his role of 'Father of the Fatherland' as the chief patron of all, and the network of power and privilege that the system gave rise to was replicated throughout the different territories. The structure of control was pyramidal, with most of the power residing with the tiny minority who made up the elite and ruling classes. Below these were a series of so-called retainer classes, types such as priests, scribes and officials, whose services were required in order to maintain the system and who were prepared to serve in return for the public status they thereby attained. Beneath these again were artisans, peasant farmers and such like, and at the bottom of the pile, making up the vast majority of the population, were the poor, day-labourers, women and children, slaves and disenfranchised foreigners – the destitute classes.[4]

Given the huge inequalities within this system, it is remarkable how infrequently social revolution occurred. This can only be due to the rigid enforcement of order that obtained and the fact that any disturbances were summarily dealt with in the most stern manner. In this regard the history of the Roman province of Judea under the procurators is a microcosm of how the Roman system as a whole functioned. Because of the strong ethnic solidarity that the Jewish religion fostered, at least in theory, the Jews in the homeland found the Roman yoke difficult to accept. It was only after two bitter wars (66-70 and 132-135 c.e.) that their sense of independence was broken and a new and very different Judaism emerged that could no longer aspire to political independence.

Thus, if Paul and his provincial companions had come to the city of Rome, Rome – in the sense of a ruling system with all the trappings of power – was no stranger to them. The hallmarks of Roman presence were everywhere to be seen, something that was illustrated superbly by the building projects of Herod the Great in Judea to honour his Roman overlords. Still today at many sites one can see the unmistakable traces of Herod the builder: a harbour, theatres, stadia, roads, aqueducts, fora, paved streets, temples, statues, bath houses. All of this elaborate building on a grand scale should be understood as the rhetoric of empire, just as eloquent as the writings of the poets and historians. The scale of many of the buildings is ostentatiously triumphalistic and speaks of Roman *majestas*; the statuary of its *gravitas*. Streets laid out in squares represent Roman order; aqueducts, harbours, bath-houses, and roads, all indicate the superiority of Roman technology. Apart from the tangible sense of presence that such buildings gave, they were also intended to service the military presence, either of a legion stationed in one of the imperial provinces such as Syria, or to facilitate an army moving through to some flash-point or other. Building projects on this scale cost money and they drained the local economies because of the amount of tribute that had to be levied. As a result, forced labour (*angaria*) was often the lot of the native, largely peasant population.

2. A Clash of Ideologies

The cultural and political significance of such tangible signs of Roman presence is captured well in a little vignette from the Babylonian Talmud reporting a conversation between three second-century rabbis:

> Rabbi Judah began. 'How splendid are the works of this people (the Romans). They have built market-places, baths and bridges.'
> Rabbi Yose said nothing.
> Rabbi Simeon bar Yohai answered him: 'Everything they have made they have for themselves: market places for whores; baths to wallow in; bridges to levy tolls'.

This conversation echoes the words of the second-century Christian apologist, Tertullian, himself a former Roman military man. However, his attitude is far more sanguine than that of the Rabbis. He proudly boasts:

> We (Christians) are but of yesterday, and we have filled everything you have – cities, tenements, forts, towns, exchanges, yes, and camps, tribes, palaces, senate, forum; all we have left to you are the temples.

At the ideological level, neither Jews nor Christians fitted easily into the Roman world, however much they may have felt at home there in other ways. It is this on clash of ideologies that I want to focus our attention for the remainder of this paper. The Jews had a long-standing arrangement with the Romans going back to Judas Maccabee in the second century b.c.e. (1 Macc 8). Subsequently, the rights and privileges associated with this treaty of friendship were confirmed in the decrees of Caesar in 48 b.c.e. These gave special status to the Jews in the homeland 'to observe their ancestral laws', and the Jews in the Diaspora cities were allowed to bring their gifts to the Jerusalem temple, have their own meeting places and observe the Sabbath. These special considerations often meant that they were the butt of anti-Jewish vilification as being idle, unsociable, and perverse. Notwithstanding these stereotypes, some Jews did have prominent positions in the imperial and provincial administration, and it was well into the fifth century c.e. before the privileges began to be rescinded by Christian emperors.

By contrast, the Christians were treated as a hated, eastern *superstitio* in Rome. Tacitus, the aristocratic Roman historian writing in the early second century c.e. has some sympathy for them because of the treatment meted out by Nero, during his persecution following the great fire of 64 c.e. Nevertheless, his account is characteristically dismissive. He writes:

> Christus, from whom the name has its origin suffered the extreme penalty during the reign of Tiberius at the hands of one of our procurators, Pontius Pilate, and a deadly superstition, thus checked for the moment, again broke out, not only in Judea, the first source of the evil, but also in the city where all things shameful from every part of the world meet and become popular (*Annals* 15, 44).

At about the same time Pliny the Elder, writing from his province of Bithynia near the Black Sea to the emperor Trajan, has an equally dismissive view of the Christians. 'The contagion of this superstition', as he calls it, had spread even to the countryside at an alarming rate and he requires instruction as to how he should deal with it, despite his conviction that the more popular slanders about the Christians, such as the claim that they were cannibals, had no foundation.

It was the refusal of both Jews and Christians to join in the civic worship of Rome that made their situation so precarious. This was to become particularly troublesome in imperial times with the tendency to count the emperor himself as one of the immortals, despite Augustus, and later Claudius demurring at such an honour. Later emperors, such as Caligula, Nero and Domitian had no such reticence, however. When Caligula wanted to have a statue of himself erected in the Jerusalem temple, the Jews protested vigorously with the governor of Syria, Petronius, as follows:

> Will you then go to war with Caesar?' demanded Petronius, The Jews replied that 'they offered sacrifices twice daily for Caesar and the Roman people, but that if he wished to set up these statues, he must first sacrifice the entire nation; and they presented themselves, their wives and heir children for slaughter. (Josephus, *Jewish War*, 2,193).

It was this same issue – refusal to sacrifice to the emperor – that had lead to Pliny's interrogation of the Christians of Bithynia. In his case the issue is very clearly stated: 'Some people claimed to have rejected their Christian faith, and proved this by 'worshipping your (Trajan's) statue and the images of the gods, and cursed Christ.' He was also able to ascertain that previously their error had merely consisted in gathering before daylight 'to sing hymns to Christ, as to a god' and returning after work to eat a common meal.

In Pliny's view it had to be either Christ or the Emperor; there could be no compromise, as in the case of the Jews, sacrificing daily on behalf of the emperor to their god, since the Christians were a *nova superstitio* and lacked the antiquity of the Jews. Yet in less than a hundred years Tertullian, that robust Roman Christian, could write as follows:

> Looking up to heaven, the Christians – with hands outspread, because innocent, with head bare … and without one to give the form of words, for we pray from the heart – we are for ever making intercession for all emperors. We pray for them long life, a secure rule, a safe home, brave armies, a faithful senate, an honest people, a quiet world, and everything for which a man and a Caesar can pray. All this I cannot ask of any other but only from Him from whom I know that I shall receive it. (*Apology* 30).

It is noteworthy that this Christian acknowledgement of the emperor, according to Tertullian is 'from the heart' and without 'any form of words'. There could be no public recognition of Caesar until Caesar first acknowledged the Christ, and that would take another hundred years before Constantine's vision of the crucifix in the sky with the writing '*in hoc signo vincis*' ('In this sign you shall conquer.'). It is tempting to suggest that this implacable Christian resistance to emperor-worship was the direct result of their own particular story. Whereas the Jews could reconcile their monotheistic faith with offering sacrifices to their God on behalf of the emperor, the Christians were faced with a choice, not between Caesar and God, but between Caesar and Christ. Both had had a similar process of deification from the human condition by their followers, and yet, within the monotheistic framework of Christian belief they could not both be acknowledged.

3. The Imperial Cult
The idea that the ruler was especially close to the gods was an old one in the Ancient Near East. Alexander the Great had exploited the idea to the full when he had himself enthroned as king in the manner of an eastern potentate, after his capture of the Persian capital, Susa. On his coins his image resembles that of Zeus, the head of the Greek pantheon. It is not surprising therefore, to find that it was in the east that the notion of the Roman emperor as a divine figure was most widely diffused, and

paradoxically, it was there that the notion caused the greatest difficulty for Jews and Christians, as we have just seen. There was no such tradition in the west, and Augustus was able to cultivate the notion of praying to his genius or spirit, during his life-time without any opposition from the conquered peoples.[6]

It is fascinating to see how the process of developing the imperial cult was achieved. Very early in his reign Octavian had seen to it that the Senate had recognised his adoptive father, Julius Caesar, as a divine figure. A comet was seen in the sky after his murder and this was interpreted as his soul ascending to the realm of the gods. A temple was dedicated to Caesar's honour in the forum, and the caption on Octavian's coins read '*Divi Filius*', 'Son of the Divine One', thereby conferring divine status on himself by association. In the east almost every major city soon had a temple in its forum dedicated to Augustus and to *Roma*. Herod the Great had one such constructed on a mound in his new port of Caesarea, and Samaria too received a temple of Augustus and a new name, 'Sebaste' (Greek for Augustus). In Rome itself Octavian was more reticent, declining to have a statue of himself added to the Roman pantheon. However, immediately on his death he was declared *Divus Augustus*, and many senators sought to become priests of the new cult of the emperor.

This process of deification of the emperor by association with a divine ancestor set a precedent, and some had little difficulty in claiming divine status even in life, most notably the emperor Gaius Caligula, and later Domitian who requested that he be addressed as *Dominus et Deus* 'My Lord and my God,' a salutation that echoes that of Thomas to Jesus in the Fourth Gospel (Jn 20, 28). The female consorts of the imperial retinue were also attributed divine status, appearing on coins in the guise of Diana, Ceres, Venus, Concordia – all members of the Roman pantheon.

While the process of divinisation undoubtedly served the purpose of consolidating imperial rule and was so intended, it also has to be seen within the context of the development of the myth of Rome, which we encountered at the outset. In this regard the military exploits of the emperors were extremely important, since the ideology of peace-making was so central to the myth of *Roma Aeterna*. This was one of the dominant themes of Augustus' *Res Gestae*, and hence the need for him to be identified with Mars, the Roman god of war, under the epithet '*Ultor*' ('Avenger'). The connection was established in a number of ways. Augustus claimed ancestry through Romulus, one of Rome's legendary founders with Mars, who was claimed to have seduced Rhea Silva, the mother of the legendary twin founders of Rome, Romulus and Remus. In addition a massive temple was built to Mars *Ultor* in the Augustan forum in 27 b.c.e. in order to celebrate his victory over the Parthians. who had been a constant threat on the eastern borders of the empire. This victory was celebrated on his coins also. Thus the emperor and the god became merged in popular perception as Ovid the poet acknowledged: 'The god (i.e. the statue) is huge and so is the structure (temple),' he writes. He beheld also the name of Augustus on the front of the temple, and the building seems to him to be greater still when he reads the name of Caesar. In addition to Mars, ancestry with Venus, the goddess of love was also established. She was the symbol of fertility and prosperity, which had become associated with the Golden Age in the poetic compositions. She too features both on the altar of Mars and on an Augustan coin with the caption *Divi Filius*, Son of Zeus, and the goddess is carrying the arms of Mars.

Not merely were Augustus' own links with the divine ancestry established through myth, legend and image. His successors also were given their place within the overall mythic framework of the new Rome. Since he had no natural son he had to seek an heir. His first two choices Marcellus and Agrippa died prematurely. He was further disappointed by the death of his two grandsons who had each been given the title '*Divi Julii nepos*', 'grandson of the divine Caesar.' He then adopted Tiberius, a son of his wife Livia and a member of the Claudian family (hence the name 'Julio-Claudian' given to the line of emperors who succeeded Augustus) whom he forcibly caused to marry Julia, his only daughter. In all this Augustus was merely following good Roman practice as a *paterfamilias*, 'father of the household.' He was also building an imperial house and endowing his successors with the same authority and majesty with which he had been able to surround his own rule.

4. Christian Responses to the Ideology of Rome

That a small Jewish reformist sect could, within three hundred years, develop to the point of being able to challenge the very foundations of this elaborately constructed system, was surely in itself an extraordinary historical achievement. Constantine's 'conversion', it is generally agreed nowadays, was more a matter of convenience than conviction. Christianity offered the best possibility for uniting a divided empire that was beginning to collapse under the weight of its own administrative system and the deep cultural fissures that were opening up between east and west. A movement such as that initiated by Jesus in the villages of Galilee might appear quite remote from Rome and its concerns, yet, as I have argued elsewhere, the most immediate historical context for understanding the Jesus movement was the occurrence in Galilee of an aggressive policy of Romanisation under Herod Antipas, represented in particular by the rebuilding of Sepphoris and the founding of Tiberias. Jesus did not have to go to Rome in order to challenge its power; Rome had come to his world and to that of every other peasant within its borders, directly and immediately, through the elaborate system of control that it had devised.

The effect of the changes occurring was a further erosion of the precarious existence of the small landowners and fishermen of Galilee and elsewhere. Jesus had exhorted resistance to such economic and social degradation, not by violence, but by a 'values-revolution' that was directly opposed to all that Roman imperialism held dear. 'Render to Caesar what is Caesar's' (Mk 12, 17) was not, therefore, the apolitical statement that is often assumed. Luke articulates the matter rather well when he has Jesus accused before Pilate on the charge of 'subverting the people' (Lk 23, 4.14). In my view Jesus' radical programme was not, as has become fashionable to claim nowadays, inspired by the Cynic philosophy, which was a counter-cultural movement of social protest within the cities of the empire. Rather Jesus' vision was grounded in the restoration hopes of Jewish eschatology which promised God's soon vindication of the righteous, peace and harmony based on justice, inclusiveness and caring for 'the little ones', that is, the socially marginalised. The images of ultimate bliss are, as we have noted already, very similar to those expressed by the Augustan poets, but the means of achieving it were very different indeed. It was God's graciousness, not human efforts, that would bring about the messianic age, the dawn of which, Jesus believed, had already begun in and through his own ministry to the poor.

On the Roman scale of things this disturbance in Judea was of minor consequence, to be dealt with locally. It was not a serious infringement of the *Pax Romana*. Indeed it often comes as a surprise to discover just how little Roman writers of the first and second centuries were appraised of, or interested in the new movement. We have seen Tacitus' views already. Suetonius, writing later still, seems to have thought that Christ had actually caused a disturbance in Rome in the reign of Claudius, leading to the expulsion of Jews from the city in 49 c.e. Thus, from a Roman perspective, Christianity for the first century of its existence, was little more than one of those pernicious eastern sects that had invaded Rome. As Juvenal, the caustic Roman satirist, puts it: 'For a long time now the Syrian Orontes has poured its effluence into the Roman Tiber'.

It is difficult to say whether or not the Jewish revolt against Rome in 66-70 c.e., leading to the destruction of the Jerusalem temple by Titus, implicated the Christians also. Probably not, at least, not directly. Nero's persecution of the Christians had occurred before the outbreak of the revolt, and it was the victory over the Jews that Titus celebrated on his triumphal arch, still today visible in the Roman forum, and on the *Judea Capta* coins which celebrate Rome's humiliation of the Jews. Even the Jerusalem Christians seem to have distanced themselves from events in Judea as early as 62 c.e after the murder of their leader, James the brother of the Lord, by the Jewish Sanhedrin. Whatever they might have thought beforehand, their experience and memory of Jesus had lead them to believe in a suffering and glorified messiah, and not in a messianic war of liberation.

One of the more plausible scenarios suggested for the writing of Mark's Gospel is that it was a call to Christians to ignore the many 'false Christs and false prophets' (Mk 13, 21f) that, according to the Jewish historian Josephus, proliferated just before the outbreak of hostilities against Rome. Instead they were to put their trust in Jesus' pacific messiahship, even if that meant persecution. Another possible scenario for Mark is the aftermath of Nero's persecution of Christians in Rome in which Peter and Paul died. According to this view, Mark had in mind particularly those Christians who had delated their co-religionists at the height of the persecution, and wished to encourage them by recalling how Peter and the first disciples had also been unfaithful when Jesus faced the Roman procurator, Pontius Pilate, but who had eventually sealed their commitment with their lives.

Whatever the precise context, this first Christian narrative Gospel also recalled Jesus' ministry of healing and benefaction (*euergeton*) to the outcasts of Galilean society in the name of the God of Israel, whose presence, he claimed, was not solely, or indeed primarily, confined to the Jerusalem temple (Acts 10, 37f). By the time of Mark's writing, such a claim would have disassociated the Christians from the ideology of the revolt as expressed on the coins that the Jewish revolutionaries had minted, bearing such captions as 'For the freedom of Zion' and 'Jerusalem the holy'. But another collection of Jesus' sayings circulated from an early date also, containing his sharp critique of prevailing Roman and Jewish aristocratic values concerning wealth, patronage, power and peace (designated by scholars as the 'Q document'). The beatitudes (Lk 6, 21-25) and the Our Father (Lk 11, 2-4) have political connotations that are highly subversive of this system of values, when read in the context of Palestinian politics of the first century c.e. Towards the end of that first century both Matthew and Luke combined these two early Christian writings (Mark and Q) with other traditions about Jesus that were in circulation to produce two new versions of the story of Jesus that must have sent alarm bells ringing in the ears of sensitive Roman provincial officials, like Pliny, charged with the task of ensuring that the emperor cult functioned properly in terms of Roman ideology of peace, order and prosperity.

Both evangelists supply a genealogy and a farewell enthronement to the Markan outline, as well as including the subversive words of Jesus from Q. While these additions have often been read in a highly romantic and/or theological manner, especially the picture of the child in the manger, it is doubtful if that was their original intention. By providing Jesus with a genealogy that traced his ancestry back to the great patriarchs of Israel, they may well have been emulating the Emperor's myth-making procedures that linked Augustus and his house with Aeneas, and eventually with Mars *Ultor*, as we have seen. The closing scenes – enthronement (Mt) and ascension (Lk) – might equally be compared with stories of the comet seen in the sky on the deaths of Caesar and Augustus. That this reading is not by any means fanciful is borne out by Luke's deliberate appropriation of the imperial rhetoric as expressed on coins and inscriptions. The birth of Jesus is heralded by the shepherds as the arrival of a *Soter* (Saviour), who will bring *eirene* (peace) to all people of good will (Lk 2, 14). His unselfish service of others is favourably contrasted with earthly benefactors (*euergetai*), implying that Jesus is the true benefactor, not the emperors or governors, who delighted in this epithet because of its importance in the honour/shame culture of the Mediterranean world (Lk 22,17; Acts 10, 38). Indeed, we might go one step further and see Luke's presentation of the first disciples in Acts of the Apostles as 'divine men', endowed with extraordinary powers, which confounded the political and religious authorities. Paul too and his companion, Barnabas, are feted as divine visitors in Lystra, where their healing powers caused the natives to identify Paul with Hermes and Barnabas with Zeus (Acts 14, 11f). Thus, Jesus' successors share in his divine status in Luke's presentation, not dissimilar to the manner in which the successors of the imperial household shared in the divine status of the emperor.

Even if Roman imperial officials did not read this literature, primarily intended for believers, they must certainly have encountered its effects when faced with the task of imposing the imperial cult. During the reign of Domitian (probably 94 c.e) a bitter persecution broke out in the province of Asia, and the Book of Revelation is a Christian response to the crisis thereby engendered. This prophetic work, so often misinterpreted by Christian readers of a literalistic frame of mind, is a highly dramatised account in mythic form of the age-old struggle between the forces of good and evil, here identified with the Christian Churches of Asia and Imperial Rome. In the end the victory is to the followers of the lamb who have been washed in his blood, no doubt a reference to the sufferings inflicted on them by 'the whore of Babylon', as Rome is described. This work becomes a defiant statement of extraordinary power and vibrancy when it is read in the light of the rhetoric of empire already discussed. The reader is taken through a series of earthly catastrophes (punctuated by scenes of heavenly worship that function as windows of hope), eventually ending in the paradisiacal condition of the new heaven and the new earth. The fact that this condition can be described spatially in terms of an architecturally perfect city (Rev 21) is a trenchant comparison of the New Jerusalem with Rome, the whore of Babylon. The author's subtle use of imperial court imagery in the opening chapters gives way to the ironic lament for Babylon the Great in chapter 18, a chapter that acknowledges Rome's great commercial achievements in terms that would have done justice to Augustus' *Res Gestae*, only to end in mock lament for the great power that has fallen.

The subsequent history of the uneasy relationship between Rome and the Christians up to Constantine cannot be told here in any detail. The literature, especially of the apologists, shows a growing sense of self-confidence, as in Tertullian's description of the Christian triumph, already cited. The relationship, never more than one of grudging tolerance on the Roman side, varied from one province to another and from one imperial ruler to another. Decius and Diocletian in the third century were the most notorious emperors in terms of brutality against the Christians, making the sudden change of fortune under Constantine all the more remarkable. The amount of pre-Constantinian Christian archaeological remains is limited, though some evidence from the stucco art of the catacombs, as well as the representation on *sarcophagi*, gives us glimpses of how Christians viewed themselves within the empire. It is remarkable how frequently certain biblical themes recur: the sacrifice of

Isaac, the raising of Lazarus, Daniel in the lion's den, the rescue of Susannah from the old men and Jonah in the whale's belly.[7] All of these are stories of rescue from potentially terminal danger, indicating the tensions under which the Christian Church in Rome considered itself to be operating. Perhaps the most interesting of all catacomb iconography is that of Christ depicted as *Helios*, which was discovered in what can be clearly identified as a Christian mausoleum under St Peter' basilica. Such a daring depiction matched Luke's politically charged language, indicating no sense of inferiority or easy syncretism, but an aggressive appropriation by the new religion of one of the most important symbols of ancient religious belief, that of *Baal Shamem*, 'the Most High God', *Helios, Sol Invictus*, the Sun God. It is interesting to note that Jews too in this period were prepared to include the *Helios*/Sun God motif on their synagogue floors amid other panels of a biblical or wholly Jewish inspiration. Were both religions in competition for this oldest and most universal religious symbol? Certainly, when paganism made a brief return under the emperor Julian in the mid-fourth century, it was the Sun worship that he sought to introduce as a replacement for the newly established state religion of the Christians, which he wished to suppress. That was the last throw of the dice for the old Rome, however. New Rome was now increasingly to become a synthesis of Church and Empire. Nowhere is this more graphically illustrated than in the famous mosaics of Ravenna, which had become the imperial residence from the early fifth century. Whether or not that synthesis has worked in the interest of both Church and Empire is a question that remains with us to this very day.

Notes

1. Peter Brown, *The World of Late Antiquity. From Marcus Aurelius to Muhammad*, (London: Thames and Hudson: 1971).
2. Alisdair Kee, *Constantine Versus Christ*, (London: SCM Press, 1982) 27-34; Timothy D. Barnes, *Constantine and Eusebius*, (Cambridge, Mass: Harvard University Press, 1981) 262-272; H. Drake,
3. For a convenient English translation of these texts see C.K. Barrett, *The New Testament Background. Selected Documents*, (Second ed. London: APCK, 1987) pp 1-9.
4. Richard Saller, *Personal Patronage under the Empire*, (Cambridge: Cambridge University Press, 1982). For a popular treatment see K.C. Hanson and Douglas E. Oakman, *Palestine in the Time of Jesus. Social Structures and Social Conflicts*, (Minneapolis: Fortress Press, 1998).

5. For a recent popular account with impressive photography and reconstructions, see Jonathan Reed and John Domnick Crossan, *Excavating Jesus*, (New York: HarperCollins, 2001).

6. Two highly significant studies on the Augustan Age are those of Paul Zanker, *The Power of Images in the Age of Augustus*, (English trans. Ann Arbor: The University Press, 1990) and Fergus Millar, *The Roman Republic and the Augustan Revolution*: Rome, the Greek World and the East, (Chapel Hill and London: The University of North Carolina Press, 2002).

7. Graham F. Snyder, *Ante Pacem. Archaeological Evidence for Church Life Before Constantine* (Macon, Ga: Mercer University Press, 1985).

3

FROM JESUS TO CONSTANTINE: JERUSALEM IN EARLY CHRISTIAN PIETY AND IMAGINATION

Jerusalem, Jerusalem, the city that kills the prophets and stones those sent to it. How often have I desired to gather your children together as a hen gathers her brood under her wings, and you were not willing. (Mt 23, 27; Lk 13, 34).

The time is coming and now is when you will worship the Father neither on this mountain nor in Jerusalem … The hour is coming and now is when the true worshippers will worship the Father in spirit and in truth. (Jn 4,22f).

These two citations from different ends of the New Testament, the one from the early Q document, which Matthew and Luke have incorporated into their later Gospels, and the other from the Fourth Gospel, encapsulate the earliest Christian attitude and ambivalence towards Jerusalem. On the one hand, as Jews, Jesus and his first followers have a deep spiritual attachment to the holy city, even though there is already a hint of opposition and rejection in the unfulfilled wish 'How often … but you were unwilling.' On the other hand the Johannine Jesus, towards the end of the New Testament period, declares Jerusalem (and Gerazim the alternative holy place of the Samaritans) obsolete, because of a new form of worship in spirit and in truth, which had been inaugurated to correspond to the new reality of messianic times that he believed had been inaugurated.

Clearly, significant changes had occurred in the seventy years between these two statements, changes to do with early Christian self-understanding and the significance of Jerusalem to these, but changes also in the external forces they had to deal with, not least the actual destruction of Jerusalem by the Romans in 70 c.e. Christians as messianic Jews had, like other branches of the parent religion, to rethink their attitudes in the light of this traumatic event, which had touched even the Roman writers such as Tacitus and Pliny, the latter describing it as 'by far the most renowned city of the ancient East' (*Natural History*, V, 14). Despite celebrating Rome's victory, the fall of a great and famous temple city could not be taken lightly in the ancient world. The event was much more traumatic for those whose hopes, beliefs and way of life were centred on God's promises for his chosen place, Mount Zion, and its pre-eminence over all the mountains of the world (Is 2, 2-4; Sir 24). A deep sense of loss and mourning pervades the literature of the period, yet despite sharing these sentiments, the early Christians were better equipped to find alternatives that were not dependent on Jerusalem's continued existence, something Matthew hints at with his comment about the magi returning to their homeland, not via Jerusalem, but by 'another way' (Mt 2, 12).

In this paper I propose to follow that other way, as it was travelled by early Christian writers from the first to the fourth century. There are three stages to the journey. The ambivalent attachment of the early period towards the earthly Jerusalem gives way to the hopes for the new, heavenly Jerusalem, itself an ambivalent symbol, only for this in turn to be supplanted by the rediscovery of the earthly Jerusalem as central to Christian claims in the wake of Constantine's gradual embrace of Christianity as the religion of the empire after 314 c.e. This journey of Christian imagination and experience with regard to Jerusalem, is a fascinating one, illustrating in a very concrete way the relationship of the new movement both to the parent religion and to Roman imperial power.

1. Jerusalem as reality and symbol in Early Christian experience

We are heavily dependent on Luke's account in Acts of the Apostles for our knowledge of the new movement immediately after the death of Jesus. Unlike Mark, Matthew and John, Luke has the disciples remaining in Jerusalem on the basis of a command from the risen Jesus, there to await the gift of the Holy Spirit and begin their ministry of witness, which was to spread from 'Jerusalem to the end of the earth.' This picture in the early chapters of Acts was indeed a somewhat idealised account, prompted by messianic expectation about the salvation that would go forth from Zion according to the prophetic promises (Is 2, 2-4; 49, 6). More solid historical ground is reached with the account of the Hebrews and the Hellenists, each with their separate cultural and ecclesial identities within the Jerusalem Church at a very early stage (Acts 6-7). Following Stephen's martyrdom, the Hellenists had to leave the city, but not before Stephen becomes spokesman for a theology that suggested that the Almighty did not need a temple in which to live. Israel's early history is recalled when their God travelled with the Israelites. Only later, and in the face of considerable opposition, Solomon had built the first temple, which ensured the subsequent status of Jerusalem as the Holy City in Israelite and Jewish tradition. The Hebrews on the other hand stayed in Jerusalem, continuing to play the role of Mother Church under James' leadership down to eve of the Jewish revolt of 66 c.e. According to the Church historian Eusebius, this Christian community migrated to Pella in Transjordan only after James had been put to death in 62 c.e.

Paul was in the vanguard of the Hellenists' world mission, but this did not mean that he felt free to ignore Jerusalem and its centrality to Christian claims. As David's city, Jerusalem was pivotal to the expectation of messianic blessings to come, and this role had to be maintained, however difficult that was to square with the fact that he and other missionaries to the gentiles were at odds with the Jerusalem Christian community. In the process of defending himself against bitter attacks from the Jerusalem Church, Paul makes his celebrated distinction between the 'Jerusalem which is in slavery with her children' and 'the Jerusalem that is above, which is free, and is our mother' (Gal 4, 25). Much has been written about this passage, and the distinction was to play an important role subsequently, as we shall see. It is part of a lengthy allegory based on Abraham's wife, Sarah, and his concubine, Hagar, in order to show that according to the Scriptures the gentile Christian community can be seen to be the child of the promise and so enjoys God's favour and protection now. In view of what Paul has to say later about his Jewish co-religionists (see. Rom 9, 1-6), it is doubtful if he intended the contrast that he draws between the heavenly and earthly Jerusalem to refer to Judaism as a separate religion over against the Christian one, something that was indeed the case a hundred years later with Paul's commentators.[1] It has been suggested, therefore, that when Paul speaks negatively about the earthly Jerusalem in the Epistle to the

TEXTS, CONTEXTS AND CULTURES: ESSAYS ON BIBLICAL TOPICS

Galatians he has in mind those 'false teachers' of the Jerusalem Christian community, who were bitterly opposed to the admission of gentiles to the new movement without their going through initiation into Judaism first, and who may have mounted a counter-mission to Paul's (Gal 2,1).

However we are to understand the contrast, it is clear that for Paul Jerusalem and the Jerusalem Christian community had a highly symbolic meaning, as is evidenced by his visits there (two according to Galatians, and three according to Acts), as well as his insistence on the collections on behalf of 'the saints in Jerusalem', analogous to the practices of Diaspora Jews in supporting the temple with their annual offerings (1 Cor 16, 1; 2 Cor 8-9; Rm 15, 26-28). This attachment transcended the actual city as he had experienced it both as a Jew and a member of the new Jesus-movement. This symbolic, eschatological significance of Jerusalem was part of his Jewish religious inheritance, without which it was impossible for him to conceive of messianic salvation. It was there that Yahweh had made his name to dwell uniquely, and it was there that future salvation would occur. As long as Jerusalem stood, the actual city continued to carry those hopes, no matter how much Paul's and other Christians' experiences of the city were at odds with the lofty expectations associated with the son of David and the Zion traditions of the Hebrew Scriptures (Pss 46; 48; 76; 84; 87; 122). These traditions spoke of universal peace, justice, prosperity and the restorations of Israel's ideal past, which would bring the nations streaming to Jerusalem, and from whence wisdom would go forth to all the earth.[2]

Paul was writing in the 50s, well before the destruction of the city by the Romans in 70 c.e., an event that put a deep question mark over Jewish hopes, giving rise to intense speculation about the future of Jerusalem. Some texts spoke of a new, restored, earthly Jerusalem of the future; others from an apocalyptic perspective, looked forward to a new Jerusalem descending from heaven; whereas others still envisaged that new Jerusalem in heaven to which the just would ascend. It is indicative of how closely early Christianity felt attached to its Jewish matrix that two quite different texts from the later writings of the New Testament, the Epistle to the Hebrews and the Revelation of John, echo these ideas.[3] The author of Hebrews develops an argument that the Jewish cult of atonement is outmoded and obsolete, as Christ the eternal high-priest, has made the perfect, once-for-all sacrifice for sin. In order to exhort his readers, probably of Jewish background, not revert to their former practices, he passionately reminds them of their new calling in terms that reflect this new thinking about Jerusalem:

> But you have come to Mount Zion and the city of the living God, the heavenly Jerusalem, and to innumerable angels in festive gathering, and to the assembly of the first born who are enrolled in heaven, and to God the judge of all, and to the spirits of the righteous made perfect, and to Jesus the mediator of a new covenant, and to the sprinkled blood that speaks a better word that the blood of Abel. (Hebrews 12, 22-24)

This dense passage draws on a variety of images of ultimate bliss from the available biblical and apocalyptic repertoire, in order to impress on the readers the finality and absolute character of the salvation in which they were already participating through membership of the Christian community. The scene of triumph, festivity and wholeness associated with the new covenant is contrasted with that of Exodus 19-24, the making of the first covenant, where a mood of awe and fear surrounds the mountain where Moses encounters God. The spatial arrangement in the Jerusalem temple, with its different courtyards for priests, lay Israelites, women and gentiles, reflected a similar situation of Yahweh's separateness from Israel. In developing an argument for the superiority of the new dispensation in Christ the author of Hebrews judges these arrangements as signs of the inferior and preliminary nature of the first covenant, and hence there is no mourning for the loss of the temple. Nor is the new temple mentioned in the above description. Instead the images of the heavenly Jerusalem and Mount Zion are deemed more appropriate to describe the inclusive nature of Christian hope that, according to the author, has now been realised through Christ's self-offering.

In contrast to this conviction of final salvation already accomplished that informs the perspective of Hebrews, the point of view of the Revelation of John is that of danger and threat for the community in the midst of a bitter persecution. The author's gaze is cast to the future, and in his final vision of consolation and hope for the readers he sees 'the holy city, a new Jerusalem, descending out of heaven from God, prepared as a bride adorned for her husband.' This city adorned with the most precious jewels stands in direct contrast to the 'whore of Babylon,' namely, Rome, that is perceived as the great enemy, and whose hoped-for destruction is celebrated in chapter 18. In keeping with the apocalyptic genre, the author receives a vision, which assures him that the chaos of the past will soon be over. God has come to dwell among his people and there will be no more suffering, pain or death. This utopian image of the new Jerusalem concludes a set of contrasting desires that run through the work, the desire of violent destruction of the enemy and the longing for an ideal world to replace the negativity of the present. The author is taken up to a high mountain where his view of the new city is unimpeded. When measured it is a perfect cube with twelve gates, twelve foundation stones, bearing the names of the twelve apostles of the lamb. There are twelve kinds of fruit growing on the 'tree of life.' Making the city a veritable new paradise where there will be no night. The author sees no temple in the city since 'the Lord God, the almighty is the temple, together with the lamb.' Thus, the destruction of the temple is turned into a positive image of God's accessibility, filling the whole city with light, life and unrestrained joy (Revelation 21). The readers can be reassured that God's final victory is imminent, even though they must return to the real world of Roman power and domination, experienced in the recent past in the destruction of Jerusalem, and in the current persecutions of the Christian Church in Asia Minor, both at the hands of two different members of the same Flavian dynasty – Titus in 70, and Domitian in the early nineties.The sense of hope and celebration that the vision of the new Jerusalem could generate has provoked the author to exploit to the full the biblical imagery in order to express the coming reversal of fortunes for the just.

Our survey of the first phase of early Christian attitudes towards Jerusalem suggests an inherent tension between their Jewish heritage, which believed that it was the city of salvation, and their own actual experience of success among the gentile cities of the Mediterranean world. This success had brought the new movement to the attention of Roman imperial power in the same generation that saw the destruction of the temple. Of all the New Testament writers, Luke is perhaps the most conscious of the political situation facing the new movement as it separates itself from the parent Judaism and launched itself on the Roman world. His two-volume work was written towards the end of the first, or early in the second century, looking back to the career of Jesus in the Gospel and forward to the mission of the Church in Acts of the Apostles. In the former work Jerusalem and its temple are at the center of the action from the outset (Lk 1, 9; 2, 22. 41) and the holy city is the divinely appointed goal of Jesus' journey (9, 31. 51; 17, 11; 19, 28). Yet the destruction of Jerusalem is explicitly mentioned in terms of a prophecy put on the lips of Jesus: 'When you see Jerusalem surrounded by an army, then know that its destruction is close at hand. ... It will be trampled on by the gentiles until the times of the gentiles are fulfilled'(Lk 21, 20-24). Unlike the other evangelists at this point, Luke does not associate that event with the end of the age, but sees it as a past historical event, the consequences of which are now playing themselves out in the missionary journey of the Church to Rome. Thus, in Acts of the Apostles Jerusalem is the place where the outpouring of the Spirit must take place, thus inaugurating the mission to 'the end of the earth' in accordance with the prophetic promises (Acts 1, 8), but the centre is shifting. By Luke's day the trauma of the fate of the actual Jerusalem had been replaced by an aggressive apologetic approach, which regarded the Christian mission as the fulfillment of the Jewish hopes for the holy city as the center of the universe. Unfortunately for the future relations, Christian self-identity is becoming entwined with Jewish misfortune.

2. Christians and Jerusalem, 100-300 c.e.

It has been claimed that the fact that the temple was not rebuilt seventy years after its destruction was even more traumatic than the actual event itself. The destruction of the first temple by the Babylonians in the sixth century b.c.e., was followed by its rebuilding some seventy years later in line with prophetic declarations. Not only was Jerusalem not rebuilt seventy years after its destruction by the Romans, the emperor Hadrian had put down a second Jewish revolt (132-135 c.e.) and established a Roman *colonia* on the ruins of the old Jerusalem. It was named named Aelia Capitolina, in honour of the Roman god, the Capitoline Jupiter. This new city had most of the architectural trappings of a Roman city – baths, theatre, nymphaea and temples, one dedicated to the Roman triad, Jupiter, Juno and Minerva on the temple mount, and one to the goddess Aphrodite at the site that later was identified as the tomb of Christ. The tenth Roman legion was stationed in the new city, ensuring no further Jewish insurrection, and a triumphal gate was erected where the *damascus* Gate stands today (i.e. on the north side), leading into a square where a dedicatory column to Hadrian stood. The *cardo* or main street ran directly south from this square, some of which can still be seen underneath the street in the Jewish quarter that was refurbished after the excavations there following the six day war in 1967. This ran into the *decumanus* or main cross street running in a west/east direction from today's Jaffa Gate to the temple mount area.[4] Architecturally this was a deliberate attempt to wipe out any memory of Jerusalem and its religious significance for Jews as the holy city of pilgrimage. Jews were prohibited from living in the city or its environs, thus giving rise to a mass exodus to the north, where Rabbinic Judaism developed and flourished until the Muslim conquest in the seventh century.

There is some evidence of Christian pilgrimage to certain sites associated with the last days of Jesus during the second century, and the names of Christian bishops of Jerusalem from the early third century are known to us. They are typical of Syriac names known to us from Palmyra, suggesting that the Christian community in the pagan city was of non-Jewish extraction. Indeed, Jerusalem was eventually to be supplanted by Caesarea Maritima as the most important bishopric in Palestine, an indication that the city's older symbolic role and association with Jesus had given way to the practical realities of the day. Unlike Aelia, Caesarea was an urbane centre of learning, and its bishop was the metropolitan of Palestine until the Council of Chalcedon in 451 c.e. Origen, the famous Christian theologian-philosopher from Alexandria, and some time after him, Eusebius, the Church historian both operated in Caesarea, and the latter was bishop in the city in the early fourth century.

More important than the minimal Christian presence in the pagan city of Aelia was the way in which Jerusalem and its fate were viewed by Christian apologists such as Justin Martyr, Irenaeus and Origen in their debates with and about Jews throughout the second and early third centuries. Justin was born and grew up in Palestine and in his *Dialogue with Trypho*, ('Trypho' being a real or imaginary Jew) we catch a glimpse of what Jerusalem could mean to Jews and Christians alike in this period. Trypho puts the question: 'Tell me then do you really believe that this place, Jerusalem, will be rebuilt, and do you expect that your people will be gathered together and rejoice with the messiah, with the patriarchs and the prophets, with the saints of our nation and those who have become proselytes before your messiah came?' (*Dialogue with Trypho*, 80, 4). This question suggests that for some Jews at least the idea of a restored Jerusalem where the ancestors would be gathered together was one answer to the crisis of identity they were experiencing in the mid-second century after the defeat and humiliation of the second revolt, the leader of which had been hailed as messiah, by one of the great Rabbis of the day, Rabbi Aqiba. Justin's reply is equally interesting from a Christian perspective: 'I and others who are right thinking Christians on all points are convinced that there will be a resurrection of the dead and a thousand year period in which Jerusalem will be rebuilt adorned and enlarged as the prophets, Ezechiel and Isaiah and others declare.'(*Dialogue* 80, 5). Some

Christians, therefore, were still sharing in the Jewish hopes of restoration here on earth to which the rebuilding of Jerusalem would be central, and Justin draws on the notion of the thousand year reign that was spoken of in the Revelation of John in order to explain how this would come about. He and Trypho differed only as to who would share in this earthly kingdom centred on Jerusalem and whether or not Jesus was the messiah who would inaugurate this future restoration.

Another early apologist, Irenaeus bishop of Lyon, had been born in Asia Minor and had travelled to Rome as a young man, and later still to Lyon in Gaul (France). Central to Irenaeus' synthesis of theology was his doctrine of the recapitulation or restoration of all things in Christ as the final act of the eschatological drama already unfolding in history, a notion that he developed from the Letter to the Ephesians, where the cosmic role of Christ, as the image of God in salvation, is outlined. For Irenaeus, however, this restoration takes place here on earth, basing himself on several passages from the Israelite prophets, especially Ezechiel and Isaiah. He even interprets Paul's reference to the heavenly and earthly Jerusalem within this framework. What Paul really meant, according to Irenaeus, was that the Jerusalem below would be rebuilt 'after the pattern of Jerusalem above,' (*Adv. Haer.* 5, 35.2), thus collapsing Paul's contrast between the two Jerusalems. Likewise, he believed that the reference in Revelation 21 to the new Jerusalem coming down from heaven really refers to a Jerusalem here on earth.

Both these early thinkers reflect a situation in which Christian theology is still greatly influenced by Jewish messianic ideas and hopes, despite the historical experiences of the contemporary Jerusalem, as a pagan city, whose ancient name is scarcely known, so successful had the Roman policy been in obliterating its memory. It must be said that neither negotiated successfully the difficulties of taking the scriptural prophecies literally, when speaking of God's final plan for the universe.

To the extent that they expected to see these prophecies realised within this world, there was a danger of restricting them to some purely historical occurrence, thereby jeopardising the definitive and ultimate nature of Christian belief about Christ and his Second Coming. It was the brilliant Alexandrian theologian, Origen, a generation after Justin and Irenaeus, who recognised the need to find a different way of understanding the ancient Scriptures and their promises about Jerusalem. As an Alexandrian he was heir to a rich tradition of allegorical or figurative interpretation of ancient texts from Homer to the Bible, which avoided the necessity of understanding all their utterances about the gods and their actions literally. This same approach had been adopted by the Jewish philosopher/theologian, Philo, in Alexandria, and Origen was familiar with his work on the Bible.

Origen was one of the outstanding scholars of his own or any age. He debated with the Rabbis, knew Hebrew as well as Greek, and recognised the necessity of understanding the meaning of texts in their original language if they are to be used for theological argument. He fully acknowledged that the Hebrew Scriptures were first and foremost about the relation of the people of Israel with the land of Israel under God. He maintained, however, that when one reads the prophecies and their elevated tones one has to ask whether they are intended solely for this people or whether they have a spiritual meaning that transcends their literal application. In several instances he develops this spiritual sense in dealing with passages of Scripture that refer to the future of Jerusalem. Thus, for example, a passage from the Song of Songs, 'I am very dark and comely O Daughters of Jerusalem' (1, 5), was used by a contemporary Rabbi to refer to builders of Jerusalem, by developing a play on the Hebrew words for daughter and builder, which sound similar, so that the passage is made to refer to the rebuilding of Jerusalem and the restoration of Israel in line with Jewish hopes. For Origen, however, the passage refers to the Queen of Sheba who came to Jerusalem to visit Solomon and receive of his wisdom: 'She came to Jerusalem, the vision of peace,' (playing on one derivation of the name from *shalom*, Hebrew for peace), he writes, 'with a great following and in great array, for she came not with a single nation as did the synagogue that was before her that was made up only of Hebrews, but with the races of the whole world ... This black and beautiful one comes to the heavenly Jerusalem, and enters the vision of peace.' He then goes on to cite Paul's reference to 'the Jerusalem that is above' from Galatians, and deduces that the Song of Songs must be speaking of the 'free Jerusalem' that calls everyone through faith. It is only she who can be the mother of us all.[5]

This spiritual interpretation of Origen was a clear break with the more literal meaning of earlier apologists and even with some of his own contemporaries. What disturbed him most was the fact that, if the literal understanding of these prophecies was adhered to, the coming of Christ could not be understood as the beginning of the messianic age. That would be unthinkable to his Christian faith, despite his appreciation of and association with the Rabbis of his day. Instead of beginning with the scriptural prophecies and understanding these literally, Origen believed that there was a more important fact to be remembered, namely, the history of Jesus of Nazareth, which was to be the key for discovering the true or fuller meaning of the scriptural texts. Thus, Origen provided a new framework for understanding the Hebrew Bible within a Christian context. He was able to do so because his own intellectual background as an Alexandrian provided him with the respectable interpretative tools to search for the fuller meaning of Scripture. In the hands of less subtle or well informed minds than his, this was a dangerous instrument, since it has provided Christian theologians down to our own day with a means of by-passing the religious experience and hopes of Israel, often denigrating them in the process. At the same time, Origen's insistence in one of his most famous works, the *Contra Celsum*, on the person and history of Jesus of Nazareth over against the fictive Jewish objector whom Celsus, a pagan writer, uses to denigrate Jesus, was to prepare the way for a different type of Christian attachment to the holy city and the land of Israel. The importance of past historical events, and not the expectation of some future fulfillment, determined the theological significance of the theatre where those events occurred. Thus arose the notion of the Christian, as distinct from the Jewish, 'holy land.'

3. The Christian Rediscovery of Jerusalem after Constantine

This brief sketch of Christian involvement with Jerusalem has so far encountered two Roman emperors and the effects of their policies towards Jerusalem on Jews and Christians alike, namely, Titus who destroyed it and Hadrian who transformed it into the pagan colony of Aelia Capitolina. The final stage of our journey has a third emperor as its focus, namely Constantine, whose victory over his rival, Maxentius, at the Milvian Bridge in Rome in 312 c.e, which was to make him the sole ruler of the empire, east and west, was reputedly achieved under the Christian sign of the Cross. The edict of Milan tolerating all religions, but favouring Christianity in particular, followed in 314 c.e. Thereafter, Christianity was to be aggressively adopted as the official religion of the empire, for political as much as for religious reasons, it must be said, and a new era opened up for Christians everywhere, especially in Palestine itself. Inevitably this would give rise to new thinking about Jerusalem and its place within Christian imagination and piety.

We are fortunate that as far as Palestine was concerned we have the detailed accounts of one of the chief participants of the events from a Christian perspective, Eusebius of Caesarea's three works, *Life of Constantine, Ecclesiastical History* and *In Praise of Constantine*. As the official court historian, Eusebius paints Constantine in the most glowing colours. His coming is seen as a divine intervention, virtually a new incarnation of the eternal *logos* – scarcely the material of sober biography. Nevertheless, the information we can glean from Eusebius about the emergence of a Christian Jerusalem is highly significant. In an early, apologetic work (*Evangelical Demonstrations*) he mentions Christian pilgrims going to Bethlehem, but their only reason to visit Jerusalem was 'not because of the glory of Jerusalem, nor to worship in the ancient temple at Jerusalem, but that they may know that the city was occupied and devastated as the prophets had foretold, and that they may worship at the Mount of Olives opposite the city.' (6, 18). In other words, at that stage Jerusalem was merely a negative symbol for Christians.

Things were to change rapidly after Constantine's success, however. Whereas heretofore emperors built temples to the pagan gods in gratitude for their victories, now churches were being built, and lavishly endowed, St John Lateran in Rome being the first, followed by St Peter's on the Vatican hill. Once his rival in the east was conquered in 324 c.e. Constantine was sole ruler of the Roman world and immediately set about building a new city, Constantinople, to celebrate his triumph, adorning it, not with images of the pagan gods, but with those of Christian martyrs. Soon he set his sights on Jerusalem, possibly under the influence of the Bishop of Jerusalem who had attended the council of Nicea in 325, and whose special status was recognised by the fathers of the Council, 'because of custom and ancient tradition.' He was determined to turn Jerusalem into a 'memorial' and a 'sign' of Christ's death and its efficacy, and Eusebius speaks of his desire 'to adorn this holy place, which from the beginning was holy and now appears more holy because it has been brought to life proud of the existence of the Saviour.' In order to underline this holiness of the places where important events of Christ's life took place, Eusebius speaks of the cave of Bethlehem where Christ was born, the cave of the Mount of Olives from where he ascended and the 'most sacred cave of his burial.' The designation of these places as caves is interesting since they are not so described in the Gospel accounts. However, caves were understood in the ancient world as 'sacred precincts' and undoubtedly, Eusebius is echoing this belief in his description of the places associated with Christ's life.[6]

However, it was through the building of churches at these caves that Constantine sought to give due honour to the new awareness of the sanctity of place in Christianity. The legend of the discovery of the cave of Christ's burial, under the pagan temple at the site, was 'contrary to every expectation,' something that seems unlikely in view of the evidence for some Christian pilgrimage to Jerusalem in earlier centuries. The likelihood must be that there were older traditions about the place of Jesus' burial, going back to the earliest Jewish-Christian community in Jerusalem, and possibly hinted at in the Gospel stories of the women visiting the tomb of Christ. Eusebius, in common with early Christian usage elsewhere about the burial places of holy people, also calls the church a *martyrion*, or place of witness. Constantine, no doubt under the promptings of Helena, his mother, who had visited Palestine shortly before her death in 329 out of motives of genuine Christian piety, told Eusebius that he wanted the tomb of the holy sepulchre to 'surpass the most beautiful buildings in every city.' Certainly, as described by Eusebius, the Church of the Anastasis, or Resurrection, as it was called, seems to have measured up to this hope. Eusebius describes it as follows:

> The interior surface of the building was hidden under slabs of multi-coloured marble. The exterior aspect of walls embellished with well-matched and polished stones, gave an effect of extraordinary beauty, which yielded nothing to the appearance of the marble. As to its roofing the outside was covered with lead, a sure protection against the winter rains; the inside of the roof was decorated with sculpted coffering, which, like some great ocean, covered the whole basilica with its endless swell, while the brilliant gold with which it was covered, made the whole temple sparkle with a thousand reflections. (*Life of Constantine*, 3,36)

The description of the place as a temple had of course a theological point to make. This new building with its imposing structure stood across the Tyropaean valley from the temple mount that now lay totally in ruins, a painful reminder to Jews of their history, and fully exploited by Christian apologists from Justin onwards as a sign of God's punishment for their obstinacy, as had been predicted by Christ. The point is that for Christians the ruins of the temple were in danger of becoming part of their own triumphalist theology of being the true Judaism or the replacement Judaism, once they began to enjoy the special favour of the Roman emperor. Even the design of the building was a subtle, but definite replication of the ordering of sacred space associated with the temple, with the notion of progressive holiness as one moves from the exterior to the interior. We can piece together the details of the layout and structure from various references in Eusebius' writings. In fact the Church of the Anastasis consisted of several buildings, comprising four main elements: 1) an entrance atrium surrounded by colonnades; 2) a basilica or *martyrion* with four rows of columns and an apse; 3) west of the basilica was an open courtyard with colonnades along three of its walls, and 4) a rotunda with twelve columns and three entrances covering the tomb itself, after the fashion of a mausoleum. Archaeological soundings underneath various parts of the present structure have uncovered various elements of the Constantinian structure, and in particular it is clear that the rock, which currently is identified as the rock of Golgotha, the place of crucifixion according to John 19, 17, was part of a large quarry that had been cut away at the time of Constantine. There is some divergence among the archaeologists as to the precise details of the rotunda and the open garden or atrium in front of it. These are due to the fact that only fragments of the Constantinian structure have been preserved, and some of these are no longer in their original positions, but have been reused in later constructions, first in the seventh century and later again in the twelfth by the crusaders. Sufficient is known, however, to allow us to discern Constantine's intentions and the importance to the original architects of both the Golgotha rock and the tomb within the rotunda (described by the pilgrim Egeria in the fifth century already). We can safely say that *for these fourth-century Christians*, this was indeed the location where the events of Christ's death and burial were believed to have occurred. It should be noted that while the site was well within the walls of Aelia, it was outside the walls of Herodian Jerusalem, as we would expect for both public execution and burials.

While the Church of the Anastasis was undoubtedly the centrepiece of the Constantinian Christianisation of Jerusalem, making its own architectural as well as theological point, the other church mentioned by Eusebius was the Eleona on the Mount of Olives, again over the mystic cave there 'as a memorial of his Ascension into heaven.' By the time of Egeria's visit (c. 400 c.e) some of the ceremonies of Easter were conducted there. Bethlehem was the third 'sacred cave' over which a church was built in the Constantinian period at the instigation of Helena. Gradually, however, other memorials were also built, as the notion of Jerusalem as a holy city for Christians began to extend itself to include the land of Israel. Sites that had no direct link with the life of Jesus were included, such as Hebron, because of its association with the Patriarchs. The influx of pilgrims to Palestine began to increase considerably and we have various accounts that give us some insights into the extent and rapidity of the change in the landscape: the anonymous pilgrim of Bordeaux (333), Egeria (c. 380) and the Piacenza pilgrim (570 c.e) as well as the letters of St Jerome. Traces of monasteries are to be found everywhere, especially in the desert regions surrounding Jerusalem. More churches began to be built in Jerusalem itself: Mount Zion already c. 340 c.e. at the alleged site of the last supper, and later the famous Nea Church dedicated by the emperor Justinian in 543 c.e. In particular the deposed empress Eudoxia, who came to Palestine in 444 c.e. after her banishment in a family feud at Constantinople, wielded enormous power and supported the monks. She herself became embroiled in doctrinal disputes about the nature of Christ, which gave rise to different theological traditions about the person of Christ in Eastern Christianity. Eudoxia was reconciled to the 'orthodox' position as defined by the councils of Chalcedon and Constantinople, and she had a great church erected to St Stephen, north of the Damascus gate, the church that is now located in the grounds of the Dominican École Biblique. Though quite foreign to our modern perceptions, the involvement of imperial power in the doctrinal disputes of Eastern Christianity tells its own story of the original reason for Constantine's acceptance of the Christian religion. The hope was that it might provide a unifying force for the empire, as pagan culture had lost its appeal for the masses and ethnic diversity began to be manifested. It is ironic that by the end of the Byzantine period these ethnic differences between Syrians, Armenians, Copts, Greeks and Latins were most obvious in the very place where unity was to be hoped for, the Christian Church. Regrettably they are nowhere more evident today than in the Church of the Anastasis, Constantine's symbol of a unified empire under a unified God. The different and often conflicting claims of these branches of Christianity to control of the building, even today, constitute a symbol of the failure of both imperial politics and ecclesiastical connivance, at the very place intended to honour the memory of him who challenged those very structures of State and Church.

Meantime, Jewish culture had begun to be revitalised in Galilee, with the emergence of many synagogue communities and Rabbinical schools after the failure of the Bar Cochba revolt in 135 c.e. The great foundation book of Judaism, the Mishnah, was edited at Sepphoris in Galilee about the year 200, and the Palestinian Talmud, a massive commentary on the Mishnah, a synthesis of Rabbinical learning and scriptural instruction, as well as various scriptural commentaries, was achieved over the next two hundred years, probably at Tiberias. This flowering of Rabbinical learning in Palestine, as well as the remains of many synagogues dating from the fourth to the seventh century, show that despite the

Christianisation of the Holy Land in the Byzantine period, Judaism was still able to flourish there. Indeed a careful reading of many of these writings suggests that there may have been much more contact between Jews and Christians than one might suspect from the polemical stances on both sides.[7] Together, Talmud and Tanach, Rabbinic teaching and Hebrew Bible, constitute the pillars of Judaism to the present day. For one brief moment in the mid-fourth century, Constantine's nephew, Julian, reverted to paganism (c. 350) and sought to embarrass the Christians by having the temple in Jerusalem rebuilt, thus seeking to falsify the prophecies on which so much Christian apologetic had been based. Julian's efforts failed, as he was killed in a battle with the Persians on the eastern frontier. Thereafter, Jewish remembrance of Jerusalem and its temple had to rely on the strength of their religious imagination. It is a remarkable fact that a large percentage of the Mishnah, which purports to lay out the details of an observant Jewish life, concerns itself with minutiae of the temple and its ritual, even though the building was in ruins and without any prospect of being rebuilt or its cult restored. Gradually also, synagogue art, forbidden in an earlier time, began to depict scenes that were reminiscent of the temple and its cult. Central to many of these representations is the of Abraham's attempted sacrifice of Isaac, an event which according to the Biblical story of Genesis 22 had occurred on Mount Moriah, a place which later Jewish legend identified with Jerusalem.

Conclusion

The account of Jerusalem in Christian imagination and piety has much to teach us, as Christians everywhere once again focus on Jerusalem in this Jubilee year. It is central to our memory and hope also, not in the way that it was and is central to Judaism and Islam also, but filled with bitter-sweet memories nonetheless. From the beginning Christianity did not see itself tied to a sacred place, even though its deep roots within Jewish piety and hope are clearly to be seen as late as the second century in the idea of a new Jerusalem here on earth. From that perspective the heavenly Jerusalem had greater symbolic potential for the inner life of Christianity, while the painful memory of Jesus' rejection in Jerusalem gave vent to bitter attacks on those who controlled its religious institutions. The rediscovery of Jerusalem for Christians in the age of Constantine was prompted by an interest in the founding events of Christianity and the memory of Jesus. Unfortunately, however, it was not the Jesus who dared to challenge the centre with the prophetic vision from the margins that was recovered. Rather, the memory was tainted from the start by the imperialist ambitions of those who propagated it, so that the Christ of the Anastasis was soon to become the *Pantocrator,* or universal ruler, whose embodiment on earth was not the humble Galilean Jesus, but the militant, imperialist Constantine. Reading the accounts of the various pilgrims, it is noteworthy that Galilee is bypassed for the most part in their journeys, partly, no doubt because of the strong Jewish presence there in the Byzantine period, as we learn from modern archaeology of the region, but also because the centre, Jerusalem, and the triumph it symbolized, was more attractive, now that Christians were in the ascendancy. The wolf and the lamb had indeed lain down together, but the latter was in serious danger of being devoured by the former.

We are creatures of space as well as of time, and memories are only possible when they are given a place to which they can be attached. It is highly important that all remembering, collective and individual, should be critical, and that we do not fall foul to the temptation of selective memory. At its most profound level the new Jerusalem is indeed a powerful symbol of togetherness for the Abrahamic religions – Jews, Christians and Muslims – and those who are influenced by the cultures they have given rise to in our secular age. As envisaged in the Book of Revelation, there are to be no divisions within the city, its gates are open and face the four compass points, ready to receive all comers. If this picture is not to be dismissed as utopian fantasy it needs the counterbalancing historical memory of prophetic voices, like that of Jesus, who refuses to allow any centre, religious or political, to obstruct the simple, but profoundly difficult, challenge of loving our neighbour as ourselves, and translating that into a caring justice for all, especially those on the margins.

Notes

1. John Louis Martyn, *Theological Issues in the Letters of Paul,* (Edinburgh: T. and T. Clark, 2000), 25-36.
2. For an excellent discussion of the symbolic significance of Jerusalem see Peter Söllner, *Jerusalem, die hochgebaute Stadt. Eschatologisches und Himmlisches Jerusalem im Früjudentum und im frühen Christentum,* (Tübingen: Franke Verlag, 1998).
3. See Sean Freyne, 'Reading Hebrews and Revelation intertextually,' in S. Draisma, *Intertextuality in Ancient Writings. Essays in Honour of Bas van Iersel,* (Kampen: J.H. Kok, 1989), pp 83-94.

4.   For a detailed account of the archaeology of Aelia in the Roman and Byzantine periods see *The New Encyclopedia of Archaeological Excavations in the Holy Land*, 4 vols., ed. E Stern, (Jerusalem: The Israel Exploration Society, 1993). The best guide with an excellent historical perspective, in several revised editions, is that of Jerome Murphy-O'Connor, *The Holy Land. An Archaeological Guide from Earliest Times to 1700*, (Oxford: Oxford University Press, 1992).

5.   Robert L. Wilkin, *The Land Called Holy. Palestine in Christian History and Thought*, (New Haven: Yale University Press, 1992), especially 65-78. Wilkin's study is a learned but readable account of the development of the idea of a Christian Holy Land, to which I am indebted for this section of the paper.

6.   Wilkin, *The Land Called Holy*, 83-100; See also the highly informative historical account of Günther Stemberger, *Jews and Christians in the Holy Land. Palestine in the Fourth Century*, (Edinburgh: T. and T. Clark, 2000), 48-85.

7.   The account by Jewish scholar, Jacob Neusner, *Judaism and Christianity in the Age of Constantine*, (Chicago: the University of Chicago Press, 1987) is a fascinating discussion of this relationship.

4

READING THE GOSPELS IN THE LIGHT OF THE 'WINDOW OF THE EVANGELISTS' AT CHARTRES CATHEDRAL

Recent studies of the Gospels have canvassed the aid of both ancient literary comparisons and modern literary theories in their efforts to define the Gospel genre more precisely. In casting their nets so widely, New Testament critics may well be guilty of ignoring the more obvious source of literary and theological inspiration available to the early Christians, namely, the Hebrew Scriptures, particularly in view of the task they undertook as 'eyewitnesses and ministers of the word'. Recently, I was reminded of that fact on revisiting Chartres Cathedral where the 'Window of the Evangelists' stands out even in such an array of stunning stained-glass creations of medieval artists. Could it be, I asked myself, that the medieval artists who designed and executed the window had a better appreciation of the Gospel writers' intentions than we modern and post-modern critics? The visit certainly prompted me to view again the Gospel stories with a fresh eye under the direction of the Chartres artists.[1]

The window consists of a circular centrepiece in the upper section that depicts the Risen Christ in glory surrounded by the twelve apostles. Underneath are five panels – a central one consists of the virgin and child, flanked on either side by two panels, each with a giant-sized figure carrying a dwarf on his shoulders. These figures are identified as prophets and evangelists in the following pairings: Mark is carried by Daniel, Matthew by Isaiah, John by Ezechiel and Luke by Jeremiah.

Two features of this depiction struck me as particularly interesting in the light of current theological discussions. Firstly, there is the conscious juxtaposition of the Jesus of history (the child and its mother) and the Risen Christ encircled by the Twelve on the central axis of the window, an acknowledgment of the common Christian confession to which David Tracy has recently drawn our attention: 'we believe in Jesus Christ with the apostles.'[2] Even more striking is the portrayal of the evangelists as dwarfs being carried on the shoulders of the prophets, depicted as giants. This provocative presentation challenges the canonical triumphalism of much early Christian exegesis, encapsulated in the dictum: 'Novum in Vetere latet; Vetus in Novo patet'. ('The New lays hidden in the Old and the Old becomes clear in the New'). The depiction was apparently provoked by a saying first attributed to John of Salisbury, (1115-80) which thereafter became a commonplace in the medieval schools, as Europe rediscovered its lost heritage after the Dark Ages: 'We today are carried forward on the shoulders of the giants of the past; we can see farther because we have been raised higher'. The Christocentrism of the Canon gives way here to a humanistic principle that all our knowledge is indeed dependent on prior knowledge, a principle that is deemed to have been as operative at the Christian 'turn of the ages' as at any other period of human history.

Such a provocative rethinking of the relationship of the New Testament to the Old prompts a further exploration of the individual pairings of prophets and evangelists. Recent discussions of intertextuality seek to avoid reducing this approach to the reading of texts in the light of other texts to source-criticism under another name. It is claimed that since all writing partakes of the pool of human language, individual authors inevitably draw on previous articulations and expressions, even when these are no longer explicitly recalled or recognised. This might appear to be stating the obvious, but critics such as Jonathan Culler are prepared to allow for some narrowing of the focus in order to make intertextual reading a meaningful exercise.[3] In the following discussion we shall follow this lead, not seeking to establish genetic relationships between the respective prophets and evangelists – though in some instances this cannot be denied – but concentrating instead on aspects of the later works that are provoked by a conscious recalling of the prophetic voices, as suggested by the designers of the window. By following the lead of the medieval artists we hope to experience the different evangelical pictures with a sharpened appreciation of their vision and perspective. From this discussion it will, I believe, emerge that however much the various Gospels can be compared with other Greco-

Roman literary productions of their period, in the first instance their writers shared in the discursive practices of the Israelite prophetic tradition, and that means partaking in the literary as well as the theological practices of those precursors.

Daniel and Mark

Markan studies have identified the apocalyptic traits of the earliest Gospel with its frequent overt allusions to the Book of Daniel. However, there has been little exploration of the various elements of the Markan story against the backdrop of Daniel, the most complete literary prototype of an apocalyptic writing within the Hebrew Bible.[4] At the level of source criticism Daniel, it is generally recognised, has drawn on two quite discrete collections of court tales and visionary accounts. At the narrative level, however, these supplement each other in terms of the overall, dramatic effect of the work.[5] In the early chapters Daniel's faithful adherence to his Jewish faith in an alien environment shares the backward-looking dimension of all narrative. Set in the Babylonian/Persian period, the central character, Daniel, shows himself to be truly wise, and his readiness to suffer for his particular beliefs marks him out as the heroic figure who is rewarded both by the gift of mantic wisdom (interpretation of dreams) and a special insight into the divine plan for history – God's secret mystery (Dn, chs 2-6). His God is 'the God of Gods' and 'the revealer of Mysteries'. Indeed, there is the suggestion that Daniel should be treated as a god because of his wondrous powers, only for him to be subsequently cast into the lion's den because of his refusal to obey the royal edict prohibiting prayer to his God. Confronted either by adulation or torture, Daniel, as the truly wise one (*maskîl*), remains faithful to his God, deeply conscious as he is that God alone is the source of his powers, and that this God will vindicate him in the end for his constancy.

Vindication does come to Daniel within the narrative in terms of the visionary experiences of the second half of the book (chs 7-12). Daniel's ascetical life-style expressed through prayer and fasting marked him out as 'a man of God', a worthy recipient of special divine communications on behalf of others, who like himself are wise (*maskîlîm*) and who endure suffering for their beliefs. Thus, his role changes from that of exemplary figure to representative. Already in the opening chapter Daniel's friends also share the epithet 'wise ones' (Dn 1: 4. 17) and in the latter half of the book their numbers are widened to those whose role it is to instruct the people in wisdom and who through suffering for their beliefs will be rewarded with astral immortality (Dn 11:35; 12:2f). Thus, the wisdom of

Daniel, though highlighting his miraculous powers in the court tales, is much more inclusive, embracing God's total plan for history, especially in regard to his elect – the people of the saints of the Most High.

When one approaches the Markan Jesus with the figure of Daniel fresh to the mind's eye certain aspects of the portrayal claim the reader's attention in a particular way. To begin with, Mark's narrative falls into two distinct sections, similar in structure to the earlier text. Jesus, like Daniel, is also a heroic figure, not in the context of a royal court, but in situations where evil powers control the lives of people. His triumphs are attributed to his wisdom (*sophia*, Mk 6, 2), and are signs of the arrival of God's kingdom and the collapse of Satan's power (Mk 1, 14f; 3, 22). The second half of the work is also revelatory, but in a way that differs from the Book of Daniel. The secret plan of God (*mysterion*, Mk 4:10) is disclosed not through revelations to be written down by the main character, but through his actions, something that is presupposed in the case of Daniel also, though not explicitly narrated. True, two apocalyptically coloured scenes, both with clear allusions to the Book of Daniel – the Transfiguration (Mk 9:2-9; cf. Dn 10, 1-19) and the farewell discourse (Mk 13; cf. Dn 7, 15) – bracket the narrative of Jesus' journey to suffering and vindication at Jerusalem, thereby alerting the reader to the triumph that will eventually ensue. Yet the revelation that the author/narrator wishes to highlight is not in the first instance that of the future victory, though that is clearly envisaged in imagery borrowed from Daniel (Mk 13:20; 14:61). Rather, the disclosure occurs in the midst of the present distress (Mk 10: 46-50; 15:39). This changed perspective from future victory to present trials was the direct result of Mark's recalling the actual fate of Jesus at the hands of the Romans, as distinct from the fictional tales about Daniel's treatment in the Persian court. Yet Mark, like Daniel, views this present as meaningful only in the light of God's total victory, which – his apocalyptically inspired faith assures him – is imminent.

Although prayer and fasting are common to both works, yet again an interesting contrast emerges with regard to the role of these ascetical practices. In the Book of Daniel they reflect the sense of awe and reverence required when confronted with the holiness of God's revealing presence (2:28; 6:11; 9:3.20; 10:2-4), whereas in Mark it is at moments of crisis that they occur. Jesus' prayer occurs not at times of divine disclosure, but at moments of failure among the disciples (1:35; 6:46; 14:32), and fasting is a necessary preparation for a successful encounter in the present with the evil one, both for Jesus and for his disciples: (1:13;

2:20 ; 9: 29). In the one instance the victory to come over evil powers is being revealed, while in the other the struggle to achieve that victory is already taking place and human agency is being sorely tried. Yet both works are confident as to eventual outcome, based on the shared belief in a God who is faithful to his promises.

Similar features of both documents highlight this shared insight, especially regarding the hidden, mysterious nature of the revelation being granted. In the Book of Daniel this effect is achieved through the frequent allusion to writing and written messages that call for decoding in the visionary second part of the book (7, 10; 10, 21; 12, 9). Yet the reader has been reassured that Daniel is capable of achieving this task, because he has shown himself to be endowed with such interpretative powers in the earlier part of the book already (5, 17). In Mark's Gospel also the need for understanding what has been written is stressed, – 'Let the reader understand' (13, 17) – an injunction that applies not just to the 'little apocalypse' (Mk 13), but to the whole work as the record of the advent of God's kingly rule in an through the career of Jesus. Throughout the narrative Jesus himself acts as the interpreting angel of the hidden meanings of his deeds and words (4, 13.33; 7, 17; 8, 14-21). As recipients of this secret revelation, the Markan disciples are expected to form an interpretative community – in deed and word – of the events they have been privy to. Their future role is, therefore, akin to that of the *'maskîley 'am'*, instructors of the people of the Book of Daniel.[6] Yet, ironically, unlike their prototypes, they show themselves to be ill-prepared for such a future role, abandoning Jesus at the hour of crisis as he is about to encounter the imperial power of Rome (14, 40), and leaving their future uncertain, shrouded in a mysterious announcement of an encounter to come in Galilee, that is couched in apocalyptic imagery (fear, white robes, visionary experience) redolent of many of the angelic appearances in the Book of Daniel.

While Mark's Gospel is thoroughly imbued with the classic apocalyptic dualism of 'present evil age' and 'future good age,' there has been considerable discussion as to how the designation 'apocalyptic' might best be applied to the work as a whole. Gospels have a backward orientation as well as a present and future dimension, whereas Apocalypses are freed from this 'historical' requirement and are totally oriented to the future.[7] Yet, the Book of Daniel too, as we have seen, does look backwards, however fictitiously, through the court tales, to the Babylonian and Persian periods, as well as being concerned with present tribulation and future vindication. Thus, the matter of defining genres precisely according to formal criteria calls for a flexible approach. Our reading of both works together suggests that they have much more in common than a mere listing of isolated allusions to the Book of Daniel in Mark's Gospel might suggest, something, one suspects, the artist who conceived the Chartres window may have been intuitively aware.

Isaiah and Matthew

Unlike the modern biblical critic, both Matthew and the designer(s) of the Chartres window read Isaiah as a single work. It is remarkable how resistant we are to thinking of the book other than in terms of First, Second and Third Isaiah, each assigned to different historical epochs. Undoubtedly, our modern historical awareness has helped enormously to illumine this collection of prophetic oracles. Yet, when read as a whole it does disclose a coherent point of view on Israel's relationship with her God – and it is this storyline that gives unity to the whole. We move from an intermingling of oracles of messianic blessing and judgment (part one), to a sense of triumphant restoration through exile and suffering (part two), to a sober reflection on the current ills that beset the community as it encounters 'let down' from the peak experience of restoration while seeking to keep alive the messianic vision for all Israel (part three). This story is embedded, loosely to be sure, in a plot that has various historical characters (Ahaz and Cyrus) and some that are not clearly identifiable (the Servant of Yahweh), but from the point of view of subsequent readers the fact that we are dealing with over two centuries of Israelite history under Assyrian, Babylonian and Persian rule, makes no difference to the unity in the message conveyed: Israel's destiny depends on her response to God's saving action, which is mediated through the historical circumstances of her existence among the nations.

Matthew, as a scribe trained for the kingdom, develops a similar line in changed historical circumstances. His plot becomes the cipher through which the same divine purpose is re-enacted. The historical rejection of Jesus and the destruction of the temple in Jerusalem, together with the subsequent world mission, are all read as one story of messianic visitation, leading to purification of a remnant through suffering, but rejection of unfaithful Israel, followed by a call to the restored community to live out the messianic ideal in the present. In bringing together into one story line the experiences of Jesus as remembered by his followers and those of his own community in the wake of the post-70 Jewish experience, Matthew achieves the same temporal ellipse as does Isaiah in its final form. From the point of view of God's purpose for Israel in history both can justifiably bring together events of different historical periods into one over-arching plot to illustrate the continuity of the divine plan at work in history.

As is well known, of all the Gospels Matthew's is the one that most self-consciously alludes to the Hebrew Scriptures, with its repeated (thirteen times in all) formula of fulfillment of Scripture. Among these texts six are explicit references to the prophet Isaiah: 3:3; 4:14; 8:17; 12:17; 13:14; 15:7, in contrast to a single mention of Jeremiah (27:9) – the only other Old Testament prophet to be mentioned explicitly. Of the other scriptural allusions, two (Mt 1:23 and 21:4) are non-attributed citations from Isaiah 7:14 and 62:11 respectively. On purely statistical grounds, therefore, we would have to conclude that Isaiah is the Gospel of Matthew's main point of reference and source of inspiration, while acknowledging that for him, the whole of 'the law and the prophets' can be read prophetically (Mt 11:17).

As in the case of Mark's Gospel an intertextual reading should, however, be concerned with more than mere statistics. Can we claim that Matthew's retelling of the Jesus story has consciously or unconsciously been shaped in its totality by his use of Isaian codes? Does our understanding of the flow of the Matthean narrative improve through a reading of the Gospel that is prompted by the prophetic text? A number of themes come to mind as controlling the whole Isaian work and they are closely interrelated and reworked in the prophetic imagination even if they may have been drawn from quite disparate traditional motifs. These are, the divine protection of Mount Zion, the emergence of a remnant that would be faithful, and the unique role that was to be attributed to Yahweh's anointed. True, this latter element is suppressed to some extent in the second and third parts of the book, but the roles of Cyrus and of the Prophet, both designated as the Lord's anointed (Is 45:1; 61:1), only serve to show how elastic the notion could be in different contexts, thus opening imaginatively the way for its unexpected application in the Gospel of Matthew. The book as a whole opens and closes with poems concerning the nations' pilgrimage to Mount Zion (Is 2:2-4 and 66:22-24, repeated at 49:18-26), there to learn the ways of Yahweh, in stark contrast to the counter image of their marching on the holy city to destroy it (Is 17:12-14; 10:27-34). The remnant theme provides the basis for the poet's on-going trust in Yahweh, and it receives further elaboration in both the Servant Songs of Isaiah 40-55 (The so-called Book of Consolation) and in the programme for the restored community's witness in the final part of the work (chs 56-66).

The profile of the ideal king that is developed in Isaiah 11:1-9 has a strong ethical dimension 'giving his verdict with equity for the poor of the land', and the law that goes forth from Zion is envisaged as having a universal significance, not just for Israel but for the nations as well (Is 2:3). Once again this theme also finds expression through the figure of the Servant who is described as a 'light for the nations', (Is 49:6). In the closing scene the gathering of the nations is presented as an eschatological reversal of the tower of Babel with the creation of a new heaven and new earth (Is 66:18-24) with all peoples gathered around the God of Israel on his holy mountain.

This thematic reading of Isaiah from a holistic point of view has interesting possibilities for the Matthean perspective also, especially in view of the very clear points of contact indicated by the list of individual citations. The Gospel of Matthew, too, has a blending of the eschatological Zion and the royal Davidic traditions, but with the adaptation that now the holy mountain where David's son, Immanuel, can be encountered, and whence the law will go forth to all the nations is in Galilee, not Jerusalem (Mt 5: 1; 28:16). The nations – Israelite and non-Israelite – gather around the mountain of revelation to learn wisdom (4:26f.), but the words of Jesus, designated as Immanuel/Son of David must also go forth from the same mountain to all peoples (28:16) – a two-way traffic of the word, as Is 2, 2-4 indicates – suggesting the openness of a genuine conversation of sharing and enquiry.

Matthew repeatedly designates the new way as 'righteousness', a term that on the basis of Isaiah, among others, calls for as inclusive an understanding as possible, comprising peace, integrity, justice in the strict sense – in a word all the values necessary to bring about a restored and renewed cosmic order (Mt 3:15; 5:6.10.20; 6:1.33; see Is 11:4; 32:1-2.15; 58:1-12). The 'messianic miracle' occurs through the achievement of this new way of righteousness, which is also the way of wisdom that is vindicated by its works (Mt 11:17). The blessing of wisdom can be described as an opening of the eyes to see and of the ears to hear (Mt 13:14f; 11:5; see Is 32: 3-4) and the new vineyard of the Lord, unlike the old, will produce abundant fruits of righteousness (Mt 21:43; see Is 27:2-5).

There are other religious themes, symbolic expressions and ethical instruction which will strike the attentive reader of both texts. Such similarities should not obscure the fact that by our modern literary sensibilities we are dealing with two very different works – the one, a collection of oracles of salvation and judgment interspersed with some scattered biographical and historical information, and the other a narrative account of the life, death and resurrection of Jesus of Galilee, told from the perspective of the Matthean community's theological vision, social situation and historical experiences. Despite such differences, there can be little doubt that the designers of the Chartres window have pointed Christian readers in a very fruitful direction as they explore the thought world and symbolic vision of Matthew, the scribe trained for the kingdom, for whom the belief in the fulfillment of Isaiah's Immanuel prophecy in the career of Jesus (Mt 1, 17; 28, 24) has a controlling theological and, we maintain, literary influence.

Jeremiah and Luke

Of the four matching pairs, that of Jeremiah and Luke appears the least obvious at first sight, particularly in view of the fact that Matthew, and not Luke, is the only New Testament writer who makes explicit reference to Jeremiah (Lk 2:17; 16:14; 27:9). Nevertheless, the historical reflection that both writers have to deal with the trauma of the destruction of Jerusalem – by the Babylonians in 589 b.c.e. (Jeremiah) and by the Romans in 70 c.e. (Luke) – provides a starting point for a reading experiment of the two works. Luke's use of the Old Testament is more oblique than Matthew's, a mosaic of biblical allusions and imitations rather than explicit citations. In fact direct allusions to Jeremiah's text in Luke are less frequent than those to Isaiah, Ezechiel or Proverbs. Yet, as in the case of the other Gospels, statistics alone can be deceptive, and as an initial exploration, the contexts in which the Jeremiah allusions occur in Luke – prophetic calls of John and Jesus (Lk 1:38; 3:2; 4:6); the judgment on Jerusalem and the temple in particular (Lk 19:42, 46); and the making of the new covenant (Lk 22:19) – should be particularly noted.

Luke's story of Jesus is that of the prophet who is rejected as he journeys through the land calling for repentance, particularly in terms of justice for the poor. This call reaches its climax in Jerusalem where Jesus virtually 'takes over' the temple, only to be rejected by the religious leaders of the people who have him removed by the Romans as a political agitator (Lk 22:3). For Luke, Jesus is the prophet par excellence, who is prefigured by such Old Testament individuals as Elijah and Elisha. Could Jeremiah also be plausibly claimed as a precursor to this Lukan Jesus?

Many scholars have remarked on the significance of prophetic biography for the over-all message of the Book of Jeremiah.[8] For the first time in Israelite prophetic literature the prophet's life and fate enter into the message in an explicit way. It is not just that the narrative of Jeremiah's life provides settings for his various oracles and symbolic gestures; rather the account of his repeated rejection helps to highlight the underlying divine plan that is working itself out in and through his life's ordeals, as he utters his oracles of woe on Jerusalem. Thus, the so-called 'Deuteronomic influence' on Jeremiah finds expression in terms of the punishments that will be inflicted on Jerusalem and its leadership because of its refusal to listen to the prophet's warning call to conversion. The fall of Jerusalem enters the larger divine plan for history, therefore, rather than being viewed as direct punishment for Israel's failure.

Jeremiah's biography is certainly that of the rejected prophet – both by his own people of Anatoth and by the powers in the land (Jr 11:18-23; 18:18). A sense of bitterness comes through clearly in many of the oracles, which hover between self-doubt and self-pity as the prophet seeks to escape the inexorable will of Yahweh with little hope of relief. (Jr 4:19; 11:18-20). Thus, we are privy to Jeremiah's own internal drama. At one moment, Job-like, he wallows in self-pity; then he looks for revenge, and yet again he begs to be free of the burden of the prophet's call. Here we encounter the new challenge facing the prophetic vocation in his day, which required different resources of mind and heart in order to continue to proclaim the message of God's control of history against all appearances to the contrary, both internal and external. Some have even spoken of his faithful scribe Baruch's account of his trials and tribulations (Jr 36-42) as the 'passion' of Jeremiah. Yet this term could give the wrong impression, as though either Baruch or Jeremiah himself, saw any positive value either in the sufferings or in the way they were borne. Rather it is the underlying sense of rebellion that comes through, as Jeremiah finds the prophetic role making its very full demands, and he is less than convinced that he is capable of bearing the burdens of the office (Jr 20: 7.9; cf. 1:7-8).

Luke's story of Jesus is that of the rejected prophet also. He is already rejected at Nazareth among his own people at the outset of his journey, and like the other rejected prophets of Israel's history, including Jeremiah, this only served to broaden his horizons to include concern for all the nations in his purview (cf. Jr 1:5-10; 50-51). Yet it was in Jerusalem that the prophet must die since his fate was ultimately bound up with that of the holy city (Lk 13:33). It is there that Jesus' exodus must occur

(Lk 9:33), and so when the divine plan finally calls he steadfastly turns his face to go to the holy city (Lk 9:51; see 19:28). There, he too will discover the full demands of his prophetic calling in his great trial or agony (Lk 20: 39-46). Like Jeremiah, the focal point of his Jerusalem ministry is the temple (Lk 19:45-48; 21:5-7), and there he is rejected by the chief priests, the scribes and the elders of the people. Indeed Luke, like the other Gospel writers, echoes Jeremiah's condemnation of the temple as 'a den of thieves', thereby underlining the social exploitation of the poor by the rich of Jerusalem in his own day, which is such a central theme of the Lukan Jesus' teaching also. Yet, Luke does not apportion blame for the destruction of Jerusalem or the rejection of Jesus in the way that later Christian apologetic was to do. Rather, he highlights Jesus' lament for the city and its failure to recognise the things 'that are for its peace.'

The sufferings of the prophet Jesus are, in the Lukan perspective, to be understood in terms of the traditional fate of God's prophet, rather than as an atoning offering for sin following the pattern of Isaiah 53. Luke (24: 25-27) explains the suffering of Jesus as being in line with that which the Old Testament prophets had foretold – a necessary part of the divine plan for the Messiah to enter his glory (see also Lk 18:31). If Luke had Jeremiah in mind he certainly does not single him out for special mention, since for him the whole of the Hebrew Scriptures is prophetic. Nevertheless, the explicit linking of the fate of Jerusalem with that of Jesus the Messiah, prompts the consideration that Jeremiah and his story must have played a more prominent role in shaping Luke's account than one might infer from the number of explicit references to the prophetic text.

Our attention is focused particularly on the passages dealing with Jerusalem and its destruction, since that played such a central role in Jeremiah's message also. Luke has Jesus weep for the city as he comes in sight of it (Lk 19:41-44), while also foretelling its destruction in terms that echo Jeremiah, especially see chapter 26 (but also Jr 6:9-15 and 10:15). In that particular account, recalling the earlier temple speech of chapter 11, Jeremiah had addressed the whole people in the court of the temple, foretelling the utter destruction of the holy place, 'like Shiloh', unless they listened to the prophetic message concerning the law. This led to the sentence of death against Jeremiah from the priests and prophets which was subsequently endorsed by the leaders of the people, while others pointed to the fact that a similar prophecy of ruin had been uttered by previous prophets without their having to suffer for it. For Luke also, Jesus is not rejected by all the people, but only by its religious and lay leaders.

It is difficult to avoid the impression that this background has in some sense provoked Luke's treatment of Jesus' lament for Jerusalem, since it did not know 'the things that were to its peace' (Lk 19:42). In an earlier passage, echoed here by Luke, Jeremiah castigated the people of Jerusalem who cried out 'peace, peace' when there was no peace, and so 'they will perish at the time of their visitation' (Jr 6:9-15). Following his lament for the city the Lukan Jesus goes on to foretell its destruction. The ravages of war (probably that of 66-70 c.e.) are an all too clear reminder for Luke and his readers of Jerusalem's failures to achieve the peace that its name had been made to symbolise in certain contemporary renderings.[9] Once again, we can detect Jeremian influences in the description of the actual Roman siege (Jr 52:4-5), as the scholarly Luke, steeped in the LXX, paints his picture with touches from a number of appropriate pre-texts (Lk 21:20-24; cf. Jr 21:7; Ez 30:3;32:9; Zech 12:9).

Jeremiah was the prophet whose life's call was 'to tear up and to knock down, to destroy and to overthrow, to build and to plant' (Jr 1:10). His life was largely concerned with the negative side of that mission, as he found himself cast in the role of prophet of doom to his own people at a time when they were prepared to play a political power game rather than trust in their God's care and protection. Luke chooses a most fitting, if tragic, setting in view of its history, namely the Jerusalem temple, to have the child Jesus designated as the one 'destined for the fall and rise of many in Israel – destined for a sign who would be rejected' (Lk 2:34). Both Jeremiah and Jesus shared in a similar call to challenge the complacency and self-centredness of their own people at critical junctures in its history, and both suffered a similar rejection. Convinced as they were that God's plan had reached its climax with Jesus, the early Christians were even more perplexed than were those who compiled the book of Jeremiah with its promises of a new covenant in the future (cf. Lk 22:19). Our reading of the Gospel of Luke against the backdrop of Book of Jeremiah suggests that in the figure of the prophet from Anatoth they found one other model in their efforts to understand the inscrutable plan of God. The fact that the Greek Bible had attributed the Book of Lamentations to the prophet only added further poignancy to the comparison, given the distinctively Lukan portrait of Jesus too, weeping for the city and encouraging others to share his sorrows (Lk 19: 41-44; 23: 26-32).

Ezechiel and John

'In the thirteenth year, on the fifth day of the fourth month, as I was among the exiles . . . heaven opened and I saw visions from God' (Ez 1:1).

'You will see the heavens opened and the angels of God ascending and descending on the Son of Man' (Jn 1:57). Both Ezechiel and John are visionaries who share a central symbol that serves to give a common focus to their visions and the ways in which they articulate their respective points of view. For both, the Jerusalem temple, the seat of God's presence to and with Israel, provides a rich repertoire of images and symbols that each can use in their distinctive manner and for their particular readerships. Both, it would seem, are writing after destruction and consciously searching for appropriate expressions of hope. For Ezechiel there are many such that can be conjured up from his predecessors in Israel's prophetic tradition, but the climax is his elaborate depiction of the new temple (chs 40-48). For John the focus is on the temple's replacement by the person of the Word-made-flesh, a perspective that can then be orchestrated with various episodes of Jesus' public career being presented in the light of the great festivals and their ceremonies – Passover, Tabernacles and Dedication (Jn, chs 2; 6; 7-8; 10; 19).

For both writers the notion of God's *kabôd* or glory is central. Ezechiel's vision includes the departure and return of this mysterious presence (Ez chs 11 and 43). Its departure from the Jerusalem temple is at once a moment of poignant loss and veiled expression of hope, since its departure is from the east gate on the side nearest to the exiles in Babylonia whom Ezechiel seeks to comfort (Ez 10:18-22; 11:22-25). It is through the east gate that the glory of God will return to fill the new temple (Ez 43:4f), whence will flow (again towards the east) the miraculous stream of water that will give a paradisiac abundance to a desert land.

Ezechiel's message of hope is tempered by his symbolic expressions of judgment. Visionary that he is, he does not hold the detailed mirror up to Israel's failures, but sees her sin rather in general terms: it is a rejection of the God who dwells in her midst, a refusal to see and to recognise that has marked the whole of the sacred history. In particular the leaders, the false shepherds, are castigated for the failures, without however exonerating each individual for their particular role in the tragic rejection. In the future, Yahweh himself will shepherd his people, gathering them together into one, restoring life where death once reigned (Ez 34). A new heart and spirit will be given (Ez 36: 22-32). The graves of the dead will be opened and the old divisions transcended in a new, united Israel that will glorify God's name among the gentiles (Ez 37). Thus, the vision as a whole, while focused firmly on Israel and its restoration, has the whole universe within its purview, despite its esoteric, priestly, inspiration.

The Johannine witness is succinctly enunciated already in the prologue: 'we saw his glory; the glory of the only-begotten of the Father, full of grace and truth' (Jn 1:16). As the narrative develops this glory or presence of God that has 'tabernacled' in Jesus is manifested in his works that lead to his disciples' belief (Jn 2:11; 11:15; 20:22). The glory that has entered history and manifests itself is, according to the Johannine perspective, distinctly reminiscent of Ezechel's images. In the midst of the temple the Johannine Jesus declares that he is the one from whom the rivers of living water will flow (see Ez 47:1f) an image that is directly related to the gift of the Spirit by the narrator (Jn 7:38). As a fulfillment of this prophetic utterance we are told that at his death, even as 'he gave the Spirit' water and blood flowed from the side of Christ (Jn 19:34). Because of his unity with the Father the Johannine Jesus can apply to himself the image of the shepherd who will gather the dispersed flock that has been neglected by its leaders (Jn 10:1-21). In another of the internal prophetic fulfillment scenarios of this work the promise that the tombs of the dead would be opened (Jn 5:19) is stunningly realised in the raising of Lazarus (Jn 11). Thus Ezechiel's vision of the valley of the dry bones coming to life again is realised (Ez 36).

Like Ezechiel, John is less interested in spelling out the specific moral demands and social failures of the Jews, God's erstwhile people. It is their blindness that is their sin, a particularly ironic judgment in view of the fact that Jesus as the light of the world is the giver of sight to the blind (Jn 8:12; 9:1-41). Both writers have a priestly perspective of the holy community (Jn 17), and hence the temple and its imagery provide a very suitable symbolic repertoire for defining the community's identity, tasks and experiences of God's saving presence.[10] Both interpret events as signs, thereby pointing to the deeper and hidden meaning of their message, which calls for a total response. Ezechiel's signs point to God's judgment on Israel's failure now as a matter of urgency, while at the same time serving to highlight future restoration. John's signs are primarily manifestations of the glory of God in Jesus (Jn 2:11; 21:25). Each writer also carries the note of separation and judgment for those who are not open to such a discovery. Thus, the emphasis within their shared perspective is different, as can be graphically seen in their very different exploitation of the image of the vine. For Ezechiel the withered vine symbolises Jerusalem's and Israel's rejection (Ez 17) whereas for John it serves as the climactic symbol of the new life that has come through Jesus (Jn 15).

Conclusion

The Chartres window has provided a suggestive model for a fresh reading of the Gospel narratives. In their different ways each pairing offered a highly creative and stimulating perspective from which to approach both the prophetic and the evangelical text. The interaction and its impact on our reading goes in both directions, it must be acknowledged. If the new is largely a recasting of images and metaphors from the old in order to express other faith-experiences, the old, likewise, takes on a new vitality when read in the refracted light of those subsequent pictures. This reflection is not intended to re-affirm canonical Christocentrism under a literary guise, but rather to suggest that Christian theology, in search of new language and images for its God-talk might well return to the whole of the Hebrew Scriptures in order to retrieve its classic but largely ignored heritage. The boldest stroke of all in the Chartres window was surely the implied contrast between giants and dwarfs, prophets and evangelists. Therein lies a challenge for contemporary Christian theologians also, both in terms of renewing their own tradition and of exploring common roots with their Jewish counterparts.

Notes

1. This essay first appeared in a collection of essays presented to Chicago theologian David Tracy, *Radical Pluralism and Truth. The Hermeneutics of Religion*, eds. J. Rilke and W. Jeanrond, (New York: Continuum, 1994) 107-20. Professor Tracy is an admirer of Chrtres and the symbolic universe created by its artists.
2. David Tracy, *The Analogical Imagination*, (London: SCM., 1992), p 237.
3. See Jonathan Culler, 'Presuppositions and Intertextuality' in *The Pursuit of Signs: Semiotics, Literature, Deconstruction* (Ithaca, NY: Cornell University Press, 1982) 100-18.
4. Howard Clark Kee, *Community of the New Age: Studies in Mark's Gospel* (Philadelphia: Westminster, 1977) 45-49.
5. John J. Collins, *The Apocalyptic Vision of the Book of Daniel* (Missoula MT: Scholars Press, 1977), especially 1-19.
6. Sean Freyne, 'The Disciples in Mark and the *Maskîlîm* in Daniel: A Comparison,' *Journal for the Study of the New Testament* 16 (1983) 7-23.
7. See William Beardslee, *Literary Criticism of the New Testament*, (Philadelphia: Fortress Press, 1970) 56-59 for some highly suggestive comments on the distinction between the two genres.
8. Gerhardt von Rad, *Old Testament Theology*, vol. 2, *The Theology of Israel's Prophetic Tradition* (London: Oliver and Boyd, 1965) 204-5.
9. Ignace de la Potterie, '*Les deux noms de Jérusalem dans l'évangile de Luc*,' *Recherches de Science Religieuse* 69 (1981) 59-70.

10. See Sean Freyne, 'Vilifying the Other and Defining the Self: Matthew's and John's Anti-Judaism in Focus', in *To See Ourselves as Others See Us : Jews, Christians, Others in Antiquity*, eds. J. Neusner and E. Frerichs, Brown Studies in the Humanities (Chico, CA: Scholars Press, 1985) 117-44.

5

MARK'S URGENT MESSAGE

None of the many studies of Saint Mark's Gospel that I have read has opened up its message for me in the way that an oral recitation of the whole text by a British actor, Alec McCowan,[1] has achieved. Unaided by any stage props the actor is able to capture the spirit of this dramatic narrative in a highly engaging manner. Tone of voice, changes of pace, facial expressions, movement – all the ploys of the actor's trade – are utilised in order to bring the text to life. Mark becomes a Gospel of great power and suspense as it draws us into its story and forces us to take sides. One suddenly recalls that it was originally written for just this kind of oral performance for Christian communities in Rome, or possibly even in Palestine.

Previous study has concentrated heavily on understanding the Gospel on its own terms – its language, its original situation, its place within the history of the early Christian literature, especially its relation to the other Gospels. Who was Mark and how did he come by the story of Jesus? Asking these and similar questions has helped enormously in our understanding of this work, even when definitive answers are hard to come by. According to early (second century) tradition, Mark was the interpreter of Peter, who wrote down the apostle's preaching for Roman Christians. In all probability this took place after the martyrdom of Peter and Paul in Nero's persecution in 64 c.e. Modern scholars have found much that is plausible in this picture, whereas others have linked the Gospel with the situation in Palestine on the eve of or during the first

Jewish revolt against Rome in 66-70 c.e., especially in the light of statements in chapter 13.

Yet when all the historical study is done, there is a danger that the Gospel could remain remote from us, belonging to first, but not twenty-first-century hearers and readers. What made McCowan's performance so memorable for me was that it was difficult to remain detached from the story. Once exposed to all of Mark's rhetorical skills, indifference to the outcome cannot be maintained. The many unanswered questions about Jesus and his purpose that punctuate the narrative are crying out for full audience participation; interaction is the name of Mark's game, and the invitation to become involved with the story and its characters is open to all honest readers.

Since Mark comes second among the Gospels in our Bibles after Matthew, most of us supply the beginning and the ending that Mark never wrote. Both Matthew and Luke introduce us to Jesus through the birth and infancy stories. We are in no doubt about the identity of the main character from the outset. At the end too, the suspense as to what happened is removed as each Gospel tells of Jesus' rejoining the group of bewildered disciples in an intimate scene of recognition. Imagine yourself trying to make sense of Mark's account without such information. Imagine early Christians in Rome or wherever attempting to do likewise. Jesus arrives in Galilee, seemingly unannounced, to begin his ministry, and at the end we are left to ponder whether or not the disciples returned to Galilee as instructed by the angelic messenger at the tomb, and if so where and how did they encounter Jesus? Do we share the women's fear? Would we return? Why Galilee anyhow?

This scarcity of advance information is deliberate. Mark wants us to be attentive readers from the start, and clever dramatist/teacher that he is, he invites us to form our own impressions as the plot develops and write the ending accordingly. How often one comes away from a good theatrical performance trying to tease out the intricacies of the plot and discern the intended 'message'. This aura of mystery hangs over Mark's whole story. Repeatedly the main character, Jesus, calls for silence about a successful healing when popular evangelism might appear to dictate broadcasting the success and it seems impossible to imagine how the crowd's enthusiasm could be contained (1,44; 3,12; 5,42). When Peter, the leader of the specially chosen group of followers, confesses that Jesus is the Christ, he is told to be silent (8,30). Shortly afterwards what might appear to be a perfectly good idea, the suggestion of making three tents on the mountain top for Jesus, Moses and Elijah, is dismissed by the author as a case of Peter being so frightened that he did not know what to say (9,5-6). Little wonder that the attentive reader is somewhat confused also!

Whatever his real purpose, the Markan Jesus is no rabble-rouser or aspirant to cheap popularity. 'And next morning (after a most 'successful' visit to Caphernaum) a great while before day he arose and went to a lonely place and there he prayed' (Mk 1,35). After feeding the multitude in a lonely place, he 'compelled the disciples to get into the boat while he dismissed the crowd,' only to rejoin the disciples on the sea when they were experiencing difficulties with the waves (Mk 6,45-52); 'He was going through Galilee and he did not want anyone to know it' (Mk 9,30). We might be forgiven for thinking that this Jesus is a 'loner', even in the midst of buzzing crowds and fussy, but uncomprehending disciples.

Sometimes this mood of secrecy and mystery passes over into a more sinister mode. Demons scream at him, declaring his name – 'the Holy One of God', or 'Son of the Most High', in what appears to be a battle of wits: knowing his name ought to mean controlling his power (1,24-25; 3,11; 5,7). But in the end they are silenced, and in a particularly spectacular and blood curdling story, a possessed man whom nobody could control ends up sitting at the feet of Jesus, 'in his right mind' (Mk 5,15). On another occasion a young boy who is possessed falls down at the approach of Jesus, 'in convulsions', so that they all said, 'he is dead' (9,14-29). Jesus, however, takes him by the hand and raises him up. Just one of the many little resurrection stories that dot the account. Jesus achieves another victory over evil, an anticipated foretaste of the great and ultimate victory that Mark and his faithful readers expected soon (Mk 13,20.24-27).

The specially chosen disciples make a fascinating study. They make an impressive start in the persons of the pairs of brothers, Simon and Andrew, James and John (1,16-20). There is a comic irony in the picture of these latter two abandoning their father and the hired servants – thus suggesting an affluent domestic situation – only subsequently to want seats of honour in the kingdom (10,35-40), or resenting the spending of money on a hungry crowd (6,36-37), even though 'they had left all to follow' and had received instruction to bring no provisions for their journey, relying instead on the generosity of others (6,8-9)! They invariably meet with Jesus privately, 'in a house' (4,19-12; 7,17), or 'on the way' (8,27; 9,30.33; 10,32), almost always to receive further instruction or have the mystery that appears as a riddle explained. Yet their progress is slow. They seem incapable of getting beneath the surface of things, recalling the external details of the feeding miracles, but not comprehending their true meaning and the identity of the one who has performed these deeds, so reminiscent of the God of Israel feeding his people in their exodus from Egypt (Mk 8, 14-21; Ex 16,9-18). Like the deaf-mute and the blind man, they seem in desperate need of having their ears truly unblocked and their eyes truly opened, in order that they might speak plainly and see clearly (7,31-37; 8, 2-26; cf. 8,18).

To add to this bleak performance despite the special coaching in Galilee, we are told that when the forces of evil closed in to arrest Jesus in Jerusalem, 'they all left him and fled' (14,50), even though they had been forewarned three times, with ever-increasing explicitness, of what lay ahead in the holy city. That is the last we hear of the male disciples as a group, though Peter makes a brief, if inglorious, entry at the trial (14, 66-72). We are surprised to learn that women have also been part of his permanent retinue, since there was no explicit mention of them through the narrative. Yet at the end there they are, standing at a distance as Jesus dies on the cross – the two Marys and Salome (15, 40-41). The same three faithful ones go to the tomb to anoint the body of Jesus when the Sabbath was over, only to have their strange encounter with a 'young man, dressed in white, seated at the right side' (16, 1-8), a subtle symbol that all is not over and that story time goes beyond plot time.

There are other individuals from the fringes of this story who also seem to out-perform the chosen disciples. Two in particular stand out. The blind Bar-Timaeus, sitting by the roadside at Jericho has his sight restored and opts to follow Jesus 'on the way', despite having been given his freedom 'to go his way' (10, 46-52). And then there is the centurion, the most unlikely candidate to grasp the full meaning of Jesus' person, who, 'seeing that thus he (Jesus) breathed his last, said: "truly, this man was Son of God"' (15,39). Thus in Mark's eyes insiders and outsiders can interchange roles very easily. There are no certainties in this school, since the God of Mark's Jesus is a God of surprises.

So what is it all about, you may well ask, as you click the button, and put away the McCowan video? At the surface level Mark's story is straightforward. The Galilean prophet manifests another face of God to the one that Jerusalem represented – a God who is not boxed in, but who is in the everyday of people's lives, overcoming the evil of the world as it impinges on and dehumanises them. Inevitably, the centre reacts negatively, and justice appears to be done and the threat is averted until God's last word is spoken, not even by the acknowledging centurion, but by the 'young man dressed in white'. 'He is risen, he is not here; go tell his disciples and Peter: "he goes before you to Galilee; there you will see him as he told you"' (16,7).

Or is this really the last word that Mark wants spoken? That depends on you and me! The story of the disciples – male and female – as well as the various individuals who come to recognise the truth about Jesus is the sub-text of the real plot that Mark intends. The journey to which the Markan Jesus summons us is not to Jerusalem or to Galilee, but to our true selves where we begin 'to think the thoughts of God, not the thoughts of men' (8,33). Only then can we begin to acknowledge God's real presence in the world of pain, suffering and oppression that so often appears to have the last word. Only then can we recognise the suffering God in the fate of Jesus and be empowered to continue with him the journey of faith, which summons us from the security of Jerusalem's narrow but safe horizons to the open-ended world of Galilee. Even then we can choose to be distracted like the Markan crowd, so impressed with power, but so lacking in real appreciation, or we can seek preferment with the male disciples and be absent at the crucial moment, or we can join Bar Timaeus in the freedom of Jesus' way , or we can be faithful to the end, if fearful, like the women disciples, or we can even seek to silence Jesus like the demons ... Mark provides us with many angles of vision; he invites us to enter the drama from several points of view, and choose for ourselves which is the best perspective on the mystery that is the kingdom of God in the world.

Praying with Mark

Unlike the other Gospels, Luke in particular, Mark does not present us with a picture of Jesus at prayer very often. His Jesus is a busy person, always on the move. The times he does choose to pray are, therefore, highly significant. They occur when Jesus is disappointed by the performance or reactions of his close associates. After a successful day of ministry at Caphernaum Jesus departs early to pray alone, and the disciples go in search of him, anxious to have their new-found status in the village as friends of the healer confirmed. But Jesus refuses to go back in that capacity (1, 35-38). Again after the first feeding miracle, the crowd and the disciples have to be separated, if real progress in understanding is to occur, and once again Jesus departs to a lonely place to pray (6, 46). Finally in the garden when the chosen four disciples fall asleep and cannot watch with him he goes away and prays to the Father in the hour of agony (Mk 14, 35). The Markan Jesus is the model of the prayer of abandonment – trust in God when human resources, especially that of the understanding of friends, fail.

Notes

1. *St Mark's Gospel*, Copyright Arthur Cantor and Alec McCowan (Arthur Cantor Productions, New York, 1990).

Some Further Reading

David Rhoads and Donald Mitchie, *Mark as Story. An Introduction to the Narrative of a Gospel*, (Philadelphia: Fortress Press, 1982)

Janice Capel Anderson and Stephen Moore, ets *Mark and Method. New Approaches in Biblical Studies*, (Minneapolis: Augsburg/Fortress, 1992).

Sean Freyne, *Galilee, Jesus and the Gospels. Literary Approaches and Historical Investigations*, (Dublin and Minneapolis: Macmillan and Augsburg/Fortress, 1988).

Richard A. Horsley, *Hearing the Whole Story. The Politics of Plot in Mark's Gospel*, (Louisville, London, Leiden: Westminster John Knox Press, 2001).

6

'IN THE BEGINNING WAS THE WORD'

A conference, held in 2000 in the Chester Beatty Library, Dublin Castle, was intended to heighten awareness of one of the jewels in the crown of this remarkable collection of Oriental and Near Eastern art and artifacts.[1] The Chester Beatty Gospel papyri, or P45 to give them their official scholarly designation, form a substantial part of one of the earliest known codices of the four Gospels, dating from the third century (c. c.e. 250). They are, therefore, a direct link with the Christian Church while it was still a persecuted sect within the Roman Empire. They put us in touch with the earliest period of a movement that was destined to shape so many facets of Western, and indeed global civilisation subsequently, though few could have anticipated this outcome at the time these documents were produced. The papyri are, then, cultural artifacts of the highest significance, of interest to the concerned secularist as well as objects worthy of respect for the committed Christian.

Like all artifacts from the past, the papyri too call for contextualisation within their own world if their significance for ours is to be properly assessed. As a Jewish reform movement, Jesus and the first Christians were heirs to the tradition of the Torah as a written collection of Israel's sacred writings. Yet, unlike some other Jewish movements of reform, such as the Essenes whose library is now known from the Dead Sea Scrolls, the early Christians were not primarily a scholastic community, at least originally.

The evangelist Luke presents Jesus reading from the scroll of the prophet Isaiah in the synagogue at Nazareth (Luke 4, 16-20), yet there is no evidence that he left any written records. Indeed Jesus' Pharisee opponents accused him of being 'unschooled' (John 7, 15). His earliest followers are also described as being 'ignorant' and 'illiterate' (Acts of the Apostles 4, 13). However, it is important to understand these statements as a standard vilifactory tactic by the small literate elite in Jerusalem, since a large part of ancient society belonged to an oral rather than a written culture, with no pejorative connotations. True, the apostle Paul used letter-writing as a way of communicating with the communities he had established in various cities, and a collection of his letters must have been made shortly after his death, an early version of which is also represented in the Chester Beatty collection (P46). The case of Paul indicates a shift in the social standing within an urban context of some at least of his new converts, as distinct from Jesus' own ministry, which was largely concentrated on the rural villagers of Galilee. Yet even Paul insists that his preference was for the spoken rather than the written word.

The impulse to produce a narrative account of Jesus' life and ministry was probably due to several factors – liturgical and catechetical needs; the death of the eye-witnesses to Jesus' life; and the shift from the Aramaic-speaking oral culture of Galilee, to the Greek speaking urban world of the Pauline mission. In this circle, history writing and biography were well-established literary genres, and thus it was necessary to produce 'an accurate account of all that has been accomplished among us, as these were handed on by those who from the beginning were eye-witnesses and ministers of the word' (Luke 1, 1-4). This statement echoes the literary practices of contemporary Greco-Roman historians and no doubt helped to maintain the credibility of the movement among its pagan competitors. Unlike its Jewish precursors, however, the early Christians adopted the relatively novel form of the codex or book rather than the scroll in publicising their message. This decision was for practical reasons such as convenience and portability for travelling missionaries, but it also helped to emphasise the movement's separate identity from the parent religion.

Modern scholarship has highlighted the fact that several different 'lives' of Jesus were produced with considerable variations even among the so-called synoptic Gospels (i.e. Matthew, Mark and Luke), who shared a common pool of stories and sayings of Jesus that had circulated orally from the very beginning. John's Gospel has always been recognised as being quite different in tone and emphasis, and others too were in circulation such as the Gospels of Thomas, Peter and Mary, as well as Gospels attributed to dissident groups like the Ebionites and the

Gnostics. The evidence points to the fact that the Fourfold Gospel, comprising our canonical four, established itself relatively early as authoritative, probably because they were attributed to known disciples of Jesus (Matthew and John) or to those closely associated with that circle (Mark the interpreter of Peter and Luke the companion of Paul).[2] It was this development that gave rise to the production of codices like the Chester Beatty one, containing the four Gospels as well as Acts of the Apostles in the one book.

Despite some recent attempts to rehabilitate the other Gospels as being early also, the likelihood is that they were derivative, and in several respects were regarded as not conforming to an emerging orthodoxy. Thus, towards the end of the second century, the Gospel of Peter was in circulation in Antioch, and the local bishop, Serapion, allowed it for private reading, but not for liturgical use in the Christian assembly.

The earliest commentators on this Fourfold Gospel, such as Justin Martyr (died c. c.e. 165) and Irenaeus of Lyon (died c. c.e. 200), were conscious of the differences between the individual accounts, possibly because pagan critics had sought to discredit them on the basis of these seeming discrepancies. Yet these first apologists stressed the deeper unity that existed between them, based on the one Spirit 'that bound them together.' Thus both writers prefer to speak of the Gospel rather than Gospels (plural), and Irenaeus justifies the Fourfold Gospel by likening it to the four cardinal points of the compass, thereby implying the universality of the message it contained. This message was 'good news' about Jesus Christ as God's final word for the human family, a conviction that had driven the movement from its inception, as Paul had emphasised for his Galatian converts. There is only one Gospel, he writes, and 'if I myself, or an angel from heaven were to preach another, we should be anathema' (Galatians 1, 8).

Others were less sure about the Fourfold Gospel and its unity as seen by Justin and Irenaeus. The Chester Beatty collection also contains another highly significant manuscript, the only known version in the original Syriac of Ephraem's fourth-century commentary on a second-century Gospel harmony, the *Diatessaron*. This work had been compiled by a Syrian monk, Tatian, about c.e. 175, who apparently was troubled by the discrepancies in the Gospels, and sought to harmonise the four into one account (hence the Greek title of his work). His concerns were more historical than theological, probably because of his desire to present a single coherent account of the 'life' of Jesus to counteract the pagan despisers, who criticised apparent discrepancies in differing accounts of various episodes in the life of Jesus.. This work was translated into various languages subsequently, but was particularly popular in Syria where it was replaced by the Fourfold Gospel only in the fifth century. Its importance lies in the fact that not all communities in the new movement, faced with the historical difficulties posed by the Gospel differences, shared the theological conviction that lay behind the Fourfold Gospel. Tatian's concerns had to await the eighteenth-century Enlightenment's preoccupation with history before they would be addressed again, and indeed they are still very much at the centre of Gospel studies to this day in the so-called quest for the historical Jesus.

There is, then, a seeming paradox at the heart of the early Christian self-understanding as this was expressed in the Fourfold Gospel. The good news is indeed one, yet its human expressions can be varied. The Word of God can never be exhausted or fully represented in the words of humans. It is for this reason that early Christian writers sought to compare the Scriptures with the Incarnation: one was the written Word of God, the other was the Word made flesh. Both modes, the written and the enfleshed, reveal and conceal the mystery of the divine love for the world. Human language, like human life, is always culturally and historically conditioned, partial and imperfect expressions of the deeper meaning of things. It calls for a special attuning of the ear to hear that deeper voice, the *lectio divina* of Christian worship and prayer.

The recognition of this surplus of meaning of the Christian story allowed Irenaeus and others after him to imagine the Christ in glory with four faces, each painted by a different evangelist. My own favourite expression of this profound idea is that of the thirteenth-century 'Window of the Evangelists' at Chartres Cathedral outside Paris. The central axis of the depiction consists of the virgin and child at the lower level (the Word made flesh), while the glorious risen Christ surrounded by the twelve apostles occupies the upper, rose section, directly above. On either side of the virgin and child are two panels, each containing a giant figure carrying a dwarf on his shoulders with an orientation towards the rose centre. What is utterly surprising about this portrayal is that the evangelists are depicted as the dwarfs and the Old Testament prophets as the giants, inverting the usual Christian understanding of the New Testament being the fulfillment of the Old. The depiction gives expression to a famous medieval saying that 'we are like dwarfs on the shoulders of the giants of the past; we can see farther because we are raised higher.' In this particular application the pairing of evangelists and prophets allows each to see the Christ in a distinctive fashion. Despite the diversity of perspective that the different panels suggest, the whole window has a harmonious unity that encapsulates the one and fourfold Gospel, and its indebtedness to its Israelite precursors[3].

In so far as we can ascertain, Christianity came to Ireland almost two centuries after the production, probably in Egypt, of the Beatty codex. By then the new movement had become the official religion of the empire, and the urgency was to spread the Gospel to the very outer regions of the known world, even beyond the borders of the empire. In the library of Trinity College, at the other end of Dame Street from the Chester Beatty Library, the great uncial manuscript of the Book of Kells bears witness to this 'triumph' of Christianity with its elaborate illumination and highly decorative calligraphy. By contrast, the Beatty Codex was written in small script by a not very elegant hand and without any illumination. It is written on papyrus, not the more expensive vellum, and each sheet is folded in two to economise and fit the text of all four Gospels into a single codex of manageable proportions. This contrast of style and execution between the two codices tells its own story of two very different moments of early Christian self-expression – the struggle for survival in a hostile environment and the high culture of triumphant Christendom.

At the beginning of the third millennium by Christian reckoning, Christendom, that is, the conjunction of Church and Empire in a single world, is now no longer a reality, even in Ireland, where, ironically, the relationship survived longer than it did within its original boundaries in mainland Europe. As we search for ways of rescuing from the jaws of the Celtic Tiger some of the more important Gospel values that shaped our culture, the moment from the past represented by the Beatty Codex has an important message. The pioneering spirit of those who produced this Christian codex and dared to live their lives by its challenging story could still serve us well today.

Notes

1. These papers, delivered by an array of international scholars, will be published in 2003 by T & T Clarke, Edinburgh, edited by Charles Horton, Curator Western Collection, Chester Beatty Library, Dublin.
2. For a scholarly but accesible discussion of this development, see Martin Hengel, *The Four Gospels and the One Gospel of Jesus Christ*, (London: SCM Press, 2000)
3. A more detailed discussion of the Gospels from the perspective of the 'Chartres Window' appears in chapter 4 of this collection.

7

CHRISTOLOGICAL DEBATES AMONG JOHANNINE CHRISTIANS

The Fourth Gospel has from the beginning been seen to differ from the other three canonical writings, whose common features have earned the designation 'synoptic', meaning a shared point of view. These divergences exercised the minds and exegetical ingenuity of Patristic exegetes from Origen to Augustine. Modern interpreters, however, are more concerned with the perceived differences within the Johannine corpus or family of writings. Style, vocabulary, and a shared theological language seem to support the traditional attribution of a number of New Testament writings – the Fourth Gospel, the Johannine Epistles, and (with less certainty) the Revelation of John – to a single authorial hand. Yet there is today virtual consensus that these writings emanated from a community or school, which inhabited a very distinctive corner of the early Christian world. Thus, despite their common traits, more than one hand has been at work in their production and hence, more than one 'Johannine' voice may be heard. Are these in fact conflicting voices, and if so what, if any, reconciliation was achieved between them?

Inevitably, these questions receive quite differing answers among modern scholars as different views of the Johannine community and its history are adopted. Should they be seen as in-house, Jewish family squabbles or as a reflection of a bitter conflict with the synagogue from which the group has been excluded, especially in view of the very negative portrayal of the Jews in this work? What one decides on these issues, the very search for answers opens up a fascinating window on a process of reflection and interpretation of the meaning of Jesus' life and ministry. Thus, it would seem, the picture of community harmony that Jesus himself is portrayed as having 'earnestly desired' in his farewell discourse, especially chapter 17, represented the ideal rather than the actual, as far as the Johannine community was concerned. On its own admission the process of reflection involved the community in remembering, waiting for the promised Spirit to lead them into all truth, and evaluating various expressions of its shared faith over a considerable period. As modern readers, we are faced with the significance of this process as we encounter it within the collection of authoritative writings of the Christian Scriptures. Are we to take this chorus of voices from the Johannine Christians as a cacophony of dissonance or as a harmonious symphony of rich texture, reflecting a variegated development? Or should we search for some mediating position?

Conflicts and Corrections

The Johannine Epistles have been described as 'reading guides' for the Gospel, so this is perhaps the best place to begin. The issues with which they deal point back to the Gospel, issues which obviously have given rise to deep divisions and have endangered the *koinonia*, or sense of close-knit community, to which the group aspires. The author of the First Epistle gives expression to these sentiments, addressing the recipients as, 'beloved', 'children', 'little children', and warmly applauding their grasp of the shared beliefs (1 Jn 2, 7-28). On the other hand the apocalyptic image of the Anti-Christ, as the embodiment of evil, is employed to condemn others who have betrayed the community by denying important aspects of its belief-system. In the author's view 'they never really belonged to us', since otherwise 'they would not have gone out from us' (1 Jn 2, 19). The author speaks authoritatively because of what he 'has heard and seen from the beginning', and he feels responsible for strengthening the bonds of unity that have been weakened by the situation that has prompted the letter.

This situation of internal conflict is the direct result of the false understanding of Jesus Christ, which certain members have espoused, something that is clearly stated more than once:

'Who is the liar but the one who denies that Jesus is the Christ?' (1 Jn 2, 22).

And again:

> 'Every spirit that confesses that Jesus Christ has come in the flesh is from God, and every spirit that does not confess Jesus is not from God' (1 Jn 4, 2f).

The issue at stake has to do with the true identity of Jesus and some must have denied his real humanity: it is Jesus (the man from Nazareth) who is the Christ and he has come in the *flesh*. This emphatic declaration echoes the prologue to the Gospel: 'The Word became flesh, and dwelt among us' (Jn 1, 14). It also explains the particular emphasis of the opening statement of the Epistle, namely, the author's claim that what he had 'touched' and 'seen with his eyes' is the subject of the message he wants to convey (1 Jn 1, 1-2). Thus, the sheer physicality of Jesus was central to the declaration, as though it had been denied or was in danger of being overlooked.

The source of such a misunderstanding can perhaps be identified through a particular emphasis in the closing chapter of the Gospel, where the community has articulated its beliefs in the Resurrection of Jesus. On the one hand Mary's desire to cling to Jesus once she has recognised him, is rejected, since he has not yet ascended to 'my God and your God'. Doubting Thomas, on the other hand, is given the opportunity of fulfilling his wish of touching Jesus' hands and side, and he humbly utters the faith declaration: 'My Lord and My God' (Jn 20, 11-29). These two appearance stories, situated back to back in the original closing chapter of the Gospel seem to be making the same point in narrative form as did the Prologue in its majestic theological tones: the Word was with God and the Word became flesh (Jn 1, 1-14). The so-called 'high Christology' of the opening statement which locates the origins of the Word 'in the beginning' with God needs to be counterbalanced with the equally emphatic statement of the Word's true humanity, if the full significance of the Christian proclamation is to be appreciated.

The starting point to the self-disclosure of God in Jesus is his earthly career. Thus, that historical moment has to be 'remembered' and affirmed in the post-Easter experience of the community (Jn 2, 22; 12,16). At the same time the fullness of truth that the promised Spirit will bring after Jesus' departure allows the community to make claims about the symbolic significance of his life in some of the most daring assertions of Christological faith to be found in the New Testament. Maintaining the tension between these two poles demanded, and still demands, a finely attuned sense of balance that avoids the temptation of opting for a crass materialism or a naive spiritualism on the one hand, or of introducing a dualism that denies any relationship between spirit and matter, on the other. The Johannine community may have been one of the earliest Christian groups to encounter these difficulties in its faith articulation, but it certainly was not the last. It has been a perennial temptation for Christian faith to take one of these options, either implicitly or explicitly, throughout history.

The orientation that the first Epistle has given us as modern readers of the Gospel, locates the debate within the Christian community, as it sought to maintain an adequate understanding of its faith-memory, faced with the dilution of the audacious claims which it had inherited. The Gospel itself makes us privy to the formation of those claims within a Jewish milieu at an earlier stage of the community's life. Here too, we can detect the sound of other voices and the noise of acrimonious and heated debates. Without deciding in advance whether these reflect the compensating claims of those who have been expelled from their 'Father's house', the parent Judaism, or the wrangling disputations of a dysfunctional family, we must first obtain a flavour of the claims and counter-claims.

After the lofty heights of the Prologue (Jn 1,1-18) we are brought down to earth for the rest of chapter one where the reader is invited to enter the world of expectation and enquiry of first century Jewish hopes. The first followers of Jesus are portrayed not as Galilean fishermen, busy about their chores as in the synoptic Gospels, but as the followers of John the Baptist across the Jordan. There John has testified first to a Jerusalem-based delegation of Pharisees that he was neither the messiah, nor any of the other expected characters of the end-time – Elijah or the prophet. This scene anticipates much more hostile ones to follow between Jesus himself and the Pharisees concerning his own true identity. The Baptist then makes a second declaration to his own followers on seeing Jesus approaching, namely, that on the basis of divine revelation he knows that Jesus is the long-awaited figure, since he is the one on whom the Spirit has descended and remains.

The sequel of the chapter presents a series of vignettes in which various characters identify Jesus according to standard Jewish expectations: he is the lamb of God (John the Baptist), the Messiah (Andrew); 'him about whom Moses in the law and the prophets wrote' (Philip); Son of God and King of Israel (Nathaniel). The series concludes with a promise to Nathaniel from Jesus himself that he will see 'greater things', namely, 'the heavens opened and the angels of God ascending and descending on the Son of Man' (Jn 1, 51). Thus, the Word that has become flesh in the first half of the chapter is now firmly anchored to Jewish hopes and expectations, a human figure, the son of Joseph from Nazareth, on whom the Spirit of God resides permanently, qualifying him for the status of the awaited figure of the end-time. And yet at the end of the chapter the other-worldly aspect re-enters the picture, described in imagery borrowed from Jacob's dream (Gn 28, 12): Jesus is not only the earthly Messiah of Israel's hopes, he is also the heavenly Son of Man on whom the angels of God reside, thus signifying direct communication between heaven and earth.

Armed with this information the reader is prepared for the disputes that lie ahead. It soon becomes clear that standard Jewish messianic expectation and symbolism is not sufficient to express the Johannine community's understanding of Jesus. At various points in the subsequent narrative this frame of reference does recur: in Jesus' dialogue with the Samaritan woman, or among the Galileans who have benefited from the feeding miracle or in discussions among the Jerusalem crowds (Jn 4, 16-26; 6, 14f; 7, 40-43) – thereby covering all three geographic areas of Jewish territorial claims, the re-establishment of which was one aspect of the Messiah's role, according to traditional hopes. However, the messianic categories merely serve as a starting point for the discussion, which quickly moves to another level. In each instance Jesus' heavenly status is affirmed either directly, or through the use of symbolism that applies to God's activity, immediately setting in train bitter disputes with his Pharisaic opponents. Jesus has blasphemed by making himself 'equal to God' in claiming to have power to judge and to give life (5, 18), or in declaring that he is 'the bread from heaven' (6, 41f), 'the 'light of the world' (8, 12), 'the good shepherd' (10, 11) and 'the resurrection and the life' (11, 25). All these utterances are resonant of descriptions for God's role in the life of Israel according to the Hebrew Bible. It is no surprise, therefore, that the Johannine Jesus eventually declares his oneness with the Father: 'I and the Father are one' (10, 30).

This unity is, however, based on a dynamic relationship of mutual love and shared life of which the Father is the sole source. At least in the first instance this unity is functional rather than ontological. Hence, side by side with the utterances that suggest equality with God are statements of Jesus' total subordination to the Father, a subordination that involves surrendering himself totally to the Father's will: 'The Father who abides in me does his works' (14, 10). In a memorable and influential phrase, the German New Testament scholar Rudolph Bultmann has described the role of the Johannine Jesus as 'revealing that he is the Revealer'. However, this statement unduly limits the scope of Jesus' life according to the Johannine narrative. In the 'Farewell Discourse' (chs 13-17) Jesus repeatedly assures the disciples that the life that he enjoys with the Father, can be theirs also by 'abiding in his love' or 'by keeping the commandments'. The Johannine Jesus is deemed to be revealing the inner life of God, and that this is available to those who follow him as 'the Way, the Truth and the Life' (Jn 14, 6). Jesus is, therefore, both the archetype and the source of union with God for believers, an experience that for Johannine Christians at least is best described in terms of knowing, seeing and loving. At this point Jewish messianic hopes of earthly restoration have been transformed into a mystical/apocalyptic interpretation that echoes also various forms of Hellenistic philosophical speculation about union with God to which the true philosopher can aspire through contemplation.

Not all the characters in the Johannine narrative share this view of Jesus and his life's purpose, however. Foremost among the opponents are the Pharisees who are often to be taken synonymously with the more inclusive 'the Jews' in this writing. They find Jesus' claims to 'be equal with God' and 'one with God' blasphemous within the framework of their strict Jewish monotheism (5, 19; 10, 33). Even the messianic claims of Jesus are rejected in accordance with their interpretation of the Scriptures (7, 47-52). The Johannine narrator often parodies their views by resorting to black irony in order to discredit their claims that they are the true interpreters of the Jewish tradition. Moses (5, 46), Abraham (8, 339-41) and Isaiah (12, 41) are all summoned as witnesses in this conflict of interpretations, and the Johannine author appears to make outlandish claims about their relationship to Jesus. Moses wrote about him; he existed before Abraham, and Isaiah saw his glory. Nicodemus, 'a teacher of Israel' is pilloried for wanting to give Jesus a fair trial (3, 10; 7, 51), yet in the end he reappears to ensure that he at least receives an honourable burial (19, 39).

Other characters within the narrative seem to represent intermediate positions. The Galilean crowds want to take him by force and make him king, perceiving him to be a prophet (6, 14f). The 'brothers of Jesus' want him to go to the Feast of Tabernacles in Jerusalem 'to show himself to the world' (7, 4). However, in both instances it is clear that the positions being espoused are unacceptable to the narrator/author of the work.

Jesus escapes from the Galilean crowd and does not accede to his brothers' request. Yet, ironically, the intention behind both episodes is realised later in the narrative: Jesus does go to Jerusalem where he makes an open declaration that he is 'the light of the world' (8, 12; cf. 7, 14. 37); and in the end he accepts from Pilate the epithet 'king of the Jews', but redefines his kingship in terms that apply to his role as revealer of the truth and not to that of earthly ruler (18, 33-38).

Even though the seamless garment of Jesus, of which the Gospel speaks (19, 23), has often been seen as a metaphor for the work itself, there is now a general acceptance that the Gospel consists of several layers, each with its own theological perspective. Despite the reworking of the material by later editors/authors, traces of the earlier perspectives can still be easily detected. Thus, the different characters and points of view can be taken as representative of the different theological views about Jesus, reflecting different stages of the community's development. These range, as we have seen, from standard Jewish messianic expectations at one end of the spectrum to the heavenly revealer figure, who can claim an intimate relationship with God, at the other. The very fact that the Johannine dialogues move from the earthly messiah to the heavenly revealer so naturally (chs 4 and 9, for example), suggests that the community was able to build on its earlier understanding as it sought to articulate its own developing interpretation of the meaning of Jesus' life.

Clearly, however, the transition was by no means a smooth one, giving rise to heated debates and recriminations on both sides of the argument. The First Epistle shows that some Johannine Christians had overstated the case for the heavenly figure to the point of denying Jesus' humanity, while in the Gospel others, like the Galilean crowds and the brothers of Jesus, seem not to have made the transition from recognition of Jesus' messianic status to an acceptance of the high Christology, which the main author espouses. The fact that both points of view, as well as the memory of the bitter disputes with those Jews who did not accept Jesus' messianic claims in the first instance, have been included in the Gospel, suggests that all points of view were important to the author, no matter how dissident the voices in question, or how painful the memory. At least they all had a right to be heard, if only to be rejected with vehemence, even vilification. Theological disputes can get nasty!

Various overarching trends can be discerned that attempt to bring order to the Johannine house. The promise of Jesus to send the Spirit that will lead them into all truth, after he has departed, points both backward to the historical life of Jesus which had to come to closure, and forward to the life of the Church in the world (14, 25f). Yet this solution was to prove at best unstable. 'Beloved, do not believe every spirit' is the ominous warning that the author of the First Epistle gives the reader, since any Spirit that says that Jesus did not come in the flesh is not of God (1 Jn 4, 1-6). Another approach by the same author was to reclaim for God the images of Life, Light and Love, which in the Gospel had been applied to Jesus, thereby putting the emphasis on a Christocentric theology rather than on a theo-centric Christology. In the larger world of the Johannine Christians, Demeter, Sol Invictus and Aphrodite represented the elemental forces of Life, Light and Love, so that the Johannine Christians required a more specific determination of each in order to retain their separate identity over against that world. The author of the Epistle was able to declare 'God is Life and Light' and 'God is Love' (1 Jn 1, 2. 5; 4, 7f), only because these were appropriate designations for their experience of Jesus.

Perhaps, however, the theologian who added the *Logos* hymn to the beginning of the Gospel had the best and most enduring solution to the Johannine dilemma. Behind this remarkable testimony stands the figure of Wisdom as this had been developed over several centuries in both Palestinian and Alexandrian Judaism. Wisdom was *both* the heavenly being that shared in God's creative power in the universe *and* the everyday understanding of life that made it possible to cope with the struggle for existence (Book of Proverbs). Wisdom was both universal and dwelling in Zion, identified with the law of the most high (Sirach 24). Wisdom was at the centre of the universe informing all life – human, animal and plant, as this could be explored by the range of human science (Wisdom of Solomon 7, 15 – 30). She was universal and local, heavenly and of the earth, Jewish and non-Jewish, transcending all boundaries and embracing all cultures. Wisdom provided, therefore, the perfect background for the Johannine proclamation that the Word became flesh in Jesus. She made it possible to maintain the fragile tension between the divine and the human as the Johannine community had experienced it in Jesus. Because wisdom was indivisible, it was possible to transform the images that spoke of Jesus' messiahship into signs of the divine glory (*kabod / doxa*) that resided in him.

In the crucible of theological debates in which all was at stake, a light has been lit that will illumine all that is in the house. Henceforth, everything that is fully human can function as a sign that there is a truth beyond our capacity fully to comprehend, and that that truth has come very close to us.

Select bibliography.

Ashton, John, *Understanding the Fourth Gospel*, (Oxford: Oxford University Press, 1991)

Ashton, John, *Studying John, Approaches to the Fourth Gospel*, (Oxford: Clarendon Press, 1994).

Ashton, John, ed., *The Interpretation of John*, (London: SPCK Press, 1989)

Brown, Raymond *The Community of the Beloved Disciple*, (London: Geoffrey Chapman, 1979).

Bultmann, Rudolph, (English translation), *The Gospel of John*, (Oxford: Basil Blackwell, 1971).

Culpepper, R. Alan, *Anatomy of the Fourth Gospel. A Study in Literary Design*, (Philadelphia, Fortress Press, 1983).

Culpepper, R. Alan and Black, C. Clifton, *Exploring the Gospel of John. In Honor of D. Moody Smith*, (Louisville: Westminster John Knox Press, 1996)

Daly-Denton, Margaret, *David in the Fourth Gospel, The Johannine Reception of the Psalms*,(Leiden: E. J. Brill, 2000)

Fortna, Robert and Gaventa, Beverly R., *The Conversation Continues. Studies in Paul and John in Honor of J. Louis Martyn*, (Nashville: Abingdon, 1990)

Martyn, J. Louis, *The Gospel of John in Christian History*, (New York: Paulist Press, 1979).

MacRae, George, 'The Fourth Gospel and *Religionsgeschichte*', *Catholic Biblical Quarterly*, Vol. 32, 122-134, (1970).

Moody Smith, D., *Johannine Christianity. Essays on its Setting, Sources, and Theology*, (Edinburgh: T. and T. Clark, 1984).

8

THE QUEST FOR THE HISTORICAL JESUS – SOME THEOLOGICAL REFLECTIONS

The debate about the historical Jesus is no longer confined to academic journals or learned books. It is repeatedly the subject of articles in the popular press both in Europe and in North America, and television documentaries continue to be made about various aspects of the discussion. If Jesus is not always 'good news' for our modern secular society, he certainly seems to be newsworthy. We are a long way removed from the climate of two hundred years ago when Herman Samuel Reimarus (1694-1768) could not publish his controversial views about Jesus. Only posthumously did they see the light of day, thanks to the Deist philosopher, Gotthold Lessing (1729-1781), who found them congenial to his own enterprise of presenting Christianity as an aesthetic religion based on the insights of a genius, but far removed from the various versions then on offer in the different Christian Churches of eighteenth-century Europe. Today, it would seem, any and every opinion about Jesus can be expressed without public concern or *odium theologicum*. It is only those who challenge the sacredness of the Islamic foundation story who must be silenced. Hollywood has taken note.

The fact that this modern interest in Jesus occurs at a time when adherence to institutional Christianity is on the wane in the industrialised, western world, is itself an interesting cultural phenomenon. It reminds us that the academic debates of the nineteenth century did not take place in a cultural vacuum either, as Albert Schweitzer's now classic, *The Quest for the Historical Jesus* (1906) so graphically illustrates. The contemporary popular interest in the historical Jesus debate, especially in North America, is the direct result of a policy of cultivation by some (The Jesus Seminar, for example, in North America) of the communications highway, which is part of our global culture. It is simply the popular front of what has been described as the third wave of historical Jesus research. In the view of one of its most notable practitioners, John Domnick Crossan, this wave differs from previous ones (both the nineteenth-century 'liberal lives' as a response to Lessing's and others attacks on orthodox Christology, and the existentialist phase associated with Rudolph Bultmann and his students in the 1950s and 60s) in three important respects: it uses a *wider range of evidence*, drawing on extra-canonical materials, either recently discovered, (for example, the Gospel of Thomas) or not properly evaluated previously (the sayings of Jesus in various Patristic witnesses); *it integrates various approaches*, literary, historical and social-scientific in dealing with the sources; its *philosophical presuppositions* are post-modern rather than romantic, liberal or existentialist, as in the case of previous efforts.

These are far-reaching claims. It is undoubtedly true that the database from which Crossan operates is expanded considerably, but in the last analysis a negative judgement is passed on much of the evidence in terms of its historical reliability, especially the canonical Gospel material. On the other hand there has until recently been a reluctance to use the interesting archaeological data from twenty intensive years' work in Galilee in the discussion of relevant sources. A greater range of disciplines are today being employed in the study of the New Testament generally, notably the use of the social sciences, but as we shall see, their application is not always unproblematic. As to the third claim, namely the post-modern context for contemporary studies of Jesus, apart from stating the obvious, it is difficult to assess its precise significance, other than to suggest that researchers seem less constrained by traditional theological claims about the definitive nature of Jesus' ministry for Christian faith than was the case with both the liberal lives and the Bultmannian phase. In the end it will be necessary to evaluate whether the current wave of historical-Jesus research has been any more successful in avoiding the pitfall of what George Tyrell at the end of the nineteenth-century described as the reflections of liberal theologians' faces at the bottom of a very deep well. In order to attempt such a judgement, however, it will first be necessary to review some aspects of the nineteenth-century efforts and the salient theological questions that may still be with us.

The Nineteenth-Century Quest in its Cultural Context

The eighteenth-century Enlightenment with its stress on the rationality and freedom of the human subject, and the scientific revolution, which sought the explanation of phenomena solely in terms of their natural causes, inevitably posed a serious question mark to the biblical stories in general and those relating to Jesus in particular. Reimarus and Lessing were Deists who denied any notion of divine revelation and posited the idea of a deity far removed from the affairs of humans. In subsequent centuries the critique of religion by Karl Marx and Sigmund Freud as either the 'opium of the proletariat' or a 'wish-fulfillment' further eroded confidence in the classical, theological claims of the Christian Churches, including those about their founder, Jesus of Nazareth. The Gospel stories about him had to be explained in ways other than simply reiterating their supernaturalist claims in an uncritical fashion. The nineteenth-century quest for the historical Jesus has to be understood against this background. The fact that it was largely conducted in the German academic world of liberal Protestantism gave it a very distinctive colouring, since many of its key practitioners were convinced that the Reformation had restored Christianity to its original simplicity. They thought of the kingdom of God as preached by Jesus in ethical rather than metaphysical terms, and saw the conditions for its realisation within cultural Protestantism, which espoused an ethical and communal form of Christianity, freed from the shackles of the dogmatic Christ of later Christian orthodoxy.

In an effort to reconstruct a plausible account of Jesus and his ministry the question of the Gospels' veracity had of necessity to be dealt with, since rationalist criticism of their supernatural claims had discredited their reliability for many. The figure of David Friedrich Strauss (1808-1874) stands out in particular in this regard, since he sought to steer a middle ground between the narrow reductionism of the rationalists on the one hand and the naive literalism of the supernaturalists on the other, by categorising the Gospels as mythical. By this designation Strauss was acknowledging that dimension of the Gospels which in principle is not open to historical enquiry, thus calling for a distinction to be drawn between different aspects of the narratives. However, with the prevailing view of history as 'things as they actually happened' and the search for objective sources that were nearest in time to those events, this acknowledgement of the mythical dimension of Christian narratives had to await the towering figure of Rudolph Bultmann in the present century before it could receive proper, if controversial attention.

Strauss did not put the results of his own analysis of the Gospels to work in terms of a strictly historical reconstruction. His account of Jesus is, rather, deeply theological and heavily influenced by Hegel's philosophy of the world spirit. Jesus is a singular, though not exhaustive, embodiment of that spirit, since 'the finite can never exhaust the infinite'. Such an account did little to inspire more orthodox views and Strauss eventually was removed from his teaching position in Tübingen. The quest for sources, however, continued unabated. Mark's Gospel, with its realistic narrative style, was deemed the earliest and most untainted and another source was identified beneath the Gospels of Matthew and Luke, a collection of sayings of Jesus that was designated simply by the letter Q (German 'Quelle' or 'source'). Thus the two-source hypothesis, still very much in vogue today, was devised in the context of the debates about the historical Jesus. *Plus ça change* ... preoccupation with the earliest sources is still the concern of the 'third wave', except that now the tendency is to replace Mark by the Gospel of Peter as the earliest Gospel, and refine the Q hypothesis with claims that the Gospel of Thomas is an early and independent source of Jesus' sayings, as in the work of J.D. Crossan.

The 'liberal lives' that Schweitzer has exposed concentrated heavily on the ethical dimensions of Jesus' teaching, in line with the liberal ideals that their proponents espoused and which were believed to be embodied in cultural Protestantism of the day. Jesus emerges as the teacher of a moral code that was 'the highest expression of the human spirit'. In the Sermon on the Mount and in the parables 'the inner power of truth immediately penetrating to the hearts of men (sic) reveals itself in its world-historical significance'. Thus Jesus' life and teaching formed a single whole that was the outer expression of the inner harmony he himself had achieved, leading to 'his complete openness to the world and perfect inwardness toward God'. One text from the Gospels, 'The kingdom of God is within you', (Lk 17,21) was regarded as expressing this unique relationship to God and to humans that was Jesus' self-consciousness, giving rise to his own gradual awareness of his messianic status and his disciples' acceptance of him as such. Unlike Strauss' Hegelian categories, the liberals had sought to safeguard the unique status of Jesus by entering into his inner life and acknowledging the truly universal dimensions of his ethical vision.

While liberal theology was still in its heyday, a new and very different emphasis was appearing in German biblical studies, namely, the History of Religions approach, which sought to emphasise the strange, the primitive and the unmodern in Jesus and in early Christianity. In contrast to the universalising tendency of the liberals, this new approach was more historically grounded, emphasising the particularity of Jesus. 'Theology was forced by genuine history to begin to doubt the artificial history with which it had thought to give life to our Christianity', as Albert Schweitzer put it later. According to this view, when Jesus spoke of the kingdom of God, he was not speaking of human, ethical possibilities, but of a wholly other understanding of God's rule that was external and cosmic in its dimensions in line with Jewish apocalyptic hopes. Johannes Weiss, in direct opposition to his father-in-law, Albert Ritschl's liberal ideas about the ethical understanding of Jesus' kingdom language, was one of the earliest proponents of this view (1892). Schweitzer developed Weiss' notion further by suggesting that when Jesus' expectation of an imminent coming of the kingdom did not materialise, he changed his mind and felt the call to take on the messianic woes that were anticipated before the end, according to the Jewish literature. While Schweitzer is quite happy to rely on Mark's outline of the career of Jesus, others such as Wilhelm Wrede went further in undermining this trust. Far from being a straightforward account of Jesus' life, Mark should be seen as a highly theological statement of early Christian apologetic in the light of the failure of the coming kingdom. However, it took the disasters of the First World War to shatter finally the liberal dream, and a new and very different voice was to emerge, namely that of Rudolph Bultmann, who would throw the whole project of the historical Jesus into question with his kerygmatic theology in an existentialist key. This is an issue we shall return to in the conclusion of this paper.

The rapid survey of some of the more significant moments of the nineteenth-century quest was intended solely to highlight some key issues that might shed critical light on the contemporary developments. Despite Crossan's disavowal of the comparison, certain issues seem clear. The question of reliable sources may not have been as refined as it is today, but it nevertheless was a real concern emanating from the purist idea of history 'as it really was', which was the dominant view of the nineteenth century. Today we may be less positivistic, but the ultimate objective appears the same. Why else would the question of stratification of the evidence be so important to the Jesus Seminar? The liberal agenda, in line with its Reformation roots, may have sought to shed later Christological formulations of the tradition but it still attempted to safeguard the universal claims about Jesus in terms of his ethical teaching. In doing so the contrast with his Jewish antecedents was over-emphasised, thus feeding into and uncritically replicating the anti-Jewish biases of nineteenth-century German academic thinking generally. These questions, too, recur in the present situation, as does the issue of either an apocalyptic or an ethical Jesus. Before condemning the latest wave, however, in terms of its antecedents' – to us – mistaken ideas, it is important to sketch the results of some of the more important findings of the present quest more adequately.

The 'third wave' of Jesus Research
It would be tedious to attempt a complete survey of all the different Jesus types that modern scholarship has thrown up. As noted already, one major contrast with the nineteenth-century 'lives' is the different context for the discussion. North America now provides the setting, partly because the centre of gravity for biblical and theological studies has shifted from Europe over the last fifty years or so, but partly also, I suspect, because that North American society today has been aptly described as a nation with the soul of a Church. In a way that is not dissimilar to liberal Protestant dreams in nineteenth-century Germany, one finds a tendency to identify Christianity with the American dream. The Jesus images emerging from such a culture will inevitably bear the marks of their origin, even if it would be misleading to suggest that that is the sole factor that is operative. I propose to sketch the picture in broad outlines only.

(i) A Jewish Jesus
New Testament studies today, like all Christian theological discourse, takes place in a post-holocaust setting. Inevitably, therefore, the *Heimholung Jesus in das Judentum*, 'the bringing Jesus home to Judaism', which has been a feature of liberal Jewish approaches to Jesus, is reflected in Christian scholarship also. The discovery of the Dead Sea Scrolls has fuelled the debate, sometimes also distorting it insofar as unwarranted, or even outlandish claims are made about Jesus and the Qumran monks, whose library the scrolls presumably represent. The impetus that these discoveries have given to studies of the Second Temple period means that we are much more aware of the variety of Judaisms that were on offer in the first century c.e., even in Palestine. Stereotypes such as the Messiah, as though all were agreed about the expected figure, or the legalism of the Pharisees, have no longer any place in responsible scholarship, and this poses a new challenge for

scholars, anxious not to replicate the mistakes of the past, by presenting a Jesus over against Judaism.

From the Jewish side the various writings of the Oxford scholar, Geza Vermes, have received most attention. In his view Jesus can be seen as a typical Galilean *hasid*, holy man or charismatic, whose life is the very embodiment of the Torah-true Jew, devoted to the ancestral religion and deeply trusting in God's care and protection. Endowed with God's spirit he can be compared with various 'men of deeds' in the Jewish sources, whose prototype is Elijah, healer and doer of mighty deeds. The various titles for Jesus, such as 'son of God', 'son of man'; even 'Lord', which occur in the Gospels can be understood as terms of address within Palestinian Aramaic without investing them with the later theological value that Hellenistic Christianity has done.

This very eirenic picture is in stark contrast with that of E.P. Sanders who concentrates on the deeds of Jesus, especially the incident in the temple, to paint a picture of Jesus as the prophet of an imminent Jewish restoration in accordance with prophetic hopes. Thus, Jesus' action in overthrowing the tables of the money-changers and his alleged threat to destroy the existing temple as a prelude to building a new one (Mk 11,15-19; 14, 58) must be seen as part of a single vision for the restoration of Israel, based on various prophetic declarations. Other deeds of Jesus, such as the calling of the Twelve, the healing of the sick and confining his ministry to Israel, all point in the same direction. At the same time Sanders does not see Jesus breaking with his Jewish heritage in any radical way. The reported disputes with the Pharisees over legal matters for the most part stem from the later Church and cannot be construed in a way that Jesus ignored the law, though in one respect he did differ from other contemporary teachers including John the Baptist, namely, the belief that God's kingdom was an open invitation to real sinners irrespective of their conversion.

Vermes' and Sanders' work, for all their differences of approach and emphasis are concerned with presenting Jesus very much within the Judaism of his own day, without breaking the mould. Other Christian scholars too, though espousing similar interests, focus more on the conflictual aspects of his ministry vis-á-vis his contemporaries. Thus, Bruce Chilton sees him prioritising personal experience over learned discussion in his use of the Scriptures, and the incident in the temple was an attempt to restore sacrificial practice to what was originally intended in the Torah, not its abolition, as Sanders maintained. Marcus Borg, sees Jesus as a Spirit-filled holy man, focusing on the present rather than the future and challenging the purity laws and their political and social isolationism by eating meals with tax-collectors and sinners. John Riches is also concerned with the purity laws in his efforts to understand the innovative dimension of Jesus' ministry. He operates with a more sophisticated notion of language as a system of signs, that though shared and conventional, takes on a personal dimension through use and association, thus enabling new and creative formulations of common ideas to be expressed. Jesus' kingdom language can thus be construed as innovative in terms of conventional understandings, thereby leading to the transformation of Judaism, to cite the title of Riches' book.

(ii) A Cynic Jesus

Under this designation it is possible to group together a number of images of Jesus that see him as participating more fully in and being influenced by popular religious attitudes within Greco-Roman society than was the case among those scholars just discussed. While, in general, proponents of 'the Cynic Jesus' stress the non-Jewish dimension of the Jesus traditions, it is important to be aware of recent developments in our understanding of the interpenetration of Greco-Roman and Jewish culture for several centuries prior to Jesus. While the encounter was sometimes hostile, this was not always the case and some Jews at least participated fully in the intellectual life of cities like Alexandria in Egypt. The specific question that needs to be discussed in this context is the degree to which such enculturation had occurred in Palestine itself, both in terms of its geographic spread and across social divisions within the Jewish temple community. The range of questions covers issues from language (Greek, Aramaic or bilingualism?) to economic and social factors, to religious practices and values. What also needs to be considered here is the bias of individual scholars, insofar as the image of a Cynic Jesus as well as the that of a thoroughly Hellenised Galilee have a certain flawed pedigree from the past that does not always seem to be appreciated by some of their modern proponents. Thus, as Hans Dieter Betz has shown, a revival of Cynicism as a world-philosophy, with Jesus as one of its outstanding examples in a deeply anti-Jewish and anti-Christian way, was espoused in the last century by no less a figure than Friedrich Nietzsche, while the notion of a Hellenised Galilee led one scholar during the Nazi period to declare that as a Galilean Jesus was, in all probability, not a Jew.

Despite such a cautionary note it is important to acknowledge that some aspects of Jesus and his followers' life-style – homelessness and the eschewing of honour and all worldly goods – do have similarities, externally at least, to what we know of the Cynics. But there are very real differences also, which risk being overlooked when comparisons are being made. Burton Mack, for example, wants to situate Jesus within a Galilee that is so thoroughly familiar with Cynic attitudes that when he speaks of the kingdom of God, this would naturally be understood by his hearers in terms of the Cynic-Stoic idea that only the wise person is truly king. This means that the personal freedom that accrues through detachment from all human needs makes one really master of one's own destiny. F. G. Downing has made a very exhaustive study of ancient Cynicism, and he too is impressed by the parallels with the Jesus tradition, arguing that it is more probable that these elements go back to Jesus himself rather than that they were introduced later, and according to him also, Cynic ideas would be perfectly at home in Galilee. At the same time, Downing is careful to acknowledge a Jewish element in the Jesus-tradition also, and notes one very important feature of Jesus' teaching absent from the Cynic sources, namely, an eschatological perspective.

The subtitle of Crossan's study speaks of a 'Mediterranean, Jewish Peasant'. All three designations are important to him in terms of his multi-faceted methodological approach, which in his view makes the present quest very different in character from the nineteenth century one. For Crossan, Cynicism represented a popular mode of resistance to ruling class exploitation in the Roman world, a form of non-violent, counter-culture, whereby those who adopted the anti-social stance espoused by the Cynics in regard to dress, begging and general demeanour, were able to ignore the otherwise harsh realities of the honor/shame ethos of the Mediterranean culture of the first century. Far from being introversionist, this vision had within it revolutionary seeds. By stressing the practical wisdom elements in the sayings of Jesus as authentic and relegating the apocalyptic as later accretions Crossan is able to present Jesus with his band of followers as Cynic-like figures, not engaged in a mission of renewal to Israel but enacting their vision of 'a brokerless' kingdom of God in the context of 'embattled brokerage' that was Roman Palestine of the first century. This message is defined as 'open commensality', or a radical egalitarianism that proclaimed 'the immediate and unmediated presence of God to each and every individual and the concomitant unmediated presence of each individual to every other individual'. Jesus' death was the direct result of the atopical, non-localised nature of his ministry of 'reciprocal exchange of meal and magic', as he wandered through Galilee. Combined with his saying against the temple, this ministry gave rise to his arrest and crucifixion on his one and only journey to Jerusalem. However, the accounts of his passion, death and resurrection in the Gospels are not based on any historical reminiscences, but are free, scripturally-based narratives serving the needs of the later Church.

For all the unconventional nature of this historical construal, not least, in my view, its marginally Jewish and overly-Mediterranean quality, Crossan's work has a genuine theological concern. There will always be a tension between a historically-read Jesus and a theologically-read Christ, he writes, and this will be reflected in the dialectic between how we see Jesus then and how we see Christ now. But for him, that tension and dialectic are creative, not distorting. There was no betrayal in the move from the historical Jesus to the Nicene formulation, in that Catholic Christianity from the start saw the historical Jesus as the manifestation of God, irrespective of how this insight was formulated. By basing his picture of Jesus on the wisdom strand of the Q source, as reconstructed by John Kloppenborg, rather than on some version of the Markan narrative, as has been customary, his Christology appears more like a 'Jesu-ology' that ignores any development in the understanding of Jesus in the light of the Resurrection experience. Its first proponents, namely the followers of Jesus in the Q-community, were living and acting in continuity with their experience of the earthly Jesus, to the point where faith in Jesus and imitation of Jesus were indistinguishable.

(iii) The social-revolutionary Jesus

Crossan's work could just as easily be seen under this heading, since for him the 'embattled brokerage' of first-century Palestinian society was the immediate context for Jesus' unique counter-cultural response. Because he regards its inspiration as arising from the cynic/wisdom rather than the apocalyptic world-view it does not engage with the powers in the way that some other recent presentations of Jesus do, however. These particular treatments are indebted to the increased interest in the social world approaches to the New Testament generally. In attempting to understand how social realities might have impacted on his public ministry, the Galilean social world of Jesus has become a matter of intense debate. How Hellenised was Galilee as a result of the circle of Greek cities? What was the nature of Galilean relations with

Jerusalem? What were the internal social tensions? These and other questions are being canvassed, on the basis of both the literary and archaeological evidence. However, insofar as such discussions are theory-driven rather than engaged in more old-fashioned social description, there is a distinct danger that Jesus may be understood solely in terms of a social reformer rather than a religiously motivated prophet. Marxist class-theory stresses socio-economic factors in social conflict, but it would be a serious mistake to reduce first-century Judaism in such a way that issues about purity, the temple, Torah-observance were seen as mere ciphers for other 'real' causes at work in the society, no matter how intertwined various aspects of life were in pre-industrial societies.

Gerd Theissen, the Heidleberg New Testament scholar, has been one of the most influential figures in this approach, analysing the Jesus-movement in terms of roles, factors and functions, in order to see how certain typical patterns within that society were replicated in this particular movement also. Jesus and his immediate followers are seen as wandering charismatics, supported by sympathisers within the local communities, who have made a virtue out of necessity by transforming certain social realities, such as poverty and violence, in a positive way, either by valuing them differently as in the case of poverty, or by internalising them as in the case of violence and aggression. Thus, while the movement can be seen as emerging from the social anomie of the society, it nevertheless functioned in an integrative way in contrast to some other responses, such as that of the Fourth Philosophy with its violent, anti-Roman stance. Richard A. Horsley, on the other hand, sees the Jesus movement in more conflictual terms as challenging the value-systems of the powerful elites by espousing the renewal of local community life, and thereby presenting an alternative vision to the predominant one, especially in terms of 'the spiral of violence,' which he considers to have been the controlling factor in first-century Palestinian society. Elizabeth Schüssler-Fiorenza applies a critical, feminist hermeneutics of liberation in evaluating oppression in first-century Palestine by developing a model of historical reconstruction to make explicit the subjugation of women, both in terms of their being devalued within the Jewish religious experience and their exploitation in the Roman imperial one. In her gender-sensitive reconstruction Schüssler-Fiorenza includes exploited males also and speaks of 'woe-man' in order to underline the inclusive nature of Jesus' community as a discipleship of equals.

This categorisation of recent discussions of Jesus and his role is very general, but hopefully it has helped to indicate the great variety of perspectives, methods and results within the current debate. Each has different strengths, but also significant weaknesses. Crossan's suggestion that the current quest differs from the first one in being thoroughly post-modern, is certainly true to the extent that no one picture of Jesus seems to dominate the horizon in the way that a liberal Jesus did in the nineteenth century. One can also see the traces of twentieth-century concerns in other respects, such as the issue of the Jewish Jesus and also the influence of contemporary social and feminist concerns, whether implicitly or explicitly. Indeed, there is a danger that Jesus himself might be vested in the post-modern garb. The focus on Jesus' words that one finds in some of the recent writing, which emphasises their enigmatic, subversive and indeterminate quality, especially his parables, is in danger of depriving him of any overall vision or intention. This danger has been well countered by James Breech who points to the story-telling dimension of Jesus' parables in particular, which though not easily yielding up the questions to which they are supposed to be answers, nevertheless, still display an understanding of human existence which calls for co-existence with others as part of an ongoing story where death is not the ultimate answer to human life, irrespective of all appearances to the contrary.

Conclusion

Breech's response to some of the dangers of the recent concern with the sayings of Jesus in isolation from his deeds, raises in an interesting manner the issue which the so-called new quest for the historical Jesus, attempted to address in the 1950s, ably documented by James M. Robinson. The 'new quest' was regarded as 'new' in relation to the nineteenth-century one already discussed, which finally collapsed with the death of liberalism in the wake of the catastrophe of the First World War. Thereafter, the towering figure of Rudolph Bultmann dominated New Testament studies with his radical existentialist interpretation of the kerygma and the denial in principle of the possibility of recovering the historical Jesus. The quest is impossible because of the nature of the sources and Christian faith is a response to the proclaimed word without any need for the support of historical research, in Bultmann's view. Eventually, however, the dangers of this radical scepticism for a genuine Christian faith were exposed by some of Bultmann's own pupils, and hence the new quest was launched, with its genuine theological as well as historical concerns. In a programmatic essay Ernst Käsemann wrote as follows in 1953:

> The question of the historical Jesus, in its legitimate form, is the question of the continuity of the Gospel within the discontinuity of the times and the variations of the kerygma ... The Gospel is tied to him, who before and after Easter, revealed himself to his own as Lord, by setting them before the God who is near to them, and thus translating them into the freedom and responsibility of faith ... He (Jesus) cannot be classified according to the categories either of psychology or of the comparative study of religion, or finally of general history. If he can be placed at all it must be in terms of historical particularity. To this extent the problem of the historical Jesus is not our invention, but the riddle which he himself set us.

This statement was programmatic for the new quest, namely, the need to establish the historical links between the proclaimer and the proclaimed, over against Bultmann's scepticism about that possibility and his disclaimer about its theological necessity. There could be no return to the old quest, however, with its biographic interests, since the nature of the sources did not allow for this. Despite this legitimate difficulty with regard to the aims of the old quest, there were problems with the new quest also, in that Käsemann and others such as Gunther Bornkamm, were too narrowly focused on the kerygma of the death and resurrection and did not take sufficient account of the narratives about the earthly life of Jesus as these too formed part of the kerygma about him. It was only with the advent of liberation theology and its stress on the accounts of Jesus' earthly life in terms of its engagement with oppressive structures, that the transformative possibilities of these narratives for Christian faith today have been properly appreciated. By contrast the Pauline kerygma of the cross/resurrection could more easily be transferred into an other worldly domain that lacks a concern for issues of social justice now as part of Christian faith itself.

If with the hindsight of history the original quest for Jesus may be seen as naive and unself-critical, it is not clear to me that the third wave has succeeded in avoiding similar difficulties. Despite all the sophisticated discussion of sources and the casting of the net for relevant data more widely, one cannot avoid the suspicion that late twentieth-century concerns have been determinative both in the choice of relevant 'historical' evidence and in the resulting pictures of Jesus. Recently,

Sandra Schneiders has called for a reformulation of the question by distinguishing between the *actual Jesus* and the *historical Jesus*. The former refers to Jesus' ontic reality, both as a being who once actually existed in this world, but who no longer does so and can only be evoked as memory, and who now exists as the risen Lord and Saviour, accessible only through faith. On the other hand, the 'historical' Jesus is a literary construct based on the actual Jesus' earthly life, but not to be equated with him, since only that which is in principle open to public investigation can be regarded as historical, and there are many aspects of his existence, not least the claim to divine status, which cannot be investigated in this way. The Gospels are interested in the actual Jesus' earthly existence, but that is not all they are interested in, since in their author's view that is not the only truth about Jesus. As such they only give us a partial account of his earthly life, that which is considered necessary in order to mediate symbolically the actual Jesus both in his pastness and in his present, glorified reality.

This formulation of the task is at once more modest and more realistic, since it means that the quest for Jesus is determined by the records about him, especially insofar as these have continued to shape Christian existence through history. Thus there are theological as well as historical grounds for giving the canonical Gospels priority over other ancient sources, which may well contain significant historical information. It is with similar presuppositions that I have also attempted to explore the Galilean dimension of Jesus' career. While the canonical Gospels' account of that aspect of his earthly existence can and should be scrutinised in terms of our burgeoning knowledge of the region from archaeological and other literary sources, in the end its theological significance must also be considered. This aspect has entered Christian theological discourse, not as nostalgic biography but as a statement of God's concern for human marginality and particularity. Our continued preoccupation with the historical Jesus is indeed justified if this aspect of the memory of Jesus is kept alive and active in our world, especially since Christian belief in his Lordship can easily de-humanise and de-personalise that memory.

Select bibliography

Betz, H.D., 'Jesus and the Cynics: Survey and Analysis of an Hypothesis', *Journal of Religion* 74 (1994) 453-473.

Borg, M., *Conflict, Holiness and Politics in the Teachings of Jesus*, Lewiston and Lampeter: 1984, The Edwin Mellen Press.

Bornkamm, G. *Jesus of Nazareth*, (English) London: Hodder and Stoughton, 1960.

Breech, J., *The Silence of Jesus – The Authentic Voice of the Historical Man*, Philadelphia: Fortress Press, 1983.

Bultmann, R., *Jesus and the Word*, (English) New York: Fontana Books, 1934.

Chilton, B., *A Galilean Rabbi and his Bible*, Glazier/Liturgical Press: Wilmington/Collegeville, 1984.

Chilton, B., *The Temple of Jesus: His Sacrificial Program Within A Cultural History of Sacrifice*. Pennsylvania: Penn State University Press, 1992.

Carlson, J. and Ludwig, R., *Jesus and Faith. A Conversation on the Work of John Domnick Crossan.*, Maryknoll, N.Y.: Orbis Press, 1994.

Crossan, J.D., *The Historical Jesus. The Life of a Mediterranean Jewish Peasant*. Edinburgh: T. and T. Clark, 1991.

Downing, F.G.,*Cynics and Christian Origins*, Edinburgh: T. and T. Clark, 1992

Freyne, S., *Galilee, Jesus and the Gospels: Literary Approaches and Historical Investigations*, Dublin: Gill/Macmillan, 1988.

Horsley, R. A., *Jesus and the Spiral of Violence. Sociology and the Jesus Movement*, New York: Crossroad, 1989.

Käsemann, E., *Essays on New Testament Themes*, (English) London: SCM Press, 1964. pp.15-47.

Kloppenborg, John, *Excavating Q: The Historical Setting of the Sayings Gospel*, Edinburgh: T and T Clark, 2000.

Lessing. G., *Lessing's Theological Writings*, ed. H. Chadwick, Stanford: Stanford University Press, 1957.

Mack, B., *A Myth of Innocence. Mark and Christian Origins*, Philadelphia: Fortress Press, 1988.

Mack, B., *The Lost Gospel. The Book of Q and Christian Origins*, New York: Harper San Francisco, 1993.

Reimarus, H.S., *The Goal of Jesus and his Disciples* (English) ed. G. Buchanan, Leiden: Brill, 1970.

Riches, J., *Jesus and the Transformation of Judaism*, London, 1980.

Riches, J., *A Century of New Testament Study*, Cambridge: The Lutterworth Press, 1993.

Robinson, J.M., *A New Quest of the Historical Jesus*, London: SCM Press, 1959.

Sanders, E.P., *Jesus and Judaism*, London: SCM Press, 1985.

Schneiders, S., *The Revelatory Text*. New York: HarperSanFrancisco, 1991.

Schüssler-Fiorenza, E., *Jesus-Sophia*, Crossword, New York, 1995.

Schweitzer, A., *The Quest of the Historical Jesus*, (English) New ed., New York: Macmillan, 1968.

Strauss, D.F., *The Life of Jesus Critically Examined*, (English) London: SCM reprint, 1975.

Theissen, G., *The First Followers of Jesus*, (English) London: SCM Press, 1978.

Vermes, G., *The Religion of Jesus the Jew*, London: SCM Press, 1993.

Weiss, J., *Jesus' Proclamation of the Kingdom of God*, (English) London: SCM, 1971.

Wrede, W., 'The Task and Methods of New Testament Theology', in R. Morgan, ed., *The Nature of New Testament Theology*, London: SCM Press, 1973, 68-116.

9

GALILEE AND JUDEA IN THE FIRST CENTURY – THE SOCIAL WORLD OF JESUS AND HIS MINISTRY

There are different emphases in the Gospels with regard to the theatre for the public ministry of Jesus. Whereas the synoptics concentrate on Galilee with one final journey to Jerusalem, the Fourth Gospel views Galilee virtually as a place of refuge from a ministry conducted for the most part in Judea and Jerusalem. Ever since David Friedrich Strauss's *The Life of Jesus Critically Examined* (1849) many attempts have been made to resolve this apparent contradiction, none of them totally convincing. In the most recent wave of historical Jesus research there has been a marked preference for Galilee, due to various factors, not least current trends among scholars interested in the social rather than the theological significance of Jesus' life. Indeed, so much has the balance tilted in that direction that some recent construals downplay the Jerusalem aspect to the extent that his death in Jerusalem is seen as purely accidental – a case of being in the wrong place at the wrong time. This is surely an aberration, since Jesus might just as easily have met his death at the hands of Herod Antipas as did his mentor, John the Baptist in Perea, had the circumstances of his ministry in Galilee so demanded. Historians of Jesus' life are missing an important clue, therefore, if they ignore the fact that it was in Jerusalem rather than in Galilee that he eventually met his fate. While these issues cannot be dealt with here, they do demand that in any discussion of the social world of Jesus, attention should be given to both regions and to the special factors that were operative in each in the first century c.e. (See maps, pp 7-8).

In the recent discussions of these topics the social sciences have tended to provide the framework for integrating the literary and archaeological evidence. In particular the model for advanced, agrarian empires developed by Gerhard Lenski has been highly influential, since it attempts to depict the social stratification that occurs in societies where management of labour is directed towards achieving a surplus rather than mere subsistence farming.[1] The Roman empire as a whole is deemed to have been one such society, and so Palestinian social life can be profitably examined from this point of view. Two major revolts against Rome, both of which can be said to have had a social as well as a religious component, have, however, convinced many scholars of the need to supplement the Lenski model with another approach that can assist in mapping the factors that give rise to social conflict and the strategies adopted by elites for its management.[2]

All models are ideal types that must constantly be revised and adapted in the light of particular situations. Yet their use can greatly assist in enabling a coherent account to be presented and in testing its accuracy in the light of the available data, thereby avoiding what has been described as the 'intuitivist' approach to the description of ancient societies. In the following account aspects of the Lenski model will be used to provide the broad framework for describing the most important aspects of Palestinian society in the first century c.e., while taking account also of those special factors that brought about regional variations as well as those that gave rise to social conflict.

Geographical and Historical Factors

As one moves from west to east, both Galilee and Judea follow a similar pattern in geomorphic terms – coastal plain, central hill-country and rift valley. On a north-south axis, however, real differences emerge, due to the different climatic conditions. The marked decrease in annual rainfall from north to south is very obvious in the landscape. Whereas the central Galilean hill country has a number of wide valleys, with rich alluvial soil and many springs running in an east/west direction, the Judean hill country has much less soil covering and tapers off quickly into the dry, arid desert region of the Dead Sea valley. In the nineteenth century Ernest Renan notoriously drew on this marked difference of landscape to illustrate the different religious mentalities of the two regions according to his particular prejudices.[3] The differences, which were recognised by ancient writers such as Josephus (*Jewish War* – hereafter abbreviated as *J.W.* – 3, 41-43; 506-21), do, however, point to some differences in lifestyles and settlement patterns in the two regions.

Historical factors played a much greater role in bringing about regional variations, however.[4] The name 'Galilee', meaning 'the circle', is derived in all probability from the experience of the early Israelites inhabiting the interior highlands and surrounded by Canaanite city states. 'Judea' on the other hand is a tribal name, which came to particular prominence in the monarchic period due to the fact that David was of Judean origin. The Galilean tribes were Zebulon, Naphthali and Asher, with the tribe of Dan migrating north later. The early accounts of the tribal characteristics and behavioural patterns especially the Blessings of Jacob (Gen 49) and Moses (Deut 33), as well as the Song of Deborah (Judg 5), suggest that the northern tribes had a more chequered career in establishing themselves in the region than had Judah and its neighbour, Benjamin, in the south. These may well reflect later situations where the issue of ethnic identity came under threat for various reasons. The northern tribes encountered much greater difficulties than the southern ones, which seem to have blended into their immediate environment more easily. Certainly the north bore the brunt of the Assyrian onslaught of the eight century b.c.e. with Tiglalthpilesar III's invasion resulting in the destruction, and possibly the depopulation of many centres in upper and lower Galilee (2 Kings 15, 29; Is 8, 23). However, unlike Samaria some ten years later (2 Kings 17, 23) there is no mention of a foreign, non-Israelite population being introduced to Galilee at that time. It was a century and a half later before Judah succumbed to the Babylonians with the destruction of the temple and the deportation of the king and the leading members of the Judean aristocracy to Babylon in 582 b.c.e. However, restoration in Judea occurred quickly under the Persians, with the edict of Cyrus in 515 b.c.e. allowing the Jews to return and rebuild the temple. Josephus acknowledges the significance of these events for later Judean history when he writes as follows: 'This name (*Ioudaioi*) which they have been called from the time when they went up from Babylon, is derived from the tribe of Judah; as this tribe was the first to come from those parts, both the people themselves and the country have taken their name from it' (*Jewish Antiquities* – hereafter abbreviated as *J.A.* – 11,173).

The subsequent history of both regions is highly significant for understanding the situation in each in the first century c.e.[5] We have very little information about the history of Galilee in the Babylonian and Persian periods, and hence different positions are adopted as to the ethnic

mix and cultural loyalties of the people there at that time. The Persian
province of Yehud, as it was officially named, remained a fairly
insignificant temple enclave for several centuries, despite the grandiose
hopes of the restoration prophets such as Second and Third Isaiah and
Ezechiel. All that was to change in the Greek period when in the second
century b.c.e. the Seleucid empire began to collapse, and various ethnic
groups, including the Judeans, were able to establish themselves within
national territories. Once the threat from Antiochus Epiphanes (175-164
b.c.e.) of forced assimilation of the Judean temple cult of Yahweh to that
of Zeus had been averted, the desecrated temple was rededicated in 164
b.c.e. and the foundation of an autonomous Jewish state was to follow in
its wake. The second generation of the Maccabees, the Hasmoneans,
initiated campaigns of expansion, which eventually lead to the
establishment of a kingdom that territorially was as extensive as that of
David and Solomon in the ninth century. For the first time in almost a
millennium, therefore, Galilee and Judea were under the same native
rulership, and significantly in the literature of the period the name
Ioudaios/ Jew begins to be used not just for the inhabitants of Judea but
for all who embrace the Jewish temple ideology and who worship in
Jerusalem.[6]

The Hasmonean state did not survive, however, as Rome's expansion
in the east had been gradual but deliberate. Eventually the treaty of
friendship that had been established between Judah the Maccabee and
the Roman senate (1 Macc 8) was put into action when Pompey, the
Roman general, then at Damascus, was invited to intervene in a
succession dispute between two sons of Alexander Jannaeus in 63 b.c.e.
One of the brothers, Aristobulus, resisted the Romans and thereby gave
Pompey the pretext he required to attack Jerusalem. Many of
Aristobulus' supporters were taken captive and there was great slaughter
in the city. The Roman general entered the Holy of Holies, but unlike a
previous invading general, Antiochus Epiphanes, he did not interfere
with the temple cult. Nevertheless, the episode left a deep impression
among pious circles in Jerusalem and is reflected in several Qumran
documents as well as in the Psalms of Solomon, a collection of Psalms
which are generally dated to this period. Hyrcanus II, one of the feuding
brothers, a weak and ineffectual character, was appointed ethnarch and
High Priest. The ousted Aristobulus II and his son, Alexander, made an
attempt at restoration, but this only led to further intervention by Rome,
this time by Gabinius, the Roman legate of Syria, who restored the
autonomy of many of the cities destroyed by the Hasmoneans, and

divided up the remaining Jewish territory into five separate districts, a classic example of the Roman principle of 'divide and rule'. Galilee, with Sepphoris as the seat of its assembly, was one of these districts, thus confirming its clearly Jewish character in Roman eyes, while at the same time giving the region a certain degree of administrative independence, which would continue to be of importance.

The demise of the Hasmoneans, despite several abortive attempts at restoration by the family of Aristobulus, as well as the civil wars in Rome that eventually lead to the establishment of the Principate, with Octavian as sole ruler, created a dangerous power vacuum in Palestine. It was a strategic territory as far as Rome's ambitions and needs in the east were concerned, and there was an extensive and influential Jewish diaspora scattered throughout the Mediterranean, and even farther afield in Parthia, Rome's potential competitor for control of the Middle East. This is the political context in which the Herodian family, an ambitious Idumean dynasty, emerged as brokers of Roman power in Palestine. Herod was appointed king of the Jews in 40 b.c.e., having distinguished himself as a young man as governor of Galilee, in dealing with a brigand band led by Hezechias. It is indeed debatable whether or not this Hezechias was an ordinary brigand or an ousted Hasmonean aristocrat who may have been driven to this type of political protest. At all events, Herod had to contend with one final challenge from this house after his return from Rome in 40 b.c.e. Antigonus, the second son of Aristobulus, gained the support of the Parthians and launched a stout resistance to the imposition of Herod on the Jews. Engagements between the two sides took place throughout the land, north and south, but with Roman help Herod was eventually able to secure his throne. Thereafter, he embarked on a period of consolidation that involved a major building project both in Jerusalem and at other centres, as well as supporting projects abroad, in a manner that resembled the benevolence of a powerful Hellenistic monarch rather than Rome's client king of a petty kingdom.

The long reign of Herod made a deep impact on both Galilean and Judean society, so much so in fact that on his death an embassy was sent to Rome requesting that none of his sons should replace him, while they competed among themselves for the honour. Augustus responded by once again dividing the kingdom between Herod's sons into three different territories, assigning Antipas to Galilee and Perea, Archelaus to Judea and Philip to Batanaea, Trachonitis and Auranitis in northern Transjordan. Galilee was again, therefore, administratively separate from Judea, something that is reflected in Matthew's Gospel, in explaining how

Jesus came to live in Galilee, though born in Judea: 'His father Joseph, hearing that Archelaus ruled in Judea in the place of Herod, his father, took the child and his mother to Galilee, and came to live at Nazareth' (Mt 2, 23). Josephus gives a broader background to this information. Archelaus had so outraged his subjects that he was deposed by Rome in 6 c.e. and thereafter Judea was ruled as a procuratorship, or Roman province of second rank, with the governor resident in Caesarea Maritima and Jerusalem acting as the temple city controlled by the priestly aristocracy.

Antipas aspired to the title of 'king', but only achieved that of ethnarch. He ruled in Galilee and Perea until 37 b.c.e., when he too was deposed and his territory was handed over to his nephew Agrippa I. Despite this lesser status, he continued with the style and policy of his father in ensuring that Roman concerns were taken care of in his territories. John the Baptist suffered at his hands, probably for the reasons given by Josephus, rather than that of the Gospels, namely that John's popularity and espousal of justice for the poor gave cause for concern that an uprising might occur (*J.A.* 18, 116-19). This would have been deemed a serious failure in imperial eyes, since client kings were tolerated only if they could be seen to ensure stability and loyalty to Rome and its values. Apart from the Jerusalem temple, Herod the Great had confined his major building projects to the periphery of the Jewish territories: Samaria was renamed 'Sebaste' (the Greek equivalent of Augustus) and a temple to *Roma* and Augustus was built there, as also at Caesarea Maritima on the coast where a magnificent harbour was developed. In the north a temple to Augustus was built at Paneas, which his son, Philip, later renamed Caesarea (Philippi). Antipas also continued this tradition of honouring the Roman overlords through monumental buildings in Galilee. Sepphoris was made 'the ornament of all Galilee' and named *autoratoris*, probably honouring the 'sole rule' of Augustus (*J.A.* 18, 27). Tiberias on the lake front was a new foundation, probably in 19 c.e, in honour of the new emperor who had succeeded Augustus.

This account of Jewish history with a focus on how events played themselves out in the different regions is crucial for a correct understanding of the social world of Palestine in the first century c.e. Historical factors were largely determinative of shifting population and settlement patterns in the different regions, thereby explaining the religious and cultural loyalties also. Economic conditions were dependent on the political realities of the day, since all ancient economies were, to a considerable extent, politically controlled. It is to these topics that we must now turn, focusing on Galilee and Judea separately, while also attempting to highlight similarities and continuities where they occur.

Galilee

Over the past twenty-five years no region of ancient Palestine has received more attention than Galilee. This interest arises from both Jewish and Christian concern with origins, since Galilee functioned as the place of origins for both religions, as the context for Jesus' ministry (the Synoptics) and the home of Rabbinic Judaism after the second revolt of 132-35 c.e.[7] In addition to the study of the literary evidence, mainly Josephus' works, the Gospels and the Rabbinic writings, the focus has been on archaeology, both at key sites like Sepphoris and in surveys of various sub-regions. The pictures emerging from these studies are varied, sometimes even contradictory, as scholars from various disciplines attempt as full a description of the region as possible in Hellenistic and Roman times. Nowhere is this tendency more in evidence than when historical Jesus studies and Galilean studies become intertwined. Ever since Albert Schweitzer exposed the anachronistic concerns of many of the liberal lives of Jesus (*The Quest for the Historical Jesus*, 1906) it has become increasingly evident that objectivity is often asserted but rarely fully adhered to as various proposals for the ministry of Jesus are put forward. In this field there is no neutral ground, since so much is at stake both personally and institutionally. In reviewing some of the recent scholarship on Jesus and Galilee it soon becomes evident that the quest for the historical Jesus and the quest for the historical Galilee are often just two sides of the same issue.[8]

Who were the Galileans? Religious and Cultural Affiliations

With these cautionary remarks the first question to be addressed concerns Galileans rather than Galilee. Who were the Galileans that we meet in the literary sources? What was their provenance, what social and economic strata did they represent, and what were their religious and cultural affiliations? Adequate answers to questions such as these, while hard to achieve definitively, can – when approached independently of special concerns – help to ground other speculations of a more theological kind and offer some criteria for evaluating different proposals. Briefly, one can distinguish three broad lines of response in the contemporary discussions to the questions posed, with minor variations to each.

The Galileans of the later sources are direct descendants of the old Israelite population, who had remained undisturbed, it is claimed, in the first wave of Assyrian conquest of the north and who had maintained their essential Yahwistic beliefs over centuries. According to Albrecht Alt, who first argued this position in a series of articles, these inhabitants of Galilee freely and naturally joined the *ethnos ton Ioudaion* (the Jewish nation) when the opportunity arose after the Hasmonean expansion to the north. This had resulted in the destruction of the Samaritan temple on Mount Gerazim and subsequently Samaria itself and Scythopolis/Beth Shean as centres of Hellenistic culture, which had separated Galilee from its natural religious and cultic centre.[9] More recently, Richard Horsley has also espoused the notion of the old Israelite population remaining undisturbed in Galilee, but he sees the situation in the Hasmonean times quite differently from Alt. He claims that over the centuries the Galileans had developed separate customs and practices that made them quite different from the Judeans, despite their sharing of the same Jahwistic beliefs based on the Pentateuch. Thus, according to Horsley, the Hasmonean expansion represented not a liberation but an imposition on the Galileans of the laws of the Judeans, laws that Horsley regards as restrictive and designed to serve the material needs of the aristocracy of the Judean temple state.[10]

The very opposite view is held by other scholars who accept the phrase 'Galilee of the nations' (Is 8, 23; 1 Macc 5, 15) as an accurate description of the population of the region and its cultural affiliations, especially from the Hellenistic period onwards. This view reached its most virulent expression with the claim by Walter Grundmann in 1941 that Galilee was pagan and that therefore Jesus was, in all probability, not a Jew.[11] Not everybody who accepts the notion of pagan influences in Galilee goes quite that far. Instead, Galileans are seen as having been more exposed to Hellenistic culture generally, so that they espoused a more open form of Judaism, influenced as they were by the ethos of the surrounding cities. Most recently this emphasis on Greco-Roman culture in Galilee has taken the form of the claim of Cynic influences on the population there. This was a counter-cultural movement within Greco-Roman society, similar, it is claimed, to Jesus and his followers.[12] Apart from the alleged evidence of the Gospels, support for this proposal is based on the fact that Gadara, one of the cities of the nearby Dekapolis, was the birth-place of an early third-century b.c.e. Cynic epigrammatist, Meleager, who subsequently was active in Tyre and on the island of Cos. Since the Cynics were an urban phenomenon, proponents of a Cynic presence there speak also of an urbanised Galilee, but with little support for such claims from the available evidence.

A third position, the one that best corresponds to the archaeological evidence, speaks of the Judaisation of Galilee from the south by the Hasmoneans, as they triumphantly marched north and east. Again, however, there are variations to this account. On the one hand some scholars such as Schürer, have accepted uncritically Josephus' version. According to him Strabo had preserved a report of Timagenes to the effect that the Hasmonean, Aristobulus I had forcibly circumcised the Itureans living in the region in 104 b.c.e. (J.A. 13, 319) These were an Arab people who had infiltrated into upper Galilee, but who have left little or no trace of their distinctive material culture in the region, and who later are to be found in Chalcis, in the Lebanon, north of Damascus.[13] Such a background, if accepted, would have made the Galilean Jews, as recent converts, suspect in the eyes of their southern co-religionists, thus explaining some later disparaging remarks by the Rabbis about the Galilean lack of piety.[14] Others on the basis of the material culture believe that Galilee was settled from the south in the wake of the Hasmonean conquests.[15] This would explain their loyalty to Jerusalem and its worship, since they would have been of Judean stock originally, but were sent to Galilee because of their support for the Hasmoneans.[16] A further variation on this notion of Galilean Jews is that which suggests a Babylonian influence there in view of some indications from the later literary sources of contacts between Galilean and Babylonian Rabbis.[17]

There is nothing to preclude in principle the Galilean population from including Israelite, Iturean, Judean and even Babylonian strands in the ethnic mix of the region in the first century c.e. Indeed it would be somewhat unreal to exclude such elements entirely. The question, 'Who were the Galileans?' is concerned with attempting to determine the dominant strand in the population in terms of cultural and religious affiliations. Certain claims can be ruled out as unlikely or over-stated on the basis of our present knowledge of the situation. Thus the case for a pagan Galilee is poorly supported by the literary evidence and receives no support whatsoever from the archaeological explorations. Nor is there any real evidence of a lasting Iturean presence in the region either, even though they may have infiltrated upper Galilee briefly before the arrival of the Hasmoneans. There are several problems with the idea of Galilean Israelites also. It is difficult to imagine a largely peasant population maintaining a separate Yahwistic identity over the centuries without a communal cultic centre. Mount Gerazim, the sacred site of the

Samaritans, who styled themselves as 'Israelites who worshiped on holy Argarizin', might have been expected to play such a role. Yet all the indications are that the Samaritans were as hostile to Galileans as they were to Judeans, especially when they went on pilgrimage to Jerusalem (Lk 9, 52; *J.A.* 20, 118-36). This possibly may be due to the Galileans' refusal to support their shrine, in view of the earlier shared history of the two regions in the divided monarchy.[18] Thus the theory of the Judaisation of Galilee from the south would appear to be the most likely hypothesis in our present state of knowledge. Surveys have shown a marked increase of new foundations from the Hasmonean period onwards, and at the same time the destruction of older sites, like Har Mispe Yamim, (between Upper and Lower Galilee), which had a pagan cult centre.[19] Excavations at such sites as Sepphoris, Jotapata, Gamala and Meiron, as well as lesser sites have uncovered such instrumentalities of the distinctive Jewish way of life as ritual baths, stone jars and natively produced ceramic household ware, all indicators of a concern with ritual purity emanating from Jerusalem and its temple and an avoidance of the cultural ethos of the encircling pagan cities.[20]

A Pyramid of Power and Social Stratification

Lenski's model envisages a pyramidal-view of society in which most of the power, prestige and privilege resides at the top among the narrow band of ruling elite and native aristocracy, if and when these are to be distinguished. Beneath these are the retainer classes who help to maintain the status quo on behalf of the elites, thereby gaining for themselves some measure of relative prestige. A further rung down the ladder, as the base broadens, are the peasants, that is the free landowners who are the mainstay of the society, but who cannot themselves aspire to going higher on the social scale. Instead, for one reason or another, they are in constant danger of being demoted to the landless poor, either due to increased taxation, a bad harvest or simple aggrandisement of property by the ruling elites for their own purposes. Such a model certainly fits well in general terms with what we know of Roman Galilee, once certain adjustments are made to this ideal picture to account for local circumstances.

While Antipas was never given the title king, but simply that of ethnarch, there is no doubt that within Galilee itself he and his court represented the ruling elite. In one sense they could be said to be retainers on behalf of the emperor, but once Antipas was prepared to accept the role that Roman imperial policies in the east had dictated for him, acknowledging that he could not even aspire to the title of 'client king' like his father, his retainer rule was assured.[21] Josephus informs us that he 'loved his tranquillity' (*J.A.* 18, 245), a characterisation that fits well with the Gospel portraits, despite his attempts to upstage the governor of Syria on one occasion in Rome (*J.A.* 18, 101-4). Augustus had decreed that he could have a personal income of two hundred talents from the territories of Galilee and Perea, and presumably he could also introduce special levies for building and other projects, especially when these were intended to honour the imperial household (*J.A.* 17, 318). Not merely did Antipas and his immediate family benefit from these concessions, but a new class seems to have emerged around Antipas whom we meet in the Gospels as the Herodians. There has been considerable discussion as to how this group should be described in terms of their social and political significance, and we must probe further in an effort to locate them more precisely on the social map of Galilee.

One passage that opens up an interesting perspective is the Gospel account of Herod's birthday (Mk 6, 14-29) where the list of those who attended is described as 'the courtiers, the military officers and the leading men of Galilee' (Mk 6, 21). The terminology used here is significant. The *chiliarchoi* are clearly military personnel of some kind, suggesting that the ethnarch had some form of permanent army, as distinct from the militia whom he might call up for a particular engagement (*J.A.* 18, 251-2). There is nothing unusual in such a force, nor does it necessarily imply a huge burden on the natives, as would be the case when a Roman legion was billeted in a region. In Antipas' Galilee there were no large-scale military operations, since the only serious episode occurred after the divorce of his Nabatean wife, giving rise to an attack by her father Aretas. But this was much more likely to have occurred in Perea, which bordered on the Nabatean kingdom. Thus the *chiliarchoi* attending the king's banquet were in all probability in charge of local policing and border posts, and for the personal protection of Antipas himself and his household, similar to Josephus' use of such a force during his period as commander in Galilee. They thus belong to the retainer level rather than the aristocratic level on Lenski's model.

The *protoi tes Galilaias* ('The leading men of Galilee') are are also known to us from Josephus' writings. Two particular incidents involving their role are significant. When the governor of Syria, Vitellius, was about to launch a campaign against the Nabatean king, Aretas, he was asked by the *protoi* of the Jews not to march his army through Jewish territory, since the Roman shields had various emblems on them, contrary to Jewish law (*J.A.* 18, 122). On another occasion of a threatened peasant strike because of the offence created by the emperor Gaius' desire to have a statue of himself erected in the temple in Jerusalem, the *protoi* of the Jews were worried that they would not have the resources to pay the tribute to Rome, and that consequently, there would be an outbreak of banditry (*J.A.* 18, 261-309). In both incidents, the *protoi* are clearly influential Jews, concerned about religious values, ostensibly at least, but they were also interested in the maintenance of law and order and the payment of the tribute to Rome. Josephus uses the expression in all seventy-five times in his writings, and in the vast majority of uses it refers to 'men who held official positions of authority among the Jews'. As such they represent an aristocracy of birth, similar to the 'well-bred and wealthy' of Roman society for whom Plutarch uses the same term. They are to be distinguished from two other groups mentioned frequently by Josephus: the *dynatoi* and the *hoi en telei*, the former referring to an aristocracy of power, as distinct from one of birth, and the latter to those holding some official office.

The third group mentioned by Mark are the *megistanes* ('great ones') whose special relationship to Antipas is underlined by the use of the personal pronoun *autou*/his. The term *megistanes* in general means 'great ones' or 'grandees'. Thus, one might be tempted to identify them as courtiers as in Dn 5, 23 (LXX). Josephus uses the term to refer to noblemen who fled from the territory of Agrippa II, bringing their horses, their arms and their possessions (*Life*, 12. 149). This seems to indicate local lords on whom the ruler could normally rely for active support at times of crisis, rather than court officials or administrative officers. It is not certain whether they could be identified with the Herodians who appear elsewhere in the Gospels (Mk 3,6; 12,13). The Latin ending to the name – *ianoi*– suggests adherents or supporters of a person, and presumably, therefore, includes a wider circle than the immediate household. Indeed at the time of the first revolt there are two people bearing the name Herod numbered among the ruling class of Tiberias, who recommended loyalty to Rome and who owned property across the Jordan (*Life*, 33f). Such a profile would fit well with that of the two *megistanes* in the same work, already alluded to. On that understanding, therefore, the Herodians in Galilee and elsewhere in the country, could be described as wealthy landowners who presumably depended on Herod the Great's and his sons benefactions for their opulence. Inevitably, they would be stoutly loyal to the Herodian house and its policies, despite the special example of the two who had deserted Agrippa for the Jewish cause, and whom Josephus for safety reasons returned to the Dekapolis region where they eventually obtained pardon from Agrippa (*Life* 149-54).

It has already been suggested that the *chiliarchoi* of Mark's list belonged to the retainer class rather than to the ruling elite. Others functionaries also appear in the literature who would fit into this same category. Mention of the *archeiai*, 'archives' in Sepphoris immediately suggests keepers of official records and scribes of various kinds, such as the *komogrammateis* 'village scribes from every village of Galilee' to whom Luke refers (Lk 5,17). Justus of Tiberias, Josephus' rival in Galilee, had a good Greek education and was in the service of Agrippa II, presumably as a high administrative officer within his realm, and likewise John of Gischala, Josephus' implacable enemy in 66 c.e. seems to have had some official role in the Roman administration of upper Galilee (*Life* 73). Given what we know of village administration from other parts of the Roman east we can presume a whole network of lesser officials within the highly bureaucratic structures that had been put in place at least from the early Hellenistic period by the Ptolemies, and which would have simply been inherited by successive regimes thereafter. In this regard, the Hasmoneans may have come to power as religious nationalists within an autonomous Jewish state, but once in power they certainly maintained the trappings of an Hellenistic-style monarchy. These officials would have included market managers (*agoranomoi*), tax collectors (*telonai*), estate mangers (*oikonomoi*), judges (*kritai*), prison officers (*hyperetai/praktores*), all of which are alluded to in the Gospels. The tax-collectors appear to be ubiquitous. This may be a distorted impression or an indication of the demands that were being made on people in that regard, not just to meet the tribute due to Antipas himself, but also the Roman tribute, the payment of which the *protoi* felt responsible, but which was dependent on the peasants insuring a harvest. This suggests payment at least of the *tributum soli*, a land tax, in kind, and it is no surpise that we hear of imperial granaries in upper Galilee at the outbreak of the first revolt. Presumably there were others throughout the region also (*Life* 71. 119). In addition tolls were important in generating revenue for local rulers and landowners, and in all probability the tax-collectors of the Gospels with whom Jesus seems to have had friendly relations belong to this category. Like some other professions, theirs was seen as dubious among the more religious circles because of suspicion of impurity, but Jesus does not exclude them from his retinue, even when this meant a certain opprobrium for fraternising with 'sinners' (Mt 11, 19; Lk 7, 34; Mk 2,16).

The issue of land-owning patterns in Galilee as elsewhere in the ancient world is difficult to determine, since the sources are either silent or ambiguous on many aspects of the problem. Undoubtedly, the tendency towards large estates, farmed by lease-paying tenants rather than free-holding peasants had been there since the Persian times already. Nehemiah had attempted a land reform in Judea, it would seem, in accordance with the older ideal of ownership of one's own plot within the land of Israel (Neh 5, 1-11). However, in the Hellenistic age, and in particular under Ptolemaic rule, this trend had been reversed at least with regard to the best land, as we learn from the account of Zenon's tour of inspection to royal estates, including Galilee in the mid-third century b.c.e. Even the Gospel parables are familiar with this pattern (Mk 12, 1-9; Lk 16, 1-9). The Hasmonean policy paid lip-service at least to the traditional patterns of small holdings (1 Macc 14, 10), even though the ruling family itself will have inherited the large estates of ousted Seleucids (J.A. 13,322). The Herodians also seem to have continued with the traditional pattern, at least in Jewish areas, perhaps in deference to religious sensibilities that they were keen to appease. Thus, for example, on the borders of Galilee allotments were given to Herodian veterans at 'Gaba of the Cavalry' on the borders of the Great Plain, close to where Agrippa II's wife Berenice had a private estate (J.A. 15, 294; Life 119-20). In Batanea, which Augustus had given to Herod the Great, Babylonian Jews were settled in villages, tax-free, suggesting strongly that they were given their own allotments in return for their peace-keeping potential in this troublesome, outlying region. (J.A. 17, 22-31). Antipas continued with the same policy. Allotments were promised to those who were forced to inhabit Tiberias, and presumably not all would have received possessions similar in size to those of the Herodians across the Jordan already mentioned (J.A. 18, 38; Life 33-34).

The results of this sketch, patchy though it is, suggest that there was a mixed pattern of land-ownership in Galilee in the first century. Undoubtedly, the trend was towards larger estates, and thus a move away from mere subsistence farming of the traditional Jewish peasant class. The foundation of Tiberias is a good example of how pressure could come on small land-owners as the ruling aristocracy's needs had to be met. In a pre-industrial situation land was the primary source of wealth, but this was in short supply in a Galilee that was thickly populated by the standards of the time (J.W. 3, 41-43). Increased taxation to meet the demands of that lifestyle meant that many were reduced to penury, thus reaching the lowest level on Lenski's pyramid, that occupied by the landless poor and the urban destitute classes (*Life* 66f). The slide from peasant owner to tenant to day-labourer was inexorable for many, thus giving rise to social resentment, debt, banditry, and in the case of women, prostitution. All these social types can be documented from the Gospels either as typical characters in the parables of Jesus or as real life figures for whom his movement offered a radical alternative to the harsh realities of daily life in Herodian Galilee.

Economic Realities: Roots of Conflict

The ancients may not have had a developed theory of economics, but they certainly were keenly aware of economic realities. The Gospels provide us with an excellent mirror of the situation in Galilee, since so much of Jesus' public ministry was conducted against the backdrop of an unjust economic system, as he saw the situation. In order to understand the full impact of statements such as 'Blessed are the poor,' or 'Forgive us our debts as we also forgive our debtors,' they need to be heard in the context of attitudes and values surrounding wealth and possessions within both Greco-Roman society and standard Jewish covenantal thinking. To be poor was both to be lacking in honour, the most prized possession of all in Mediterranean society, as well as to be cursed by God according to the Deuteronomic principle that the good will prosper and the wicked will perish. Yet Jesus is not a starry-eyed romantic wandering around a lush countryside with an idyllic view of life and its demands. Wealthy people who can lend money and then exact it back with interest are part of the landscape of his ministry, and thieves are a constant threat for those who seek to hoard their money. The poor or the destitute are never far away and they are the frequent characters in his parables. On the other hand it is important to recognise that this picture may be somewhat distorted because of the particular emphasis of Jesus' ministry. Certainly, not everybody who was attracted to him was in this category. Indeed the relative failure of his message as far as the majority of Galileans was concerned, both during his life-time and immediately after his death (cf. Mt, 11, 19-21), shows that many Galileans found his message too radical and did not opt for his alternative life-style. Thirty years later we are given another glimpse of Galilean social conditions through the lens of Josephus' *Life*, and there we encounter villagers who are happy to pay temple tithes and at the same time can be relied upon to provision a large native militia that supports Josephus in his struggles with other native 'big men' in the region who are vying with him for control of the revolt against Rome.

In order to avoid a highly impressionistic picture of the economic situation, therefore, there is need for a more systematic analysis. This can best be achieved by attempting to identify changes occurring within the economic system and the factors that have brought these about. In recent scholarship much has been made of the importance in cultural terms of the two new city foundations of Antipas within the region, Sepphoris and Tiberias, but little attention has been given to their significance in terms of economic changes. The hypothesis suggested earlier, namely, that the development of these two new foundations in Antipas' Galilee brought about a rapid economic change, which left some people more marginalised than previously and whose plight Jesus seeks to address in and through his ministry.[23]

According to the proposed model the signs of rapid economic change are developments on three fronts occurring concurrently. These are: changes in the market or modes of production, changes in the means of exchange, mainly through the introduction or increase of money in the economy, and changes in prevailing values and attitudes. The available evidence from Galilee would suggest that, in fact, all three types of change were happening in Antipas' Galilee just at this time. It is not that the region had never experienced such changes previously, they had occurred before, most notably in the early Hellenistic period (300-200 b.c.e.) when the Ptolemaic overlords sought to maximise their control of all Palestine as 'royal lands'. The reign of Herod the Great must also have seen rapid changes occurring, though, as previously noted, Herod's main building projects took place in the south, or in the non-Jewish sectors of his kingdom such as the coast or in Samaria. What was different about Antipas' rule was that changes were now taking place within the Galilean heartland, thereby disrupting the patterns of village settlements that the Hasmoneans had opted for and that even Herod seems to have been anxious to foster in the territories across the Jordan, which he had received from Augustus as a reward for his loyalty. We must briefly indicate the evidence for each of the three elements in the model for Antipas' reign.

Changes in the Market
The market can be described as an exchange arena where goods and services are exchanged for the benefit of buyers and sellers alike. The notion of an arena recalls the *agora* or market place that was such a

central feature of Roman towns. There the complex network of supply and demand came together, either to meet local needs or on a larger regional or inter-regional basis. Galilee's location and potential resources meant that it was in an ideal position to meet demands on a wider scale than the purely domestic. The overall fertility of the region was ensured by the prevailing climatic conditions. The lake was also an important natural resource, which appears to have been fully exploited with many breakwaters, harbours and fish pools dating from the Roman period.

It is no accident that weights inscribed with the title *agoranomoi* 'market supervisors' have been discovered at both Sepphoris and Tiberias, thus indicating that these places also functioned as important market/collection centres within the Herodian economy, something that the numerous silos found at Sepphoris would also seem to indicate. In addition we hear of imperial corn in upper Galilee and corn stored at Herodian estates near Besara in lower Galilee when Josephus took over control of the region in 66 c.e. It is important to understand these scattered pieces of evidence in the context of Roman grain policies in the imperial period. Augustus had brought order to what was a chaotic situation in the supply system through the *lex Iulia de annona*. This measure meant that the state guaranteed an annual corn dole to the citizens of Rome itself, thus creating a demand that the Italian peninsula could not meet. This amounted to the introduction of a state mobilisation programme, which inevitably restricted greatly the free sale of corn by individual suppliers. As Peter Garnsey writes: 'The grain that found its way to Rome was, in the first place, state grain, coming in the form of taxes in kind from tribute-paying provinces, or of rents in kind from tenants of the *ager publicus* or imperial estates.'[24]

In the light of such a policy one can see that Galilean peasants, like peasants elsewhere, were unlikely to have much surplus for personal profit, once family requirements and the demands of the tribute were met. In addition there were the temple taxes and offerings as well as the need to lay aside some seed for the next year's sowing. We cannot be sure of the exact amount of grain that Antipas was expected to supply, but in all probability it was determined by the decrees of Caesar some fifty years earlier, which stipulated that '... in the second year (possibly every second year) they shall pay the tribute at Sidon, consisting of one fourth of the produce sown, and in addition they shall pay tithes to Hyrcanus and his sons, just as they paid to his forefathers' (*J.A.* 14, 203). Clearly, these demands created difficult conditions for the Galileans and one can readily understand why there was resentment of the ruling elites who represented, and in many instances acted as agents for Roman imperial demands. Again, Josephus' account in *Life* indicates that much of the Galileans' ire was directed against Sepphoris and Tiberias, thus suggesting that the reign of Antipas had intensified an already fraught situation.[25]

A rapidly changing market situation also calls for increased specialisations. Unlike subsistence living, where individual families have sufficient basic skills to supply immediate needs, a more developed market situation calls for greater intensity of production, thereby providing a disposable surplus of goods. This also means a greater skill level and a more concentrated use of labour. It does not seem possible to date such specialisations as can be detected in the Galilean economy directly to the reign of Antipas, but it is a fair assumption to make that the greater numbers of new elites living in the two major centres led to an increase of demands for various goods and services of a more specialised kind than heretofore. These would include craftsmen of various kinds, skilled in monumental building techniques, as well as potters, weavers, smiths, scribes and others with various technical skills associated with a court life-style. Often this meant that certain villages became associated with providing a particular item or service, as was the case in Galilee with Kefr Hanania and Shikhin, which became associated with the ceramic industry.[26] These two centres provided all the household wares of Galilee and competed with other production centres farther afield, such as in the Golan. Gischala (Hebrew, '*Gush ha-lav*', literally 'fat soil') was associated with olive growing reflecting its name, thereby explaining the many olive presses in the region generally, as well as the possibilities for exploitation by middle-men entrepreneurs, such as John of Gischala. According to Josephus he was able to avail of the great demand for oil among observant Jews living outside the land in the territory of Caesarea Philippi, by buying up a large supply and selling it on at a hefty profit to his co-religionists, anxious to use only kosher oil (*Life*, 74f; *J.W.* 2, 591f).

As already mentioned, the lake provided its own demands and opportunities. The fish industry had been highly developed, probably from the Ptolemaic period, since Josephus mentions that a particular type of fish, the coracin that was found in the lake was elsewhere characteristic only of the Nile (*J.W.* 3, 506-8).[27] Indeed, 'Tarichaeae', the Greek name of Magdala, is presumed to refer to the salting of fish for export. Magdala has been identified with 'Migdal Nunnaya', 'Fish Tower', mentioned in the Talmud (b. Pesh. 46b). Bethsaida, 'House of

Fish', an important site at the northern end of the lake, also has specific reference to the fish industry in its name. This latter village had been elevated to the status of a city, and renamed after the emperor's wife as Bethsaida Julias by the third of the Herodian brothers, Philip. Presumably, therefore, its population would have been increased somewhat, and since it was strategically located to control the fish industry the ruling elite there would have been the first to benefit. The new retainers that this development inevitably introduced into the region would all have to do with the control and management of the fish industry – tax and toll collectors and license controllers, and beneath that level a whole range of craftsmen – sailors, boat-makers, stone masons for provision of harbours and anchors, weavers of sails and net-makers.[28]

These indications of the impact that the development of new Herodian foundations had on the economic situation of Galilee are sufficient to suggest that there were appreciable changes occurring there, which inevitably would have adverse implications for the peasants. It remains to assess these developments further in the light of other aspects of the model.

Modes of Distribution

In the ancient world different modes of distribution as well as production existed side by side. These included barter, that is reciprocal exchange of goods – which had to be on a local level given the difficulty of transportation, redistribution, or state controlled monopoly, and free market. The extent to which this latter operated has been debated, especially in view of Rome's virtual control of the grain trade. While there undoubtedly was a lot of state intervention and control, nevertheless, it seems highly likely that there was indeed some free trading.[29] The sources speak of merchants, travelling salesmen, ship owners and other types who prosper in a free market situation. In addition, the increasing supply of money favours this mode of distribution also. Not merely was there imperial coinage, used for paying the army, there was also city and regnal coinage in circulation, at least to a limited extent. The importance of money in a developing economic situation is that it represents a generalised value that can be stored and used subsequently to obtain goods or services elsewhere or from a supplier other than the person with whom the original transaction took place. Inevitably, therefore, its diffusion went with greater mobility and favoured those who could travel rather than the traditional peasant tied to a plot of land, and engaged in the daily chores of mixed farming in order to provide basic needs such as food, clothes and shelter for himself and his family (cf. Q Lk 12, 22-31/Mt 6, 24-34).

The monetary situation in Galilee appears to have been quite developed despite the absence of any Roman army in the region until after the first revolt, as payment of soldiers was one of the main reasons for minting coin in antiquity. The Gospels testify to the fact that money was in circulation, even at the most impoverished level of the population, widows and day labourers for example (Mk 12, 42; Mt 20, 9). People are presumed to have money, either to provision themselves or to meet an emergency (Mk 6, 36-38; Lk 10, 35). Even imperial coins, which were of greater value, were available to Herodians challenging Jesus in a Jerusalem setting (Mk 12, 16f). The coin profiles of the most important excavated sites show a combination of Phoenician city coins, mainly Tyrian, Hasmonean coins of lesser value, and not as large a quantity of Herodian coins as one might have expected.[31] Only three known strikings of Antipas' coinage can be documented – for the years 19/20, 26/27 and 38/39 c.e. Not even his father, Herod, was allowed silver coinage, so Antipas' coins are all bronze, but of a large size (16 grammes). All three strikings were minted in Tiberias, bear his name as ethnarch and have no animal or human representation, but rather have various decorations of a palm branch or a reed, a wreath, and on a final striking, a bundle of dates as well. One can detect in these coins somebody who is caught between the religious conservatism of his largely Jewish subjects and his subordination to imperial fiscal policy, yet who is anxious to honour his patrons and facilitate small-scale local trade, possibly between the two parts of his territory.[32]

As mentioned, Tyrian coins predominate at several of the important sites of Galilee, as well as in various hoards that have been discovered. This fact has given rise to a lively debate on the extent of trading links between Galilee and Tyre, an important naval city, but one which lacked its own natural hinterland in the interior due to the geographical features of the coastal plain at that point. Throughout history it either relied on various supply centres, including Galilee, or actually encroached on the interior in order to secure its important trading links with the east (Ez 27, 12- 25; J.A. 14, 297-99). The popularity of its money generally may be merely a matter of more Tyrian coins in circulation than those from other Phoenician cities, because of the importance of its trade; or it may be that Tyrian money was particularly prized, because unlike other currencies, it remained remarkably consistent in value throughout several centuries.[33] Another factor that made for its popularity in a Jewish context was the fact that the Tyrian half shekel was 'the coin of the sanctuary' with which all male Jews were expected to discharge their annual offering for the temple. Presumably this meant that there were more Tyrian coins in circulation in Palestine than would otherwise have been the case. Does this explain the quantity of Tyrian coins discovered in hoard-finds at Tiberias, Migdal and Carmel? They possibly result from collection of dues from the Diaspora that were being brought overland to Jerusalem as described in the Palestinian Talmud (P. Ta'an. 4, 69a). Independently of such considerations, there is good reason to believe that some trading links did exist between Galilee and Tyre. For one thing there were Jews living in the city itself at the time of the first revolt, and presumably Jesus' visit to the region was to co-religionists in various villages within Tyrian territory (*J.W.* 2, 478; Mk 7, 26).[34] As observant Jews they would have sought out produce from the land of Israel where possible, thus giving rise to an inner-ethnic trade. In situations where no threat of assimilation or idolatry was present there was no objection in principle to trade with non-Jews also. Mark envisages conditions in Galilee where goods where bought and sold at local village market places and fields (Mk 6, 36. 56), and presumably it would be at such places that middle-men such as John of Gischala would have purchased produce to be sold on to larger markets. In this respect it is interesting to note that John traded in Tyrian shekels according to one account of his conduct of the oil monopoly in Galilee (*J.W.* 2, 592).

This account of modes of distribution in Roman Galilee has concentrated on the evidence for the increased use of money as symptomatic of developments in the economy generally in the Roman period. It is significant that only one saying of Jesus', which may have been proverbial, reflects a situation of barter: 'the measure you give is the measure you receive' (Q Lk 6, 38/Mt 7, 2). This situation was not entirely new with Antipas, but it certainly received a major impetus with the foundation of the two centres in lower Galilee. Indeed the rivalry between Sepphoris and Tiberias was in large part due to the financial benefits accruing to the former, once Tiberias and its territory was transferred to Agrippa II by Nero in 54 c.e. Justus of Tiberias bemoans the fact that the royal bank and the debt records were in the rival city, because this meant that the money-making possibilities that banking entailed for the wealthy elites were also now at Sepphoris (*Life* 38). Undoubtedly, the resentment for both places and the elites who inhabited them in at the outbreak of the revolt 66 c.e. was largely due to the sense of exploitation that the Galilean peasants experienced over the previous fifty years. In these clashes we sense two competing sets of values and assumptions at work, the third element in the model to be investigated.[35]

Competing Values and Attitudes

The values that the Roman authorities propagated were for the benefit of the elite, suitably masked in the rhetoric of *pietas*, or love of fatherland. Augustus had initiated a reform in terms of a return to the ancestral values that had brought Rome to its position of dominance as ruler of the world. In the *Res Gestae* he boasts about the peace that had been established during his reign, and the court poet, Virgil, sang of the advent of an era of justice in language that rivalled the description of the messianic age in any Jewish writing of the period. In the prevailing covenantal theology of Judaism based on Deuteronomy, the good are deemed to prosper and the wicked to suffer. Thus the dominant ideologies of religion and state coalesced insofar as the poor and the marginalised were deemed shameful and accursed. Nevertheless, the religious tradition did have other voices, particularly those of the prophets who called for justice for all in Israel, especially the marginalised poor and the stranger in the midst. Even within the legal corpus, institutions such as the Jubilee and Sabbath years and the poor man's tithe were intended to emphasise the communal nature of Israel's existence in the land and restore the egalitarian balance of 'all Israel'. While many of the stipulations relating to these institutions were honoured more in the breach than the observance, the fact that they formed part of the heritage of Israel and were seen as the ideal to be attained in some of the prophetic pronouncements of the post-exilic period, meant that not every development of Hellenistic and Roman culture that was to their immediate benefit was welcomed by the religious establishment. Indeed it was this ambivalence that ultimately lead to their participation, however reluctantly, in the first revolt that had both social and religious roots. Even then, however, their lifestyle and conduct had created such deep alienation within Palestinian society (*J.A.* 20, 181-206f) that the country peasants joined with the lesser priests in Jerusalem in ousting those who had lived with double standards, establishing in their place an egalitarian alternative, however short-lived (*J.W.* 2, 242-47; 4, 147-48).

Thus the symbolic role of the temple and its institutions was unable to cloak indefinitely the deep divisions within Palestinian society, divisions that had first emerged in the Hasmonean period when the new ruling class had opted for a combination of Jewish religious loyalty on the one hand, and the opulence of the Hellenistic life-style on the other. As previously mentioned, the desire for a just king who would rid the nation not only of foreigners, but of injustice in the ruling family began to be expressed in pious circles such as the Pharisees who produced the Psalms of Solomon. The Essenes also may be seen as a protest, counter-cultural group opposed to the cities and the breakdown of communal loyalties that urban life-style and affluence had brought about. Fictive kinship groups such as these two movements, as well as the Jesus 'family' (Mk 3, 31f), were one type of response to the erosion of more traditional values within Jewish society in the Roman period. Another, more sinister sign of the same phenomenon was the rise of banditry, some of which may have had a social revolutionary component, but which for the most part was symptomatic of the loss of control by the traditional institutions and their agents.[36] Power resided more and more with local strongmen who challenged the ruling elite's claim to loyalty, but who themselves offered little to the peasants harassed by the double bind of Roman imperial values and aristocratic Jewish religious claims.

The former was more overt because it eventually resulted in the revolt, whereas the latter was cloaked in a shared symbolic world, proclaimed by the Jerusalem aristocracy, but which was becoming increasingly fragmented and sectarian. Josephus, the Jewish apologist, represents the more benign face of this Jewish aristocratic elite. His repeated calls for *homophulia*, that is, 'shared kinship', sound somewhat hollow as he himself tries to defend his own role and that of his ilk in the revolt, while at the same time having to acknowledge that he had been betrayed by the Jerusalem council that had sent him to Galilee in the first place. Equally, however, he had failed in his efforts to be fully accepted in Galilee, as local 'provincials' resented his intrusion in their affairs and his imposition on them from the centre.

The competing values and loyalties in Galilee that come into clear light of day at the outbreak of the first revolt were not entirely new, however. The situation must have begun to surface already some thirty years earlier as the refurbished Sepphoris and the newly founded Tiberias introduced new, heterogenetic types into the Galilean rural landscape.[37] These types espoused values that were alien to the Jewish peasants living in the villages, and disturbed the fragile fabric of the social network of the region. It was not a case that their values were totally new and unknown in Galilee, but now the symbols of the outsider were clearly visible in the very landscape. Peace and justice, perhaps, but for whom and at whose expense, and how were they to be achieved? This is the context within which the Jesus movement came into being, offering its version of the 'values revolution' that Roman rhetoric had proclaimed, but with a very different emphasis and strategy for its achievement.

Judea/Jerusalem

As was mentioned at the outset there is a real difference of emphasis between the Synoptics and the Fourth Gospel in regard to the locale of Jesus' ministry. This latter makes Judea and Jerusalem in particular the main focus, whereas the former have him active in the villages of Galilee (Mt 4, 23; Mk 1, 39; Lk 4, 44) with the single final journey to Jerusalem. The argument of this article is that while still in Galilee Jesus was for the most part active among *Ioudaioi*, that is adherents of the Jerusalem temple and its laws. Yet the social ethos he would have encountered in Jerusalem would have been considerably different. It was not just a matter of the general differences operative everywhere between provincials and residents of the national capital, but something deeper than that because of the particular character of the Jerusalem as the holy city of Jews everywhere. The pre-eminence of Jerusalem was recognised even by pagan writers and Herod the Great had sought to enhance this by his building projects, which included not merely the temple mount but also palaces, streets, an aqueduct and other public buildings such as a theatre, a hippodrome and an amphitheatre (*J.A.* 15, 267-91).[38] At the same time he had also developed other cities within the realm, most notably Caesarea Maritima, with its altar dedicated to *Roma* and Augustus in 10 b.c.e., as well as its impressive new harbour. Thus, when direct Roman rule was imposed in 6 c.e. with the deposition of Herod's son, Archelaus, the Roman procurator had a suitable location in which to establish the trappings of Roman administration, leaving Jerusalem to the Jews as the religious, but not any longer the administrative capital of the province.[39]

This separation of the religious and administrative centres points to a deep cleavage in Judean society of the first century between the ruling elite and the native aristocracy, something that did not occur in Galilee. While Herod had enhanced the physical splendour of Jerusalem, he succeeded in taking control of the most important institution of the temple state, that of the high priesthood. Early in his reign he had appointed a young Hasmonean, Aristobulus III, as high priest, only to realise quickly that this was a major political mistake because of popular support. Aristobulus was done away with, and thereafter Herod appointed various Diaspora Jews to the office, first a Babylonian, and then an Alexandrine, thus introducing a new dynasty into Judean life, the Boethusians, whom he could control at will (*J.A.* 15, 22.39-41 and 320-22). Not merely did this send a signal to the Diaspora Jews that he was the real ruler of the Jews, it also eroded the effectiveness of the office for inner-Judean life. Likewise, Herod replaced the Hasmonean lay nobility with Hellenised Idumeans who were loyal to him, apportioning to them some of the best lands in the district described as '*har ha-melek*', 'the king's mountain', because there were royal estates in the region (probably in north-west Judea) that had fallen to Herod.[40]

Thus, when the Romans introduced direct rule they discovered a native aristocracy, religious and lay, who lacked credibility with the Judean populace and were, therefore, devoid of the authority to play the role that Rome expected from their ilk effectively, namely, to render the population of a region amenable to its rule. The failure of the aristocracy in this regard is most clearly evident in the fact that they were forced unwillingly into a revolt against Rome that they really did not want, simply to retain some credibility with the people as a whole, in a last desperate effort to cling to power. This situation of a disaffected peasantry and an ineffectual native aristocracy had, as Martin Goodman has persuasively argued, deep roots in the social realities of Judean life. None of the usual status criteria of Greco-Roman society, such as wealth or claims of noble lineage could cloak the historical realities. In Galilee, it was the Herodian ruling class emanating from Sepphoris and Tiberias that were resented, but in Judea the aristocracy was supposed to share a common symbolic system with all the people, one which in theory meant that all shared in the fruits of Yahweh's land. Ostentatious wealth was, therefore, unacceptable, yet as the recent excavations in the Jewish quarter of the city clearly demonstrate, the Jerusalem priestly aristocracy lived a life of luxury, even when this meant violent action in the villages in order to ensure that the offerings were paid to them rather than to the country priests (*J.A.* 20, 180-1,206-7). In this instance, therefore, the imbalance between rich and poor that was a feature of all ancient economies was greatly exacerbated because in Judea/Jerusalem it was directly at odds with the shared religious ethos described in the national saga, the Torah of Moses.

As a temple city, Jerusalem generated considerable revenue, both in terms of gifts for the sanctuary and as service provider for the many pilgrims who visited annually. Herod's refurbishment was a major boost, not just for the citizens of Jerusalem itself, but for Jews in the Diaspora also (*J.A.* 16, 62-65). The indications are that the number of pilgrims increased greatly from the first century, not all of whom would have been adherents of the Jewish faith, and lodgings were necessary for these, as the Theodotus inscription illustrates with its reference to the provision of lodgings. Thus the picture that is given in the opening chapters of Acts of the Apostles of Jews from the known world as well as proselytes and God-fearers present in the holy city, is not just an idealisation. The rebuilding project continued throughout the first century, and provided work for twenty thousand men. In addition to the various ranks of cultic ministers residing in or near Jerusalem, there were many different 'lay' functions associated with the temple and its daily rituals, requiring specialisations of various kinds: wood-cutters, incense-makers, market inspectors, money-changers, water-drawers, providers of doves and other sacrificial animals and the like. Many of these were looked down on by the elites and several of them feature in the various lists of despised trades that appear in Rabbinic literature, due to suspicion with regard to purity.[42] This form of social segregation meant that Jerusalem had more than the usual share of urban poor. Thus, despite all the obvious advantages, the economy of Jerusalem was out of balance. The wealth of the temple itself was non-productive, and its benefits did not flow back into the country. Those who stood to gain most from the temple-system were its immediate guardians, the aristocratic priestly families, who jealously sought to protect their privileged status because of their religious role (*J.A.* 15, 247-8). In contravention of the biblical ideal that the tribe of Levi should have no share in the land, the best lands in the Judean countryside were in the hands of the priests or their wealthy (Sadducean) supporters (*J.W.* 6, 115).[43] Yet the attempt was made to cloak this anomalous situation in terms of religious loyalty, as is evident from Josephus' own posturing in Galilee, while freely admitting that he also owned lands adjacent to Jerusalem (*Life* 63.80.348.442).

It is not surprising, therefore, that the first century saw an increase in social turmoil of various kinds in the Judean countryside: banditry, prophetic movements of protest, and various religious ideologies, which can be directly related to the prevailing social conditions. Thus, the Essenes' practice of the common life in the Judean desert away from the city and the Pharisees' espousal of a modest life-style (*J.A.* 18, 12.18) represent the classic counter-cultural response to the prevailing aristocratic ethos, by treating poverty as an ideal rather than as shameful. However, it is in the various revolutionary groups and their strategies, which come into full view at the outbreak of the revolt in 66 c.e., that one can best judge the resentment felt towards the aristocracy and its elitist behaviour. The refusal to pay the tribute, the cessation of 'the loyal sacrifice' on behalf of Rome, and the burning the debt records (*J.W.* 2, 404. 409. 427), were all acts prompted by hatred of the Roman governor, Florus, yet they had a strong social and class component also.[44]

From the outset the chief priests had sought to calm the populace outraged by Florus' behaviour in introducing extra Roman troops to Jerusalem who were allowed to pillage the city. Josephus tells us that the chief priests, by a display of public piety, which was as contrived as it was personally motivated, sought to no avail to persuade the people to accept the Roman troops (*J.W.* 2, 321-4). Their real reasons for trying to placate Florus were revealed later to Agrippa, 'being men of position and as owners of property they were desirous of peace' (*J.W.* 2, 338). As the faction fighting increased, various alliances were formed between the lesser clergy, the country *sicarii*, the Idumeans and the groups lead by various 'strong men' such as Simon bar Giora and John of Gischala, all jostling for power as though the nation as a whole was not embroiled in a revolt against Rome.[45] In fact a political revolt had become a social revolution in which the chief targets were the high priests and their immediate followers. Thus, in 67 c.e. as Vespasian advanced on Jerusalem, supported by 'brigands' from the countryside, the zealots occupied the temple, and elected by lot a country villager with no legitimate credentials to replace the high priest Ananus, whom Josephus describes as 'a most wise man, who might possibly have saved the city, had he escaped the conspirators hand' (*J.W.* 4, 151). Ananus was in fact murdered a little later by the Idumeans who had been secretly admitted to the city in order to assist the zealots besieged in the temple. The comment of the aristocratic priest Josephus on these events tells everything about the manner in which this class saw their role at this period of crisis for Jerusalem and its inhabitants: 'I should not be wrong in saying that the capture of the city began with the death of Ananus; and that the overthrow of the walls and the downfall of the Jewish state dated from the day on which the Jews beheld their high priest, the captain of their salvation, butchered in the heart of Jerusalem.' (*J.W.* 4, 318). One suspects that his opinion was not shared by too many of his contemporaries.

Judea, like Galilee, was a rapidly changing society and one must avoid projecting back to the earlier part of the century the situation that emerged clearly at the outbreak of the first revolt. Nevertheless, when all due caution is applied, it still seems clear that the systemic causes of the breakdown of Judean society, so graphically illustrated during the revolt, were already operative in the early provincial period. To some extent these were the legacy of Herod the Great's domination of the religious institutions of Judaism for his own political ends. He was able to contain any show of dissent by his strong-arm tactics, to the point that no protest was possible. The reaction among the Jewish people on his death and the failure of Archelaus to maintain order are clear indications that Judean society was already in turmoil in a way that Galilee was not. This was the world in which Jesus grew up and which shaped his distinctive understanding of Israel's destiny and his own role in it. Within the broad contours of the Gospels' portrayals and allowing for their later kerygmatic concerns, it is possible to discern two different though related strategies operating in the career of Jesus. In Galilee he sought to address the social needs of the village culture, whose lifestyle and values were being eroded by the new level of Herodian presence there as a result of Antipas' presence.[46] However, as a *Jewish* prophet he had also to address the centre of his own religious tradition in Jerusalem, like other country prophets before and after him, whose unenviable task it was to proclaim judgement on the temple and the city.[47] Thus in their separate ways both the Synoptics and John have retained different, but plausible, aspects of a career that spanned both Jerusalem and Galilee.

Notes

1. Gerhardt Lenski, *Power and Privilege. A Theory of Social Stratification*, (New York: McGraw-Hill, 1966).

2. Richard Horsley, *Sociology and the Jesus Movement* (New York: Crossroads, 1989), is critical of Theissen's use of a functionalist approach in his application of sociological models to the study of early Christianity. Cf. Gerd Theissen's *Sociology of Early Palestinian Christianity*, (Philadelphia: Fortress Press, 1977) and *Social Reality and the Early Christians. Theology, Ethics and the World of the New Testament*, (Edinburgh: T. and T. Clark, 1993).

3. Ernest Renan, *The Life of Jesus*, English trans. (New York: Prometheus Books).

4. Sean Freyne, *Galilee from Alexander the Great to Hadrian. A Study of Second Temple Judaism*, (Reprint Edinburgh: T. and T. Clark, 2000); Raphael Frankel, 'Galilee: Prehellenistic,' in the *The Anchor Bible Dictionary*, ed. David Noel Freedman, 6 vols. (New York: Doubleday, 1992) vol. 2, 879-94.

5. For a detailed account of this history, see Emil Schürer, *The History of the Jewish People in the Age of Jesus Christ*, (Revised edition, Edinburgh: T. and T. Clark, 1973-84), especially vol.1.

6. Sean Freyne, 'Behind the Names: Galileans, Samaritans, *Ioudaioi*,' in *Galilee and Gospel. Selected Essays WUNT 125* (Tübingen: J.C.B. Mohr 2001), 114-131.

7. A number of important collections of essays have appeared based on two international conferences: Lee I. Levine, ed., *The Galilee in Late Antiquity*, (New York-Jerusalem: The Jewish Theological Seminary of America, 1992); Douglas Edwards and Thomas McCollough eds., *Archaeology and the Galilee. Texts and Contexts in the Greco-Roman and Byzantine Periods*, (Atlanta: Scholars Press, 1997); Rebecca Martin-Nagy and Eric Meyers, eds, *Sepphoris in Galilee. Cross-Currents of Culture*, (Raleigh, NC: NC Museum of Modern Art/Eisenbrauns, 1997); Eric Meyers ed. *Galilee through the Centuries. Confluence of Cultures*, (Winona Lake: Eisenbrauns, 1999).

8. Cf. my essays, 'Archaeology and the Historical Jesus,' and 'Galilean Questions to Crossan's Mediterranean Jesus,' in *Galilee and Gospel*, 160-182 and 208-229.

9. Albrecht Alt, 'Galiläische Probleme 1937-40' in *Kleine Schriften zur Geschichte des Volkes Israels*, 3 vols, (Munich: Ch. Beck, 1953-64), vol. 2, 363-435.

10. Richard Horsley, *Galilee, History, Politics, People*, (Valley Forge, Pa.: Trinity Press Interntional, 1995).

11. Walter Grundmann, *Jesus der Galiläer und das Judentum*, (Leipzig: G. Wigand, 1941).

12. Burton J. Mack, *A Myth of Innocence. Mark and Christian Origins*, (Minneapolis: Fortress Press, 1988); John Domnick Crossan, *The Historical Jesus. The Life of a Mediterranean Jewish Peasant* (New York: Harper San Francisco, 1991; F. Gerald Downing, *Cynics and Christian Origins*, (Edinburgh: T. and T. Clark, 1992),115-168. For a detailed criticism of the hypothesis see Hans Dieter Betz, 'Jesus and the Cynics. Survey and Analysis of an Hypothesis,' *Journal of Religion* 74(1994) 453-475.

13. Schürer, *History of the Jewish People*, vol. 2, 7-10, 561-73.

14. Adolf Büchler, *Der Galiläische 'am ha-'aretz des zweiten Jahrhunderts* (Reprint Hildesheim: Olms, 1968).

15. Mordachai Aviam, 'Galilee: the Hellenistic and Byzntine Periods,' in *NEAEHL* vol 2, 455-58; Jonathan Reed, *Archaeology and the Galilean Jesus*. (Harrisburg Pa: Trinity Press International, 2000), especially 23-61.

16. Sean Freyne, 'Behind the Names,' in *Galilee and Gospel*, 114-131.

17. Etienne Nodet, 'Galilee from the Exile to Jesus,' in Etienne Nodet and Justin Taylor, *The Origins of Christianity*, (Collegeville: Liturgical Press, 1998) 127-64.

18. Freyne, 'Behind the Names,' in *Galilee and Gospel*, 116-119; A.Thomas Kraabel, 'New Evidence for the Samaritan Diaspora has been found on Delos,' *Biblical Archaeologist* 47(1984) 44-46.

19. Raphael Frankel, 'Har Mispe Yamim – 1988/89,' *Excavations and Surveys in Israel* 9(1989) 100-102; Raphael Frankel and R.Ventura, 'The *Mispe Yamim* Bronzes.' *Bulletin of the American School of Oriental Research 311* (1998) 39-55.

20. Reed, 'The Identity of Galileans: Ethnic and Religious Considerations, Archaeology and the Galilean Jesus, 23-61, is the most detailed and up-to-date report of the evidence.

21. The most detailed study of Antipas is Harold Hoehner, *Herod Antipas*, (Cambridge: Cambridge University Press, 1972).

22. David Fiensy, *The Social History of Palestine in the Herodian Period*, (Lewison/Lampeter: the Edwin Mellon Press, 1991).

23. Sean Freyne, 'Herodian Economics in Galilee: Searching for a suitable model' and 'Jesus and the Urban Culture of Galilee,' in *Galilee and Gospel*, 86-113 and 183-207.

24. Peter Garnsey, 'Grain for Rome,' in Peter Garnsey, Keith Hopkins, C.K. Whittaker, *Trade in the Ancient Economy*, (Cambridge: Cambridge University Press, 1983), 118-30, especially 120.

25. Sean Freyne, 'Urban-Rural Relations in First-Century Galilee. Some Suggestions from the Literary Sources.' In *Galilee and Gospel*, 45-58.

26. David Adan-Bayewitz, *Common Pottery in Roman Galilee*; (Ramath Gan: Bar Ilan University Press, 1993).

27. Mendel Nun, *Ancient Anchorages and Harbours around the Sea of Galilee*, (Ein Gev: Kinneret Publications, 1998).

28. K. C. Hanson, 'The Galilean Fishing Economy and the Jesus Tradition', *Biblical Theology Bulletin* 27(1997) 99-111.

29. With reference to Galilee this conclusion has been challenged by Richard Horsley, *Archaeology, History and Society in Galilee*. (Valley Forge: Trinity Press International, 1996), 66-87. See however the detailed study of Zeev Safrai, *The Economy of Roman Palestine* (London: Routledge, 1994) pointing to the Jewish sources which presume such free exchange between individuals and villages.

30. Denis Oakman, *Jesus and the Economic Questions of his Day*. (Lewison/Lampeter: The Edwin Mellen Press, 1986); K.C. Hanson and Denis Oakman, *Palestine in the Time of Jesus. Social Structures and Social Conflicts*. (Minneapolis: Fortress Press, 1998), especially 99-130.

31. Richard Hanson, *Tyrian Influence in Upper Galilee*, (Cambridge, Ma: ASOR Publications, 1980); Joyce Raynor and Yaakov Meshorer, *The Coins of Ancient Meiron*, (Winona Lake: Eisenbraun, 1988). Dan Barag, 'Tyrian Currency in Galilee,' *Israel Numismatic Journal* 6/7(1982/3) 7-13, and Danny Syon, 'The Coins from Gamla. An Interim Report,' *Israel Numismatic Journal* 12(1992/3) 36-55.

32. Gerd Theissen, *The Gospels in Context. Social and Political History in the Synoptic Tradition*, (Edinburgh: T. and T. Clark, 1992), 28-37.

33. Ariel Ben-David, *Jerusalem und Tyros*, (Basel: Kyklos Verlag, 1969).

34. Theissen, *The Gospels in Context*, 61-80.

35. See Sean Freyne, 'The Revolt from a regional perspective,' in Andrea Berlin and Andrew Overman eds. *The First Jewish Revolt. Archaeology, History, Ideology*, (London: Routledge: 2002), 43-56.

36. Richard Horsley and John Hanson, *Bandits, Prophets and Messiahs. Popular Movements at the Time of Jesus*, (New York: Winton Press, 1985); B. Shaw, 'Tyrants, Bandits and Kings. Personal Power in Josephus,' *Journal of Jewish Studies* 44 (1993) 176-204.

37. See Freyne, 'Urban-Rural Relations in First-Century Galilee.' in *Galilee and Gospel*, 45-58.

38. Ehud Netzer, 'Herod's Building Projects,' in Lee Levine ed. *The Jerusalem Cathedra I*, (Jerusalem: Izhak Ben-Zvi Institute, 1981) 48-62; Peter Richardson, *Herod, King of the Jews and Friend of the Roman* (Columbia: University of South Carolina Press, 1998)174-215.

39. Doron Mendels, *The Rise and Fall of Jewish Nationalsim*, (New York: Doubleday, 1992) 277-331.

40. Fiensy, *Social History*, 49-55.

41. Martin Goodman, *The Ruling Class of Judaea. The Origins of the Jewish Revolt against Rome, A.D. 66-70*, (Cambridge: Cambridge University Press).

42. Joachim Jeremias, *Jerusalem at the Time of Jesus*, (London: SCM Press, 1969) 303-17.

43. Menahem Stern, 'Aspects of Jewish Society: the Priesthood and other Classes,' in *The Jewish People in the First Century (Compendia Rerum Judaicarum ad Novum Testamentum)* Philadelphia: Fortress Press, 1992, vol. 2, 339-356.

44. Goodman, *The Ruling Class of Judaea*, 152-197.

45. David M. Rhoads, *Israel in Revolution 6-74 C.E. A Political History based on the Writings of Josephus*, (Philadelphia: Fortress Press, 1976), 94-149, for an excellent summary of the different groups and their shifting alliances.

46. Sean Freyne, 'Jesus and the Urban Culture of Galilee' in *Galilee and Gospel*, 45-58.

47. Sean Freyne, *Galilee, Jesus and the Gospels. Literary Approaches and Historical Investigations*, (Dublin: Gill Macmillan, 1988) 224-39.

10

MILLENNIUM, JUBILEE AND JESUS

Throughout Christian history both the Millennium and the Jubilee have had an inherent fascination for believers, yet neither has been properly interpreted in the light of the biblical witness. In the Roman Catholic tradition, in line with its preoccupation with sin and confession, the Jubilee was associated with the granting of indulgences by those who made a pilgrimage to Rome during certain designated 'holy years', the intervals between which varied at different times from a hundred to fifty to thirty-three years. The Millennium on the other hand has had a special attraction for Reformation-based Churches such as Anabaptists, seventeenth-century German Pietists, and in more recent times, Mormons and Seventh Day Adventists, whose literal approach to Scripture has lead to the identification of various events in history with the return of Christ. Indeed, so widespread is this kind of thinking that millennial and millenarianism are now technical terms among secular social scientists for groups who anticipate the imminent advent of some cataclysmic event and who, as a result, adopt behavioural patterns that are deemed to be strange and counter-cultural.

In this paper I do not want to separate our discussion of the Jubilee from that of the Millennium, since it will emerge that there are close and important associations between the two notions, once they are understood in their proper, biblical settings. As a Jewish reform movement, early Christianity was heir to a rich repertoire of images, symbols and ideas that described the ideal society and embodied future hopes and expectations. The repeated failure of various earlier reform movements in Israel gave rise to a transference of many of these images to the future messianic era that was hoped for, when the arrival of an ideal king would ensure that Israel would realise all her dreams and conform perfectly to God's will and plan for history. The Jubilee was one of those expressions of Israel's ideals that was picked up by a number of the later prophets, especially Isaiah, who combined it with the outpouring of the Spirit which was hoped for in the coming messianic age (Is 58,6; 61,1-2). Jesus and the early Christians also found that it provided an appropriate set of categories for their ideals as they proclaimed and awaited the definitive establishment of God's reign over the universe. Thus, as we shall see, Jubilee and millennial thinking were kept in an active tension, the one giving concrete expression to the deepest values that Israel aspired to for her life under God in the land, and the other providing the symbolic and mythological horizons within which it remained possible to go on hoping for such an ideal future, despite repeated failures and disappointments.

Biblical Reflections on the Millennium and the Jubilee

The Millennium

It is interesting to note that insofar as the religious aspect of the millennium is adverted to at all in present discussion, it is supposedly to celebrate the birth of Christ. However, as is widely known, such a dating is quite inaccurate. Our present calendar is based on a twelfth-century miscalculation of Christ's birth. This event, we know from the Gospels, must have taken place prior to the death of Herod the Great, which is to be dated to 4 b.c.e. by our current reckoning. Thus we are anything from four to six years late for a two thousand anniversary celebration of the Nativity. As a Christian event, however, the millennium celebrates the second coming of Christ, not his birth. The notion is based on the passage from the Book of Revelation (20, 4-6) where the thousand year reign on earth of Christ together with the martyrs is predicted, prior to the final consummation of all things as envisaged in both Jewish and Christian standard scenarios for the end of the world.

This particular understanding of world history being divided into two ages – the present evil age and the future good age – is rooted in the apocalyptic interpretation of God's ultimate dominion over his creation, despite the apparent presence, and even dominance of evil in the world. As Paul expresses it, God will eventually 'be all in all'. It is important to be clear that this is a theological, not a scientific, understanding of history, based on the belief that Yahweh would never abandon his covenant with humankind in and through the election of Israel (Ex 19). It has been a constant temptation for some well-meaning, but misguided, forms of Christian piety to take that account literally, predicting the imminent end of the world at various moments of history, only to be sadly and often tragically disappointed. This form of literalism ignores the particular character of apocalyptic literature with its deeply mythological and poetic style of expression. The genuinely apocalyptic mindset acknowledges the deep mystery of the universe, while confidently believing that it is in the care of a good God, even when this is neither obvious nor easily explicable. 'Lo, I tell you a mystery; we shall not all die, but we shall all be changed', Paul tells his Corinthian converts, before uttering his triumphant cry: 'Death, where is your victory? Death where is your sting?'

In an earlier section of this same chapter (1 Cor 15) Paul paints his own picture of the end-time scenario, in which he clearly envisages an interim stage following the Resurrection of Christ, before even the Son, having conquered every ruler and every authority and power, is himself made subject 'so that God may be all in all'. This is only one of many variations on the theme of the end-time triumph of God which are to be found not just in the New Testament, but in other Jewish Restoration literature also.

It is against this background that we must try to understand the passage from the Book of Revelation on which all talk of the millennium should be based. Here too an interim stage in the manifestation of God's victory over evil is envisaged, but unlike the Pauline scenario, this stage is represented as taking place here on earth, not in some other realm. The thousand year reign of Christ and his saints is part of a pattern of contrasting sets of images which punctuate this highly symbolic narrative, culminating in the final scene of the new Jerusalem descending from heaven as part of 'the new heaven and the new earth'. The various oscillating sets of images of good and evil – seals, bowls trumpets, beasts – convey a sense of the ongoing struggle between the forces of good and evil engaged in the final cosmic war, in which victory for the saints is assured, due to the triumph of the lamb who has been slain. By sealing their commitment with their blood the martyrs will reign with Christ, and the second death will not touch them, unlike other Christians who must continue to struggle against the forces of evil within the world.

This highly creative work must be read in the context of the persecutions of the first Christians in the province of Asia during the reign of the emperor Domitian in the last decade of the first century c.e. A defiant response has been given to the might of imperial Rome, 'Babylon the Great' as the author calls it, whereby those who remain faithful are reassured that despite the apparent triumph of Evil, in the end their steadfastness will be rewarded, since victory is already assured. The distinctive and original contribution of the author is the fact that the thousand year reign is *on earth* and is meant to convey a sense of reassurance for those who have not suffered martyrdom, and who must therefore continue to endure ongoing oppression. The totalising language of the apocalyptic genre with its strange, even bizarre images is not a flight of utopian fantasy, but a call to resist injustice and evil in the present, no matter how hopeless the situation might appear. The author invites his readers to exercise their imaginations in order to envisage the triumph that has already been procured. Jesus Christ, the lamb who has been slain, is the alpha and omega, God's final word to all in search of hope within the structures of an evil world, and the thousand year reign of Christ and the martyrs is the guarantee that all can share in that victory even now.

The Lord's year of favour for Israel

Moving from the highly charged atmosphere of the Book of Revelation to the seemingly mundane world of the Book of Leviticus one could be forgiven for considering that their authors inhabit different planets. The rhetoric of Revelation is highly symbolic and evocative, whereas the legislation of Leviticus is precise, measured and earthy. Yet despite these real differences, theologically speaking, both visions are fashioned out of the same beliefs and hopes in a God of justice who is ultimately in control of his created world.

The legislation concerning the Jubilee is seen either as reflecting very early social conditions in Israel, or alternatively as a late idealisation of the hopes of the restored community, depending on one's dating of the Book of Leviticus (Lev 25). Either way it represents an extraordinary vision of Israel's self-understanding based on the intimate relationship between God, people and land. On the one hand the right to private property is acknowledged – Israel is to be a community of small land-owners, each charged with the responsibility to acknowledge Yahweh's blessings through the offerings of agricultural produce at the central sanctuary. At the same time nobody is permitted to benefit from another's misfortune by acquisition at the expense of their neighbour, since 'the land is mine, says the Lord' (Lev 23, 25), and 'you are tenants in the land'. Thus personal responsibility is affirmed while strict limits are imposed on the extent to which that right can be exercised within the community that is all Israel, living in Yahweh's land by Yahweh's favour.

The Jubilee legislation is based on the priestly understanding of Israel as a nation established in the land around a central sanctuary, yet it has a deeply prophetic inspiration that is dissatisfied with the status quo of a static order. The Jubilee was to be proclaimed by the priests on the Day of Atonement every fiftieth year. It thus formed a cyclical reminder of Israel's failure to live up to its founding vision and constituted a renewal of purpose and vision for the future. The fiftieth year came immediately after the 'seven times seven' cycle of years, seen as a perfect order, so that the beginning of the new cycle also represented a new beginning. The tribe of Levi who were in charge of the priestly responsibilities had no share in the land, but were dependent for their existence on the offerings of the other tribes, thereby symbolising their total trust in God's provident care. In the Jubilee year all Israel was expected to share in this condition, allowing the earth to go fallow, releasing prisoners who were incarcerated for non-payment of debts and remitting outstanding debts. Thus the original order of a truly egalitarian society was restored and God's care for his people was once again affirmed and gratefully acknowledged.

The regulations of the Jubilee were fashioned in the context of a society of small land-owners, engaged in subsistence farming in a pre-industrial, peasant economy. Over the centuries the invasions of the Assyrians and the Babylonians had caused serious disruption to this older pattern of life. Indeed the rise of the monarchy in the tenth had already produced a court aristocracy who owned the best lands and seriously violated the older ideals of a shared land, perfectly exemplified in the story of the forced acquisition of Naboth's vineyard by Ahab and Jezebel (1 Kgs 21). It is against this background of the changing social and economic patterns in Israel that such prophetic voices as Amos and Hosea, and later still Isaiah were raised in protest at the treatment of the widow, the orphan and the stranger in Israel, contrary to the almost utopian ideal that had been expressed in the law codes. There was further polarisation between rich and poor in the Persian and Greek periods, with the policies of establishing Greek-style cities, the colonisation of conquered territories and the abandonment of many of early Israel's ideals. In these circumstances it is not surprising that the evidence for the observance of the Jubilee is scant, though not entirely lacking (1 Macc 6, 49). Ideals and reality did not match, but interestingly, those ideals were not abandoned. Instead they became part of the future hopes of Israel, and this was true of the Jubilee also (Is 58, 6; 61,2).

Thus the Jubilee and the millennium share common horizons of hope and responsibility. God's graciousness – the year of favour – as the ground for hope becomes a present reality in the concrete realisation of Israel's ethical ideals. Paradoxically, the future millennium is not deferral, but presence in and through the realisation of these ethical demands. It was in a Jewish synagogue on a Jewish festive occasion, that the Jewish Jesus, reading from the Jewish Scriptures issued that stunning challenge: 'Today, this scripture is fulfilled in your hearing.' We must examine this proclamation more closely in a second step of our biblical reflections.

Jubilee and Millennium as Horizons for Jesus and his Ministry
Luke's portrayal of Jesus

> He (Jesus) unrolled the scroll and found the place where it was written:
>
> The spirit (*pneuma*) of the Lord is upon me because he anointed (*echrisen*) me
>
>   *a* to announce the good news (*euaggelizein*) to the poor
>
>   *b* he has sent me to proclaim (*kerussein*) release (*aphesia*) for captives,
>
>   *c* and sight for the blind,
>
>   *b1* to send away the dowtrodden released (*en aphesei*)
>
>   *a1* to proclaim (*kerussein*) the Lord's year of favour.
>
> (Lk 4: 17-19; cf. Is 58:6; 61: 1-2).

Unlike Matthew who presents Jesus as the great law-teacher or John for whom he is the other-worldly being who has become incarnate, Luke thinks of Jesus as a prophet of justice on behalf of the poor and the marginalised. This role was already foreshadowed in his mother's prayer of praise as Luke reports it: 'He (God) has put down the mighty from their seat and exalted the lowly; he has filled the hungry with good things and sent the rich away empty' (Lk 1, 52f). The presentation by Luke of Jesus' visit to his home-town synagogue, Nazareth, is very much coloured by this perspective. It is intended as a programmatic statement of Jesus' ministry to follow, something that is echoed at various points in the subsequent narrative, e.g. 6, 22-25; 7, 22-23. The account is realistically but subtly crafted to capture our attention and admiration and to highlight the authority of Jesus: he stands while all are seated; the scroll of Isaiah is handed to him, but he himself unrolls it and finds the place(s) he wants to read; when he has completed his reading which in fact comprises two different passages, he rolls up the scroll, gives it back to the attendant and sits down. The eyes of all are expectantly fixed on him, but it is his utterance that appears to draw a favourable comment from his townspeople: 'they wondered because of the words of graciousness that came from his mouth.' As well as the studied suspense that Luke cleverly evokes, their is also deep irony in the people's reaction here. The passage of Scripture he has just cited and applied to himself has as its central statement that he will 'open the eyes of he blind', and their eyes are fixed on him. However, their reaction soon shows that their hearts are closed: they acknowledge his *gracious* words', but not, however, the year of grace, that is, the Jubilee that has just been proclaimed, and its radical implications for them.

According to the Leviticus account it was the priests at the temple on the occasion of Yom Kippur that were to proclaim the year of Jubilee, but in Luke it is a local country prophet who arrogates this role to himself in the synagogue and on the Sabbath. Not only that, but he dares to broaden the scope of God's year of favour to include outsiders as well as Israel. For the Lukan Jesus, the Jubilee has universal application, though its centrality for Israel is maintained. The chosen texts are significant also, belonging to the last section of the book of Isaiah, where they express the millennial hopes of the returned exiles from Babylonia in terms of good news for the poor and release of those enslaved, combined with the expectation of the outpouring of the spirit in the messianic times (Is 58,6; 61,1-2). Significantly, there is no mention of leaving the land fallow for the year, yet in his parables and imagery Jesus is deeply conscious of the natural fruitfulness of the land and the mysterious processes, whereby the earth 'of itself' can produce a rich harvest, while humans are dumb bystanders. (Mk 4, 26-29). Thus from the rich tradition of the Jubilee, the Lukan Jesus, just like the Isaian prophet before him, felt free to choose those elements that were applicable 'today'; there was no need to implement slavishly other aspects of the Jubilee that were no longer appropriate or operable. For him there were other ways to respect and embody the values associated with leaving the earth untilled, as we shall see.

As already suggested the central statement of Jesus' scriptural citation is the phrase 'giving sight to the blind', an emphasis that might appear to be at odds with Luke's concentration here and elsewhere throughout his Gospel on practical social action. True, the blind are frequently mentioned in his lists of marginalised characters – the poor, the blind, the maimed the lame – that is, those, who according to Leviticus (Lev 21, 17-24) were precluded from full participation in temple worship due to their physical blemishes, are to be included at the table of the kingdom in Jesus' vision. Yet there seems to be another, deeper aspect to this centring of 'sight for the blind' in his scriptural reading. Elsewhere, sight is compared to a lamp that lights up and illuminates the whole person, 'so that there is no darkness at all' (Lk 11, 33-36). Once illumination occurs then the rest of Jesus' radical demands become totally intelligible in the deeper understanding of God that Jesus' reflection on the Jubilee and its implications had uncovered. The Jubilee is at once a statement of God's care for all, but also a manifestation God's justice on behalf of the marginalised and the disadvantaged. God is both a caring judge and a just carer, just not by the standards of distributive justice, but by those of unbounded love for all, irrespective of, wealth or physical stature. In the Mediterranean world within which Luke's Jesus operates, the status and honour that these public attributes brought were the most prized possessions of the rich and powerful, whereas disgrace and shame were the lot of the poor, the marginalised and the maimed. However, in Jesus' 'values revolution' it is the poor and hungry that are blessed and the wealthy and well-fed that are shameful. Thus, according to Luke, the charge on which Jesus was arrested and tried was not a threat to the temple, but rather in subverting the people, 'stirring up the nation from Galilee to this place' (Lk 23, 3-4). This same charge is subsequently levelled at the Christian communities of the Greco-Roman world in Luke's second volume, Acts of the Apostles: 'They turn the world upside down, refusing to obey the decrees of Caesar' (Ac 17,19).

Jesus and the Millennial Jubilee

Luke chose to present Jesus in the guise of a radical prophet of social justice, not primarily for Roman ears, but for those very communities of resistance and hope that had emerged in the various Mediterranean cities mentioned in Acts. Theophilus, the addressee of both volumes stands for such Exodus communities, to borrow Edward Schillebeeckx's description. Christianity had become a house-church movement, gathering in their homes for the breaking of bread, in Corinth, Philippi, Ephesus, Thessalonica and Rome itself. As more wealthy god-fearers and others joined it was in danger of forgetting its origins in the Galilean villages of Jesus' ministry. Luke clearly wanted to keep alive the dangerous memory of that Jesus, who had challenged not only the values of Roman imperial power, but those of the temple religion with its Deuteronomic theology which proclaimed God's favour in terms of prosperity for the good and rejection of the wicked, with its dangerous social implications within a flawed theological system.

In recent times there has been much discussion as to the source and inspiration of Jesus' own vision, with his abandonment of home, family and possessions. Was he motivated by the ideal of the popular Greco-Roman philosophy of the Cynics whose anti-social posture was also intended as a counter-cultural attack on the Roman value system of the day? Or was Jesus enacting a dream that was dreamt in the heart of his own Jewish piety and reflected in its Scriptures? Clearly, it is impossible to enter this debate here, but I want to suggest that a plausible case can be made for the claim that Jesus was prompted by the values of the Jubilee and their underlying theology of God's caring and inclusive justice, especially as this was expounded by the prophets, while at the same time maintaining the millennial dreams that he shared with his Jewish contemporaries. While we have been presented with many different images of Jesus in modern scholarship, surprisingly, the notion of the Jubilee and its programme has rarely been suggested as the background for the shape and motivation of the Galilean ministry. There is fairly widespread agreement today that Jesus was originally a disciple of John the Baptist, sharing John's millennial beliefs in the imminent coming of God's judgement and calling on all Israel to repent and undergo his baptismal ritual in the Jordan to prepare for the coming kingdom (Jn 3, 22f). Subsequent to John's arrest he went to Galilee, abandoning the desert and its call for a ministry of healing and making whole among the outcasts of the Galilean village communities.

What prompted this change of emphasis from outright millennialist to prophet of the Jubilee? When Jesus was a young adult two major symbols of Roman imperial power were being erected in lower Galilee, namely the cities of Sepphoris and Tiberias, both of which were intended to honour the Roman overlords of Herod Antipas. These were intended to celebrate the achievements of the emperor Augustus and his step-son Tiberias, who had brought peace to the empire after a long period of civil war. Yet these cities were not just symbols of an alien power in the heartland of Jewish life, their establishment also meant a social revolution in terms of rapid economic and cultural change through the development of a politically controlled economy in favour of the wealthy. More than their modern counterparts, pre-industrial cities were heavily dependent on their immediate hinterland, making serious inroads into local resources. Land was appropriated, a new elite had to be accommodated and other resources, natural and human were exploited in the interests of a small but powerful elite. This social revolution provides us with the best and most immediate context for understanding Jesus' ministry, since it points to the corrosion of the values that were part of the Jewish village culture and which were enshrined in and enjoined by the Torah, values based on close-knit kinship relations and which were supportive of the weak and the marginalised.

It is plausible to understand the shift in Jesus' perception of his own mission and destiny against the background of this concrete situation. In a word, he tempered his millennial dreams for the future with the Jubilee values for the here and now. He recognised the need to resist openly these new and corrosive forces by embarking on a life-style that radically opposed the values of the new elite. One of Rome's court poets, Virgil, in his famous *Fourth Eclogue* had lauded the achievements of Augustus as the ushering in of a new era of world peace marked by fertility in nature: 'Justice returns; returns old Saturn's reign', he wrote, Saturn being the old Roman god of agriculture. The poet envisaged a restoration of harmony in nature, unprecedented fertility of flocks and land, independently of any human intervention or labour. The language and imagery is not dissimilar to that of the Hebrew prophets, especially Isaiah, writing about the messianic age to come (see Is 9, 1-6; 11, 1-9). Virgil writes: 'He shall receive the life of gods and see heroes and gods commingling, and himself be seen of then, and with his fathers worth, reign oe'r a world at peace.' Yet because of the prevailing pyramid of power, all this prosperity would benefit only the ruling aristocracy; the masses would have to make do with bread and circuses.

Jesus too spoke of peace, justice and God's bountiful blessings. His wandering, homeless life-style was an embodiment of the values he proclaimed in the name of Yahweh's *basileia* or kingdom, not Rome's *imperium*. The difference was that his notion of peace was grounded in hearts that could find ways to love one's enemy; his justice was for the poor; all, and not just the elite few were to share in God's bounty of the land. His was a revolution from below, whereas Rome's was imposed from above. His community would be based on kinship values of caring and sharing, since his followers from many different backgrounds and social strata could be described as relating to him and to each other as brother, sister and mother. The taboos associated with sickness and physical disability were set aside, and Jesus' healings were not just cures, but the restoration of dignity and status to those who were deprived of any by the prevailing political and religious ethos. Jesus' call to replace all anxiety with a total trust in the God who cares, expressed through the images of searching for food, drink, clothing and shelter, is merely carrying to its logical, though radical conclusion the Jubilee ideal (Mt 6, 25-33; Lk 12, 22-34). The questions Jesus puts on the lips of the anxious by-standers in this passage, 'What shall we eat and what shall we drink, and wherewith shall be clothed?' are a direct echo of the Israelites' query to God in the Jubilee legislation: 'What shall we eat in the seventh year if we may not sow or gather in our crop?', to which God replies that he will give his blessing in the sixth year so that the crop will be sufficient for three years (Lev 25, 20-22). Now, however, the Jubilee values were not to be operative for just one year in fifty, but were to be adopted as a permanent lifestyle. Such a radical vision was scarcely understood by his intimate followers, let alone the Galilean crowds who seem to have been attracted by his healing ministry. It was he, not they who eventually paid the price in Jerusalem, not just because he was accused of betraying his own religious tradition, but because he dared to confront Roman imperial values with those of the Jubilee, which was grounded in utter confidence in God's coming kingdom. It can be said that Jesus dared to live the Jubilee values because he believed utterly in the millennial dream of God's victory over evil in all its manifestations.

11

THE APOSTLE PAUL, THE FIRST CHRISTIAN MYSTIC?

The paradox at the heart of the mystical experience has been well stated as follows:

> Experience proves ineffable and incontestable. It knows that it is being put in question, but it is vowed to silence. If this experience undertakes to speak of the God who visits it, it appeals, at the heart of the most profound subjectivity, to a truth and objectivity which are those of God himself ... It has to confront the otherness of the word of God, and he way in which it is brought to bear in the community of believers.[1]

The mystic is faced with an experience that is by definition unspeakable, and yet in order to authenticate the event as genuine, and not self-delusory, has to attempt to justify it before the court of the community's rule of faith as defined by Scripture, Tradition and Teaching Authority. Perhaps that paradox may explain why the mystics and their messages have been regarded with suspicion, if not downright scepticism, at best as curiosities who have little to say to 'ordinary' believers. I have to acknowledge that as a white, western male, I too am naturally suspicious of the more exotic forms and expressions of religious sentiment. Most of us have been socialised by the institutional, seeking to be 'good and respectable' citizens, and therefore, avoiding the seemingly exotic in belief as well as in life. In these justice-conscious days one can also point to the lack of social concern and the reactionary trends that are often associated with some modern forms of the charismatic movements, as a rationalisation for such negative attitudes. The mystics seem to belong in that camp rather than in the aesthetically cold and increasingly irrelevant world of our middle-class Churches. Either we seek to appropriate them to our modes of thinking or banish them to the margins in our desire for order, neatness and sobriety in our worship and in our lives.

What are we to do with the mystics, therefore, if, as we are told, the mystical is what we all have to aspire to as 'members of the mystical body of Christ'? In contemporary Roman Catholicism, at least, the institutional, with its appeal to authority within a rigid and hierarchical framework, is in grave danger of stifling the spirit. Do the mystics with their personal authority based on their extraordinary experiences not have something special to offer in such a repressive climate? If there is any truth in the stereotypes of the masculine as cold and rational and the feminine as free-spirited, emotional and even irrational, could not the mystics have something to offer to a Church that is so alienating for so many women? Could we find a place for the ecstatic as part of what we consider to be 'the normal' in the Christian life? Can the mystics and the mystical be reconciled to the mutual enrichment of all of us?

In attempting to address these questions I have chosen to look at the apostle Paul and his writings. The question mark in my title does not refer to the fact that I doubt that Paul did have genuine mystical experiences. Indeed, Paul may not have been the first mystic within the new movement. Jesus should logically be a contender to the title, but we simply do not know enough about his own personal spiritual life to be able to decide with any degree of certainty. The author of the Fourth Gospel undoubtedly depicts Jesus as a mystic, but this seems to tell us more about the milieu of that work than it does about the historical Jesus. The unnamed 'beloved disciple' who appears to be the prime contender for the authorship of the Fourth Gospel purports to speak on behalf of a community: 'we have seen his glory' (Jn 1, 14). Yet in this work and we do not experience the same intense personal feelings of a troubled author as in the case of Paul and his writings, where the autobiographical seems to play a very important role in the making of the personal experience and the theology. It is for this reason that Paul is constantly appealed to when it comes to talking about the nature of Christian identity. So intriguing a personality is he that he has been variously categorised in terms of contemporary psychological understanding. One could develop a plausible character portrait of him as being troubled, neurotic, misogynist, irascible, impatient, self-centred – almost the whole gamut of counter traits to those that he himself lists as the fruits of the spirit! (Gal 5, 22f). We must avoid modernising Paul in the way that we are constantly modernising Jesus in our attempts to make them both relevant for our times. By allowing them to emerge as people of their own time and within their own worldview rather than ours we may be surprised to find just how contemporary they become in addressing some of our own most pressing problems.

I propose to proceed in three steps: firstly I want to introduce, however briefly, the idea of what constituted the mystical experience in the world of Paul, in order to attune ourselves to his language and imagery. Secondly, I want to examine the case for Paul the mystic by focusing on a few key passages that seem to correspond to those traits, which are today associated with the mystical experience. Finally, I shall sketch aspects of Paul's understanding of our communal Christian existence that have often been described as 'Pauline mysticism'.

Mystics and Mysticism in the World of Paul

The *Age of Anxiety* is the description used by ancient historian E. R. Dodds to describe the mood of the ancient world in the early centuries of the Common Era.[2] The causes of the anxiety were manifold – political, social and religious – but the symptoms manifested themselves particularly in the increasing desire of individuals to be connected or reconnected with the forces that were deemed to rule the world. Union with the gods was paramount and various techniques and methods were in vogue in order to achieve that end. In particular the mystery religions were deemed to provide the kind of spiritual nourishment that the state religion of Rome could not offer.

The root word is *muo*, 'to be silent,' from which comes the word mysterion, meaning that which is hidden or secret. It is this meaning that gives rise to the description of many Greco-Roman cults contemporary with Early Christianity as mystery religions. Through the media of ritual and myth individuals were initiated into the hidden secrets of the universe, often focusing on the nature of the afterlife. This initiation and its attendant rituals gave rise to a deep sense of union with the deity in question – Isis, Dionysus, Cybele, Mithras, Serapis – and a feeling of direct encounter with, and participation in the experiences of the particular god, as this was described in the myth or story that gave rise to their worship. Afterwards one returned to everyday life refreshed and consoled.

Very often the transformation of the individual is described in terms of a heavenly journey in which the initiate is transposed from earth to heaven, there to encounter the god face to face. We have a very moving account of one such initiation rite/journey from a slightly later period than Paul, but it is no doubt expressive of the emotional support that many displaced people in the Greco-Roman world experienced through participation in such a ritual. The account is of an initiation rite into the cult of Isis, described as 'the mother of the universe.'

> Lo I am with you Lucius, moved by your prayers, I (Isis) who am the mother of the universe, the mistress of all the elements, the first offspring of time ... My single godhead is adored by the whole world in varied forms in differing rites and with many diverse names. ... I (Lucius) approached the boundary of death and treading on Proserpine's threshold I was carried through all the elements, after which I returned. At dead of night I saw the sun flashing with bright effulgence. I approached close to the gods above and the gods below and worshipped them face to face. (Apuleius, *Metamorphoses*, Bk 11).

Many of the elements that we shall meet again later in considering Paul's heavenly journey are present here and are typical, as described in other sources also – the journey theme itself, the secret and unutterable message, the partial loss of personal identity in conjunction with a changed state of consciousness, and a different perception of the world around. Some scholars have been so impressed by the similarities between these mystery cults and early Christianity, especially in its Pauline form, that they have judged it as just another such mystery cult. The fact that it succeeded in surviving to become a 'world religion' whereas others did not, was merely an accident of history and was not due to any intrinsic differences between it and those other cults.[3]

There is undoubtedly some basis for the comparison, even if the conclusion is often grossly overdrawn. At the end of his *magnum opus*, the Epistle to the Romans, Paul speaks of his meditation on Christ's role in resolving the great cosmic drama of good and evil as follows:

> I do not want you to be ignorant of this mystery which has been hidden for ages and has now been revealed ... 'O the depths of the riches of the knowledge and wisdom of God ... All that is comes from him, exists through him and for him. To Him be glory for ever Amen.' (Romans 11, 25.33-36).

In other letters also (especially in 1 Corinthians and Ephesians) Paul (or his disciple in the case of Ephesians) uses terminology that suggests that he and his readership were quite at home in a world where intimate union with God could be achieved through special ritual, bringing with it consolation and a sense of superior, intuitive knowledge of reality itself.

Despite these similarities between Paul and the mystery religions, which I do not want to underplay, there is, however, another strand of thinking in antiquity to which Paul was heir, and which, undoubtedly, played a formative role in his spiritual and theological development.[4] This is the strand of mysticism associated with Jewish apocalyptic thinking. Apocalyptic, both as a literary genre and as religious worldview is often denigrated in theological discussions as being out of tune with our modern, progressive view of the world and human achievement. Whatever about the validity of some of these claims, it still remains true that it provided the framework for the early Christians' self-understanding, and it deserves our close attention if we wish to understand their religious and theological point of view. The heavenly journey is an important element in this corpus of writings also.[5] The accounts, often couched in vivid images and describing strange phenomena, are not primarily concerned with end of the world scenarios, but are intended rather to describe the most immediate and direct encounter with the God of Israel that was considered possible. This encounter usually took place at a moment of crisis, and though intensely personal in the description of the experience, it nevertheless had a communal function of reassurance and hope for a larger group.

The origin of the heavenly journey motif in Judaism is usually associated with the prophet Ezechiel's vision of the fiery chariot drawn by creatures, part animal, part human, part angelic. Above the chariot is a throne on which is seated a being that looked like a man, and this is identified with something like the glory of the God of Israel. This is the famous *Hekaloth* or 'chariot' vision, which made a profound impact on subsequent Jewish mystical speculation, down to the middle ages and which the rabbis tried to control or even repress.[6] Though much of this *Hekaloth* speculation seems to have gone underground and did not surface in literary form until much later, there is good evidence from the Qumran documents as well as from Paul and others that it played a very important role in certain pious circles of Judaism in the centuries leading up to the common era. In particular the Book of Enoch (a composite work in its present form) seems to have been greatly influenced by this motif. According to tradition Enoch walked with God and 'God took him' (Gn 5,18-24), giving rise to speculation that Enoch had not died but was taken up to heaven.

This idea was to stimulate the imagination of pious Jews later. In the opening section of the book, usually described as 'The Book of the Watchers' (chs 1-36) Enoch acts as intermediary on behalf of 'the watchers' (usually identified with the Jerusalem priesthood) who have a sentence of judgment hanging over them because of their defilement. Enoch goes to Mount Hermon in the north to intercede for them, and while there in a dream is transposed to heaven where he is taken to a heavenly temple and presented before the throne of the Great Glory, 'whose cloak was like the appearance of the sun and whiter than much snow.' The Great One reassures Enoch, addressing him as 'righteous man' and 'scribe of righteousness', while confirming the sentence of judgment on the wicked priests (I Enoch 14). While the scene has many elements of later accounts of mystical experiences, not least Enoch's terrified reaction, within the context of the book as a whole its functions is to establish Enoch's authority, thus providing an interesting point of comparison with Paul's vision, as we shall see.[7] Subsequently he begins a tour of the heavenly regions guided by an angel. The purpose of this tour is manifold, displaying God's wisdom and power, but also confirming Enoch's own wisdom, which is recognised as a gift from God. It also provides a context for understanding the order that pervades the cosmos despite the disorders of the watchers and their lifestyle. While the treatment is certainly unique, one can recognise here also another purpose of the heavenly journey as developed in later apocalypses, namely the revelation to the elect of the hidden plan of the world, which no human wisdom can comprehend.

In the section of the book known as the Parables of Enoch (chs 39-71) Enoch is again depicted as ascending to heaven reciting hymns and blessings; his face changes as he is overcome by the splendour of the throne room (ch 39) and he sees the blessed (not God); later his whole body is transformed and he himself is seated on the throne and addressed as the Son of Man and given assurances that God will take care of him (71, 1). He is thus promised the immortality that was associated with the stars according to the Book of Daniel (12, 2f). He describes the transformation in terms that are typical of the mystical experience as it is known to us from other sources:

And it came to pass after this that my spirit was translated and I ascended into the heavens and I saw the holy sons of God. They were stepping on fire, their garments were white and their faces shone like snow ... And I fell on my face and my whole body became relaxed and my spirit was transfigured and I cried with a loud voice, with the spirit of power and blessed and glorified and extolled ... Then an angel came to me and greeted me and said to me: 'You Son of man who art born in righteousness and upon whom righteousness has dwelt, the righteousness of the Antecedent of Time will not forsake you' (1 Enoch 71).

It is not absolutely clear whether, in the author's view, the second description refers to the end of Enoch's life. What is significant is that he is transformed and is admitted into the heavenly realm where other mortals also dwell, but without ever directly encountering the living God, but only God's messengers.[8]

This aspect seems to be an essential feature of Jewish apocalypses of this type, namely there is never a direct encounter with God, but only with some god-like being or something reflecting God's reality, such as God's glory or presence. The motif has its rationale in the Book of Exodus where Moses is not allowed to see the face of God:

You cannot see my face; for man shall not see me and live – While my glory passes by I shall put you in the cleft of the rock and I will cover you with my hand until I have passed by; then I will take away my hand and you shall see my back; but my face shall not be seen. (Exodus 33.18-23).

This passage was crucial in all subsequent Jewish speculation about the human encounter with God. The God of Israel can never be encountered in God's self, not even in the most awesome and mystical settings. God can only be encountered in the glory, that is, some some emanation of God's power and presence, or in some being, angelic or human (such as Enoch or Adam) who has been transformed.

In later speculation Moses too can represent the living God, especially in his role as law-giver, when his ascent to Mount Sinai is transformed into an ascent to the throne of God, where he is conferred with the status of a divine being. This speculation also takes its point of origin from the biblical text:

When Moses came down from the mountain of Sinai – as he came down from the mountain, Moses had the two tablets of the covenant in his hands – he did not know that the skin on his face was radiant after speaking with Yahweh. And when Aaron and all the sons of Israel saw Moses the skin on his face shone so much that they would not venture near him ... And when Moses had finished speaking to them, he put a veil over his face. Whenever he went into Yahweh's presence to speak with him, Moses would remove the veil until he came out again (Exodus 34, 29-34).

Philo, the Alexandrian Jewish philosopher, interprets this and other texts (e.g. Ex 20, 21; 24, 18) in which Moses is said to have responded to God's invitation to visit him on the mountain, in terms of the prevailing philosophical tradition. In order to maintain God's otherness and perfection Moses cannot encounter God directly in line with Jewish thought. Yet the Hellenistic philosophical environment demanded an intermediary of some kind. The concept of the *Logos* as adapted from the Stoics by the Middle Platonists provided Philo with the ideas he required to bridge the gap between heaven and earth. His Logos is no divine spark innate to all creatures as the Stoics thought, however, but virtually a second God, with whom Moses is united through contemplation. This, for Philo was the true ascent of Moses to God. Thus in his *Life of Moses* he can declare that Moses shared the communion with God to such an extent that he also shares the same names 'God and king.' Philo continues: 'Moses, we are told, entered the very darkness where God was, and there beheld what is hidden to mortal nature.' (*Life of Moses* I, 158). Later he describes Moses preparation for the ascent in terms of a purification of the passions so that he might be ready to receive the divine oracles. Commenting on the passage from Exodus, cited above, which describes the descent from the mountain with the two tablets, Philo writes:

> For we read that by God's command he ascended an inaccessible and pathless mountain, the highest and most sacred in the region ... then after forty days he descended with a countenance far more beautiful than when he ascended, so that those who saw him were filled with awe and amazement. (*Life of Moses* II, 70).

It has often been said that Paul, like Philo, was a person of two cultures, equally at home in the Greek and Jewish worlds of thought. It should be noted that the heavenly journey motif is common in Hellenistic and Roman literature also. But there was another strand of mystical thinking current among those Greeks who were heir to Plato's philosophy. They could speak of the soul's journey to God as its source, and the mystical-philosophical task was to rid oneself of all bodily or material sensations so that one could enter into the stillness that was God. According to Plotinus, the most prolific representative of this tradition from a later time, the desired union can only be prepared for and awaited. His pupil and biographer, Porphyry, declares that his master was lifted four times in his life to the primal and transcendent god, through meditation and use of other methods of philosophical thinking suggested by Plato in the *Symposium*. Plotinus describes the experience as follows:

> The soul sees God suddenly appearing within it because there is nothing between; they are no longer two, but one; while the presence lasts, you cannot distinguish them. It is that union that earthly lovers imitate when they would be one flesh. The soul is no longer in the body, or of itself as having identity ... When in this state the soul would exchange its present condition for nothing in the world, though it were offered the kingdom of all the heavens; for this is the Good and there is nothing better. (Plotinus, *Eneads* Bk 7, 34, 12ff).

One cannot help but notice the real difference between this description of the mystical union and the Jewish experience as articulated in the theme of the heavenly journey, even in Philo's spiritualised version. Unlike Plotinus, there is no theory of the soul as a separate and separable part of the human person, whose true desire is to be re-joined to the one source of its being in the Universal soul. Paul, as we shall see, is overwhelmed by the gifted nature of his experience, whereas for Plotinus this state of union, though ultimately to be awaited for, nevertheless can be hastened by intellectual exercise. According to E.R. Dodds, 'it has no physiological or sacramental aspects, no breathing exercises, no naval brooding, no hypnotic recitation of sacred syllables and no ritual.'[9] The end is the union of contemplation in which the soul loses its total identity, freed from the shackles of the body. For the Jewish tradition generally, on the other hand, it is the transformation of the body-self into a new mode of existence that is similar to that of the One who is encountered, but without ever losing oneself totally in the All that is God, no matter how intimate the relationship may be.

Paul's Mystical Experience

> I know a man in Christ who fourteen years ago – whether in the body or out of the body I do not know, God knows – was caught up to the

third heaven. And I know that this man – whether in the body or separate from the body I do not know, God knows – was caught up into Paradise and he heard unutterable words which are unlawful to speak. (2 Cor 12, 2-4)

Before attempting to set this text in the larger context of Paul's autobiographical utterances, it is important to note the way in which its significance has been downplayed by Pauline scholars.[10] Some have claimed that Paul is in fact disparaging such ecstatic phenomena as a way of countering his opponents who claim similar experiences (2 Cor 12, 1). In terms of his apostolic authority, which he wishes to vindicate, such experiences are of no importance. Other commentators point to the fact that Paul speaks of his heavenly journey having taken place many years previously, and that it is now recalled by way of an afterthought. Or again, it is suggested that it is the experience of his own weakness that Paul considers as paramount (2 Cor 12, 9f; 13, 4). In all of these various suggestions one can rightly suspect that we are hearing the voices of Christian scholarship that is distrustful of such experiences, rather than Paul's own views on the matter.

The context for the description of the heavenly journey (2 Cor 10-13) is his defense of his own authority as an apostle over against other missionaries who have arrived in Corinth after Paul had written the first letter to the Cointhians, which dealt with several internal problems within the community. Some of these problems included issues to do with the abuse of charismatic gifts and claims of revelatory experiences (1 Cor 12; 14). Far from downplaying his own ecstatic experiences, Paul compares them with those of his opponents, by speaking of an actual ascent to heaven in contrast to their mere pneumatic occurrences. This forms part of his commendation by God, thus validating his apostolic authority. His weakness is not itself a sign of apostolic calling, but rather a reminder of the inability of humans to achieve anything before God. This contrasts with Plotinus' confident claims for human reason and the control of the passions.

The argument of these chapters is complex and not easy to follow in view of Paul's use of irony, parody and sarcasm in order to discredit his opponents in line with best rhetorical practice of the period.[11] What is important is the context in which Paul feels it necessary to recall his heavenly journey, namely his desire to legitimate his claim to be an authentic apostle, whose word is the word of God not that of humans. Elsewhere, Paul can rely on a more institutional type of argument when he is not under direct attack with regard to his apostolic claim. His encounter with the Risen Christ means that he is included in the list of official apostolic witnesses alongside Peter, James and the other apostles (1 Cor 15, 2-8). It is noteworthy, however, that when his apostleship is challenged as in Galatians, it is to his mystical experiences, described as an *apokalypsis Iesou Christou*, that he has recourse – experiences that put him in line with such Hebrew prophets as Ezechiel and Jeremiah (Gal 1, 12.15f; 1 Cor 9, 1).

It is reasonable, therefore, to assume that the reference to the heavenly journey in 2 Cor may have a similar intention. To begin with, Paul, while using the third person, 'a man in Christ', contrasts his own ecstatic experience of the past with the ongoing 'thorn in the flesh' that he must constantly live with, despite his desire to be free of it. Two quite contrasting states are thereby indicated, and the fact that earlier Paul has given a detailed list of his ongoing tribulations (2 Cor 11, 23-29) suggests that these daily signs of his weakness are much more pressing than his ecstatic moments. As noted already, the fact that the specific incident of the heavenly journey occurred fourteen years earlier has been interpreted to suggest that it was of no great significance in the overall context of his life. Yet this interpretation ignores the very pointed double use of the present tense of the verb 'I know' (*oida*), which strongly suggests that this is an ongoing and present condition, resulting from a past event of singular importance. Paul is utterly convinced of the experience, which was so intense (*hyperbole* v. 7), and so potentially beguiling, that he accepts the thorn in the flesh as God's way of striking the balance – possibly in contrast to the opponents – by bringing him back down to earth, both literally and metaphorically.

The double utterance in the text – 'I know a man ... whether in the body or outside the body, I do not know, God knows' – raises the question as to whether 'the third heaven' of v. 2 and the 'Paradise' of v. 3 are identical, or whether a two-stage journey is intended, climaxing in Paradise, the abode both of the just and the throne of God, according to certain Jewish texts.[12] This is the more likely scenario, and the two-stage journey merely distinguishes Paul's experience from those of the others. It is probably for this reason also that he mentions the 'unutterable' things, which are unlawful to mention. This last phrase suggests the milieu of the mystery religions where the initiates are prohibited from sharing the secrets of the group with outsiders. From a Jewish perspective, however, the unutterable things point in the direction of the mysterious nature of God, which cannot be comprehended by human reason. 'It is not the nature of the One who Is to be named, but to be,' is Philo's profound interpretation of the refusal of God to disclose his name to Moses (Ex 3, 14). Despite Philo's own philosophical leanings, which suggested that union with God could be achieved through contemplation, in this instance, Philo, like Paul, is more a Jew than a philosopher.

Despite Paul's reserve, it is possible to infer the impact that this inexpressible experience had on his self-understanding and his theology. Much of Jewish mystical speculation was based on Moses' experience as reported in Exodus. While Moses could not look directly on God and live, he was nevertheless transformed to such a degree that he had to wear a veil over his face subsequently when speaking to the people of Israel. Earlier in 2 Cor Paul uses the same image of the veil to suggest that the people of Israel were blinded from seeing the true reality of God, whereas Christians endowed by the Spirit are being transformed 'from one degree of glory to another', in accordance with Paul's Gospel (2 Cor 3, 12-18). His assurance of this and of his own apostolic ministry with regard to the role of Jesus in the transformation of all the baptised, is the direct result of his own personal encounter: 'For it is the God who said, "Let light shine out of darkness," who has shone in our hearts to give the light of the knowledge of the Lord in the face of Christ' (2 Cor 4, 6). Paul is quite sure of the source of his extraordinary experience – that of the Creator God – but the object of that experience is not God directly, but rather the transformative glory (or power) of that God in Christ. The veil that has been removed for Paul is the awareness that in the transformation of Jesus God's glory has made him into the very eikon or image of God. If Paul cannot speak openly of God, he can speak with passion and conviction of Christ's glorified status, and hence his assurance of his own and his converts' transformation by the Spirit into the same glorious (i.e. God-like) status.

Pauline Mysticism and Christian Existence

The argument of this paper so far has been to suggest that the mystical experience that Paul, under pressure from opponents, reluctantly speaks of, played a much more significant role in his understanding of his apostolic ministry than is usually recognised by scholars. I have suggested that the experience itself should be understood in the more general context of the heavenly journey as this is described by several Jewish writers. Such a journey was deemed anticipatory, a foretaste granted to a few, of the transformation that all the just could hope for. Central to such journeys is the reserve that is the cornerstone of Jewish theology, namely, the radically mysterious nature of God, not because God has chosen to be distant and aloof, but as a reaction to the reductionist tendencies that rendered the very notion of God problematic. It is a reverential, not an agnostic stance, the primacy of the *apophatic* over the *katophatic*, to employ the language of medieval theology, and which in the end makes all Jewish theology mystical. In the Jewish tradition, the person who undergoes the heavenly-journey experience encounters some representative of God, who themselves have undergone the transformative process. The visionary is thus given a foretaste of their own and others transformation. In Paul's case this explains the centrality of Christ in his theology, giving rise to what has been described as Pauline mysticism.[13]

Various definitions of 'mystical' as applied to Paul's theology have been proposed, most famously, that of Albert Schweitzer:

> We are always in the presence of mysticism when we find a human being looking on the divisions of earthly and super-earthly, temporal and eternal, as transcended, and feeling himself, while still externally amid the earthly and the temporal, to belong to the super-earthly and the eternal.[14]

Others have offered different descriptions, but all are agreed that in Paul's terms what is significant is his use of the phrase 'in Christ', his notion of the 'body of Christ' and his understanding of the role of the Spirit in Christian life. These three themes are interwoven in Paul's mind, to form an almost seamless robe, whereby the Christian 'put on' Christ. Through faith and baptism believers can be said to be 'in Christ' and to have the Spirit of Christ indwelling in them, and together they form the body of Christ. Moderns, so attuned to the individualistic thinking that is the hallmark of the Enlightenment, find such descriptions of Christian existence incomprehensible and meaningless. Indeed, so removed have we become from that world of corporate identity in our religious, as distinct from our economic existence, that most Christians operate with the notion of Christ as an exemplary figure only, and think of God as remote and detached from their everyday existence. With God removed to the outer reaches of the universe and our own highly individualistic culture, we could scarcely be more removed from the ancient Mediterranean notion of what has been described as the 'dyadic personality'. By that is meant an understanding of the self as essentially, not just accidentally, related to the group, whether this is constituted by ties of real or fictive kinship – family, clan, tribe, or free association.[15] From our modern perspective there is a logical gap between the conclusion that if one man has died, then all have died, but for the first-century Mediterranean person on the other hand this connection is both immediate and obvious.

'If anyone is in Christ there is a new creation' (2 Cor 5, 17). This is one of Paul's many expressions in which the formula 'in Christ' is used. Mention of the new creation immediately provides a context for the expression within the ambit of Jewish apocalyptic hopes for the renewal of all things. In Paul's opinion this event is already in train, as 'the whole creation is groaning in travail until now', awaiting the redemption of the children of God, who already are enjoying the fruits of the Spirit (Rm 8, 22-24). Being 'in Christ' means that the believer has already entered into that sphere of divine transformation, which God has inaugurated in and through Christ's death and resurrection. This is not just an ethical or psychological transformation; the very mode of being of the believer is being 'metamorphised' into the mode of being of the Risen Christ who as Spirit shares in the glory that is God.

This shared transformation is made possible in Paul's view through his understanding of the body of Christ, that most illusive, yet suggestive, of Paul's metaphors. Unlike the Greeks who supposed a real separation between soul and body, the latter being regarded as a disposable part of the human person, the Hebrews understood bodiliness as a shared reality of the human condition that constitutes the self as a body-person, that is, the self can only be understood as an external communal being in the world. To lose one's body is to cease to exist; to exist differently from one's present corporeal existence is to be a different body-self. Christ, as the Risen one who has entered into the mode of being of God is the first human to achieve this status as a spiritual body-self, but in this he is a representative figure, a new Adam, 'a life-giving Spirit' (1 Cor 15, 45-49; Rm 5, 12-19). The Christian enters this new spiritual existence through faith and baptism, that is, through a surrender of the old self both personally and ritually, thereby entering into Christ's death/resurrection as a way of participating in his body-self that now includes the whole of redeemed humanity (Rm 6, 1-11).[16]

A discussion of the spiritual body introduces the third strand of Paul's mystical language, namely the gift of the Spirit. How is the Spirit's role to be understood? Sometimes the Spirit is scarcely distinguishable from the Risen Christ. The Spirit dwells in us and Christ dwells in us; if Christians are to be in Christ, they are also to be in the Spirit; the Spirit plays a role in our resurrection, just as Christ does. These and other parallels have convinced some that, for Paul, the notion of the Risen Christ loses all its specificity, becoming identified with the universal spirit of the Hellenistic age and its modern counterpart in Hegel's philosophy. Thus Paul can actually declare: 'The Lord is the Spirit' (2 Cor 3, 17). However, such a conclusion undoubtedly goes too far. For Paul Christ or the Lord is not some universal abstraction but the crucified and risen one whom he has encountered, a concrete historical being whose historical personhood is now continued in the person of the glorified Christ (Philippians 2, 6-11; 3, 20f). In Paul's thought it was through this historical figure, not through an impersonal spirit, that God has redeemed us, by giving his only son for us. In Paul's system the Spirit functions not as an independent and parallel force, but as the Spirit of Christ. Thus, the notion of the Spirit that the believers share, enables Paul to describe the new mode of existence that Christ already enjoys to the full and that believers participate in as the pledge of final salvation.

Conclusion

Paul understands the Christian life as union with Christ, and we have briefly suggested various strands of his thinking and expression of this reality that was so intimate for the apostle himself, that he could declare: 'It is no longer I who lives, but it is Christ who lives in me' (Gal 2, 20). Christians who share the Spirit of Christ can be said to form the body of Christ (Rm 8, 8-11). Is this union mystical, or better still, is it helpful and accurate to describe this union as mystical? If the contention is correct that Paul's heavenly journey played a much more important and lasting role in his spiritual development than is usually recognised, then to describe his theology as mystical, in the sense of breaking the boundaries between heaven and earth, seems altogether apposite and illuminating. At the end of his *magnum opus*, his Epistle to the Romans, Paul speaks of his Gospel as the revelation of 'the mystery kept secret for endless ages, but now manifested, so that it could be proclaimed to the gentiles everywhere' (Rm 16, 25-27). Here Paul's language reflects the milieu of the mystery religions, and yet is firmly grounded in the Jewish apocalyptic notion of the divine plan for the universe that lay hidden until the appropriate time. Paul straddles two cultural worlds in his terminology, but his experiences of the Risen Christ is so intense that it not only breaks down the cultural barriers of Jew and Greek, it also bridges the gulf that humans have always experienced between heaven and earth, between God and his creation.

Notes

1. Yves Cattin, 'The Christian Rule of Mystical Experience,' in *Mysticism and the Institutional Crisis*, Concilium (1994) 1-16.

2. E.R. Dodds, *Pagan and Christian in an Age of Anxiety*, (Cambridge: Cambridge University Press, 1965).

3. For a detailed description and evaluation see Hans-Josef Klauck, *The Religious Context of Early Christianity. A Guide to Greco-Roman Religions*, (Edinburgh: T. and T. Clark, 2000) especially ch. 2 'The Fascination of the Mysterious: The Mystery Cults,' 81-154.

4. See Alan Segal, *Paul the Convert. The Apostolate and Apostasy of Paul the Pharisee*, (New Haven: Yale University Press, 1990), especially 34-71.

5. See John J. Collins, *The Apocalyptic Imagination. An Introduction to the Jewish Matrix of Christianity*, (New York: Crossroads, 1984), especially 26-28 on the heavenly journey motif in Greco-Roman and Jewish perspectives. See also James D. Tabor, *Things Unutterable. Paul's Ascent to Heaven in its Greco-Roman, Judaic and Early Christian Contexts*, (Lanham: University Press of America, 1986), especially ch. 3. (pp. 57- 98), 'The Heavenly Journey in Antiquity,' which offers an informative typology of such journeys in terms of their different functions.

6. For a full discussion see Gersholm Scholem, *Major Trends in Jewish Mysticism*, (New York: Schocken Books, 1946).

7. Collins, *The Apocalyptic Imagination*, 41f.

8. Segal, *Paul the Convert*, 46-48.

9. Dodds, *Pagan and Christian*, 86f.

10. Tabor, *Things Unutterable*, concludes that there is nothing either in the context or the report that indicates that Paul disparaged such an experience. On the contrary, he believes, that the vision of the heavenly glory would have closely correlated with the core of Paul's message, namely, his expectation of the glorification of the many Sons of God (44f).

11. See Jerome Murphy-O'Connor, *Paul, A Critical Life*, (Oxford and New York: Oxford University Press, 1996) 317-22.

12. Tabor, *Things Unutterable*, 113-119.

13. For an excellent discussion see James D.G. Dunn, *The Theology of the Apostle Paul*, (Edinburgh: T. and T. Clark, 1998) 390- 412.

14. Albert Schweitzer, *The Mysticism of Paul the Apostle*, (London: Adam Black, 1931), 1. See also Alfred Wikenhauser, *Pauline Mysticism. Christ in the Mystical Teaching of St. Paul*, (English trans. Edinburgh-London: Nelson, 1960)

15. Bruce Malina, *The New Testament World. Insights from Cultural Anthropology*, (London: SCM Press, 1981) 51-70.

16. Rudolf Schnackenburg, *Baptism in the Thought of Paul*, (Oxford: Blackwell, 1964), especially 139-169.

12

FAITH AND CULTURE – REFLECTIONS ON THE EARLY CHRISTIAN EXPERIENCE

It is commonplace in various introductions to the New Testament to point to the advantages that the Hellenistic age and Roman administration offered the new movement that began its life as missionary. Indeed, as Amos Wilder has remarked, early Christianity represented an extraordinary outburst of creativity in terms of new forms, new images and new speech-patterns.[1] While this assessment may be somewhat exaggerated, there is no denying that the first Christians showed great originality, flexibility and energy in undertaking the task of sharing good news for all of humanity, as they saw it, throughout the Mediterranean world. Undoubtedly the way had been prepared for them in a number of respects. There was a common language, travel was frequent and widespread, Jewish communities existed throughout the Diaspora and provided a social structure, a set of ancient texts to which appeal could be made, and an ethical system based on monotheistic belief which was attractive to pagan sympathisers.[2]

As a cultural and religious force Hellenism did not provide early Christianity with the support that is sometimes claimed, however. By the first century c.e. Roman imperialism had attempted to revive the older religion as a form of state religion, and philosophies such as Stoicism and Epicureanism, which had originated shortly after Alexander's conquests as an expression of the universalist mood of the times, had been considerably transformed. Under Roman imperial rule the cities had lost a considerable amount of their autonomy, and this inevitably led to a redefining of freedom as an inner spirit of detachment rather than a civic and political right and privilege. Under Nero in particular resistance to state imperialism was dangerous, as Stoic philosophers as well as Christians were to learn. Pessimism in religious terms was in the air according to that most religious of Romans, Seneca, and consequently there was a spiritual void that was partly filled by the mystery religions and partly by astrology, magic and other means, devised to negotiate the hazards of life with as little trouble as possible. The popularity of guilds to ensure a seemly burial at the end for those who had often enough very little out of life, is a stark reminder of the social and religious situation of the average Greco-Roman of the first century, despite the official state rhetoric about the Augustan age as one of universal peace and harmony.

In particular Hellenism had been perceived as an alien force by many Jews whose way of life had given rise to a very distinctive culture and identity. Despite the material benefits that some Jews had sought to experience in the wake of Alexander's one-world ideals (1 Macc 1, 11), the two Jewish wars against Rome can be seen as the collective and climactic expression of this people's will not to be swamped by the prevailing Great Tradition. A later rabbinical tradition describes the opposition to assimilation thus: 'neither their women, their language nor their oil' (p. Shabb 1,3c; b. Shabb 17c). Religious belief in terms of messianic hope and apocalyptic longings played a vital part in the resistance, with its strong political and nationalistic expressions. In this respect at least many early Christian groups could be seen to have accommodated themselves to the wider culture in a way that other Jewish groups in Palestine had not. This was due, no doubt, to a complex set of factors – the example and memory of Jesus in terms of his teaching on non-violence and his expressions of universal care, as well as the considerable re-interpretation of messianic and apocalyptic hopes on a cosmic plain that had occurred, even within Jewish Christianity, in the wake of the successes of the Gentile mission. Thus, those very symbols that had fuelled the fires of revolt against Rome on the one hand, could also provide the interpretative framework for Paul and other early Christian missionaries in dealing with the issues of redemption and salvation that were so dominant in the prevailing culture.

Thus far the argument has been that, faced with the attempts to impose a uniform culture on the Mediterranean world through Roman imperial power, apocalyptic and messianic hopes had provided some Jews with the possibility of resistance that was cultural as well as religious and was quite unique by the standards of the day. The question we are now left with is how far these same categories could provide the early Christians with a similar possibility for resistance to a unicultural tyranny, and how in fact did they respond to such a challenge in the light of their memory of Jesus' universal care and their own missionary task, as this was understood?

With the rapid increase in the number of converts to Christianity the movement quickly transcended the ethnic boundaries of its Jewish origins and different ways of accommodating had to be developed. Cultural diversity became part of the new movement itself, and local circumstances varied from one city to another, as even a superficial reading of Acts of the Apostles makes clear. At the same time the imperial presence made itself felt everywhere. Roman *ordo* found expression in the very layout of the city streets; Roman *majestas* was exemplified by the size and grandeur of the monumental architecture; the statues of the emperors, which adorned the fora and basilicas, spoke of Roman *gravitas*.[3] Any local cult or ethnic group that challenged this self-image of grandeur and power, thereby disturbing the *pax Romana*, would be summarily dealt with, as the Jews were to learn in the wake of the two revolts. The Christians were in an even more precarious position, not enjoying any rights as a *religio licita*, being deemed instead a 'pernicious *superstitio*', as Tacitus, the Roman historian describes the movement.

Hellenists and Hebrews: Early Christian Praxis of Inculturation

It was through the development of a missionary praxis that the first Christians were most directly and immediately confronted with the problem of faith and culture. It should be remembered that the mission originated, not with the Twelve but with the Hellenists who were driven from Jerusalem in the wake of Stephen's attack on the central symbols of Jewish faith – the temple and the Torah. The divisions between this group and the Hebrews must have gone much deeper than disputes over the welfare service as depicted in Acts of the Apostles (6,1-7). Martin Hengel has argued that the designations 'Hebrew' and 'Hellenist' in the first instance refer to different language patterns, but this brought with it other cultural assumptions and horizons also.[4] Not that we should regard the Hellenists as lax Jews who were prepared to abandon ancestral ways for the new faith. It was among their own ranks, 'men from the synagogue of the Freedmen and of the Alexandrians and Cyrenians and those from Cilicia and Asia', that the charge against Stephen originated. Paul too seems to have shared their view, if the evidence of Acts of the

Apostles is to be accepted. The Hellenists were zealous Jews, as Paul also describes himself subsequently (Phil 3:6), yet significantly their names betray a Greek rather than a Jewish upbringing. Their presence in Jerusalem must surely indicate a very genuine search for an authentic expression of Jewish faith, and some among them found this in the Jesus movement, whereas others clung fast to the received interpretation of their Jewish faith-symbols.

Their primary significance, from our current perspective, is the attitude towards Greco-Roman culture that they manifested. On the one hand their upbringing and education made them culturally mobile in the Greco-Roman world (one was a proselyte from Antioch), yet they were seeking an expression of Jewish faith that seems to have brought them to Jerusalem on a quasi-permanent basis. Their embracing of the Jesus' way and their readiness to break the traditional boundaries between Jew and Greek subsequently at Antioch (Acts 11,19-31) cannot be interpreted as any form of syncretistic accommodation of faith and culture, therefore. According to Martin Hengel it is among these first Christian missionaries that the major adaptations and developments in Christological thinking occurred, even prior to Paul, by the adoption of categories and images current in the Greco-Roman world, but yet firmly anchored to the memory of Jesus (cf. Phil 2:6-11).[5] Hellenistic Judaism in the Diaspora had provided the intellectual framework for such a contribution – witness Philo's *Life of Moses*, for example, – yet heretofore there was no indication of any missionary zeal comparable to that portrayed by the Christian Hellenists among such Jews. The driving force for this activity was almost certainly the apocalyptic urgency that originated from the earliest Christian understanding of the significance of Jesus' death and Resurrection – the importance of which was shared by both Hebrew and Hellenists alike, it seems (See Acts 3:19-21).

We can reasonably assume that The Epistle to the Hebrews represents a later, post-70 version of the theology of this circle of early Christian Hellenistic-Jewish missionaries. This writing combines the same critique of the exclusivity of Jewish temple rites that was echoed in Stephen's speech, the apocalyptic framework of the present and future ages as well as the sole, once-for-all role of Jesus in bringing about a juncture between these two worlds. The language, rhetoric and style breathes the air of Greek rhetoric and philosophy, the anxiety about suffering and death is typical of Greco-Roman religious concerns (2:10. 14-15; 5:7-10), and yet the story of the historical Jesus ('the days of his flesh') remains firmly in place as the starting point for the author's typological reflections on its eternal and lasting significance.[6] It is in this insistence on the memory of the historical Jesus and his role in salvation, against the spirit of Alexandrian Greek theology and philosophy, but which yet was couched in the language and style of argumentation of that tradition, that we capture a glimpse of early Christian mission praxis with regard to the larger culture. The desire to communicate with that culture is very real, but this does not compromise the essential element of the Christian story as this had been received, namely, the centrality of the life and death of Jesus for understanding the meaning of human life in the world.

We are less well informed about the other group within the Jerusalem Church, the Hebrews. Acts of the Apostles portrays them as remaining in Jerusalem, but this should not obscure their concern for Christian mission, which stems from their belief in the Zion prophecies that a restored Israel would bring about the conversion of the nations also (Is 2,2-4; 49,6). This belief explains the symbolic importance of the Restoration of the Twelve in Jerusalem for Luke's account also (Acts 1, 12-26). However, according to Gal 2, 9-10, the Jerusalem apostles divided the *oikumene*, or inhabited world, into two spheres, they concentrating on the circumcised, and Paul and his companions on the uncircumcised. Thus, the missionary impetus was maintained, even if serious theological differences were to emerge between the two sides. Nor does the division of labour appear to have been rigidly adhered to. Luke insists that Peter opened the Gentile mission by receiving Cornelius into the new movement (Acts 10), whereas Paul emphasises his concern for his Jewish co-religionists (Rm 9.1-5; 1 Cor 9,20).

It is more difficult to discern how their mission praxis may have differed, but we can infer certain things from their differing theological standpoints. To insist on the continued necessity for Torah-observance meant that the Jewish way of life as this was practised among Diaspora communities continued to be observed. Inevitably this lead to differences with regard to the ways in which communal life was organised and larger cultural patterns could be adapted and adopted. Jewish Diaspora communities did indeed practice various degrees of enculturation within the larger Greco-Roman society, as John Barclay's detailed study has cogently argued.[7] Nevertheless, there were certain non-negotiable boundaries and aspects of lifestyle that had to be maintained: the celebration of the Sabbath and other festivals; the practice of male circumcision and the observance of the dietary and other purity laws. These and other aspects of the Jewish way of life are echoed in various features of Greco-Roman anti-Judaism, indicating that no matter how much Philo and other intellectual Jews attempted an accommodation of the Mosaic dispensation to Greek philosophical categories, the more general perception was that Jews were indeed different and were perceived to be so within their pagan environment. Nor should it be forgotten that there was a large non-Greek speaking Jewish Diaspora in Syria and Babylonia also. Presumably the processes of enculturation were different in these regions to those in the western Diaspora, and this would have applied for the early Christian movement also, especially the Hebrew (Aramaic) speaking section. The emergence later of a distinctive Syriac-speaking Christianity is one indication of how language patterns could have wider implications in terms of liturgical and ascetic forms as well as in theological positions, which presumably should be traced back to the earlier generations, and may be reflected in such New Testament writings as the Gospel of Matthew and the Epistle of James.[8]

Much has been written about the authorship and anti-Pauline tendencies in The Epistle of James. Even if, as most commentators believe, the work does not come from James the brother of the Lord, the head of the Jerusalem Church, it does represent a very different theological tendency to that of Paul. The collection of moral exhortations have a theocentric rather than a Christocentric motivation. Indeed some have gone so far as to argue that the work was written to counteract not just Paul's theology of justification by faith rather than works (Jas 2,14-17), but also his busy travelling on various missionary journeys suggested by such passages as Jas 4:13. The author appears to be well versed in such Greek rhetorical devices as play on words, alliteration and the use of an imaginary interlocutor as in a Greek dialogue. Yet the work is addressed 'To the twelve tribes of the Dispersion' (1,1), thereby aligning itself with the view of the Hebrews in terms of the need for the prior restoration of Israel. Visits to the synagogue are mentioned (2,2) and there are echoes of the *Shema*, that uniquely Jewish prayer (2,19; 4,12). The work breathes the air of Hellenistic Jewish instruction, yet lurking in the immediate background are clear allusions to the teaching of Jesus, especially as these are recorded in the so-called Q document. This is not a xenophobic work that is reacting negatively against its environment, but one that is extremely critical of certain social and economic realities of that world in the light of its own understanding of what constitutes 'true religion'. The 'dangerous memory' of Jesus is recalled in a context in which the economic and social realities of the Hellenistic world are clearly making inroads into the Christian community's life in a way that the author sees as contrary to the spirit of

Jesus (Jas 2,1-12; 4,13; 5,1-6), and he rails against it.[9] The pattern seems to be similar to that which we have seen for the Epistle to the Hebrews, namely, a distinctive vision, ethical rather than soteriological in the case of James, based on the memory of Jesus' lifestyle and sayings, yet expressed in the language and form of popular Greek didactic literature and critical of the very environment whose forms and modes of expression are being employed.

Thus far our limited soundings of early Christian mission have revealed a diversity of approaches, arising from different cultural backgrounds. Both Hebrews and Hellenists had, however, a quite distinctive point of view based on their memory of Jesus that they wish to share with others in the larger cultural milieu – a point of view that concerned social and economic as well as religious realities as these were experienced within that world. Adaptation and creativity abounded as a sense of urgency derived from an apocalyptic worldview impelled these first preachers of the good news. That same world view also enabled them to look critically on that culture and its values, irrespective of how much 'at home' within it they might otherwise have felt.

Faith and Culture in Paul's Missionary Praxis

Paul, of course, is our main witness to early Christian mission praxis, and here we can only sketch the outlines of an answer to our initial question. In what might be deemed an ideal manifesto for a mission Church Paul declares:

> Free from all, I made myself a slave to all to win over more of them. To the Jews I became like a Jew in order to win over Jews; to those under the law, being like one under the law (though I am not myself under the law) to win over those under the law; to those free of law like one free of law (though I am not free of God's law, but am bound by Christ's law) to win over those free of law (1 Cor 9: 19-21).

In all his letters Paul repeatedly expresses himself globally, as we might say, in terms of the two cultures he was familiar with – Jew and Greek. He is deeply conscious of the different presuppositions, and attitudes of these two cultures, even if his formulation of both – Jew and Greek – is somewhat undifferentiated in terms of the great varieties of outlook that were present in each. In the Epistle to the Romans he confronts a typical representative of both cultural spheres in order to challenge both to a sense of their own standing before God, as preparatory to his proclamation of the good news of the Gospel for all (Rm 1, 18-3, 31). For Paul that task was all-consuming. Cultural affiliations, as in his own case, were quite secondary:

> I became all things to all men, so that somehow I might save some. I do everything for the sake of the Gospel so that I may become its partner (1 Cor 9:23).

The tradition of the Hellenists to which Paul was heir had already engaged in a cultural translation of quite massive proportions in making Christianity an urban religion, despite its rural, Palestinian roots. In view of the ancient hostility between city and country this was quite a daring venture, something the later apologist Luke clearly perceived with his finely tuned sense of Greco-Roman taste, by telling the story of the Palestinian peasant Jesus in terms that were accessible to his urban readership.[10] As Wayne Meek's study has shown, this translation was to affect every aspect of the community's self-understanding – ritual, government, beliefs and value system – and this process can be clearly seen at work in the Pauline letters, with Paul himself actively directing the venture at Thessalonica, Corinth, Philippi and Galatia.[11] Gerd Theissen's study of Christianity in Corinth is highly instructive in this regard.[12] He points to the changed socio-political, socio-economic, socio-ecological and socio-cultural factors that brought about a very different missionary strategy to that practised by Jesus and his first followers as echoed in the Synoptic tradition. Not all Christian missionaries followed Paul's style of course and he is critical of those wandering charismatics who look for support from local communities (see e.g. 2 Cor 2:17). Paul and Barnabas were conscious of being cast in the role of missionary charlatans, and hence in the time-honoured fashion of the true philosopher, refused to accept any payment for their efforts, working instead with their own hands. Paul's claim to have achieved a degree of personal freedom (*eleutheria*, Gal 2:4) and self-sufficiency (*autarkia*, 2 Cor 9:8), which were the hallmarks of the detachment cultivated by rival philosophic missionaries such as the Cynics, take on a whole new significance once they are situated in the context of Paul's missionary world-view.[13]

This adaptation concerned not just the style, but the very content of Paul's Gospel, according to Theissen. Missing are the familiar ideas of 'the kingdom of God' and the critique of wealth – both linchpins of the Jesus' movement's proclamation in the Palestinian setting. The theocratic implications of the former were to lead to a dangerous and counter-productive confrontation with Rome for other Jews. Had Paul an inkling of this already and realised that it might be counter-productive? And yet his constant use of the title *kyrios* for Jesus had its own political innuendoes that were not likely to be lost on provincial Roman establishments. The question of wealth and poverty was another matter. Paul's allusion to the social origins of the Corinthian community – 'not many of you were wise according to worldly standards, not many were powerful, not many were of noble birth' (1 Cor 1,26f) – implies that some at least were of such a background.[14] Paul was not adverse to using the social standing and affluence of those who were for his own ends on behalf of the Gospel while retaining his freedom to critique their behaviour when it threatened the koinonia of the community, as his handling of the episodes of the meat sacrificed to idols and the revelries at the eucharistic meals at Corinth makes clear.[15] His 'love-patriarchalism', to use Theissen's phrase, appears to endorse the household as the correct social setting for the Christian community in a way that Jesus' critique of the values associated with the settled, stable way of life in the Palestinian context does not. In this regard, Paul's social critique seems to be somewhat muted, less direct, unless we view it in the broader context of his challenge to the Greco-Roman value system and its cultural and religious assumptions, something we shall currently examine.

Space does not allow for any further exploration of the details of Paul's missionary strategy in adapting to local socio-cultural settings. Hopefully, enough has been said to at least raise the question as to how it was possible for Pauline Christianity to retain any wider sense of identity, in view of the radical adaptation to local cultural needs which we have glimpsed. That this experience of common identity, despite local diversity was part of early-Christian self-understanding is clear not just from a later apologist like Luke in his account of early Christian mission in Acts of the Apostles, but also from Paul's own letters. The network included not just those Churches founded by Paul, but others also (Rome, for example) as well as the Mother Church in Jerusalem, despite all the difficulties that he had with that centre. This sense of *koinonia*, or *community*, was achieved in a number of practical ways, not least by Paul's intensive correspondence to the various foundations with their references to the reception he was receiving elsewhere (1 Thess 1,9) and the injunction to have his letter passed on to other Churches (Col 4,16). Then there was the network of co-workers who acted as official companions/ambassadors for Paul in establishing and maintaining the links between the Churches when he himself was absent. In this regard the greetings that Paul addresses to the various Churches show how much he wants to foster a sense of communal identity for the various local groups. The Corinthians receive greetings together with 'all who invoke the name of our Lord Jesus Christ in every place' (1 Cor 1,2). We hear of the Churches of different provinces – Galatia, Asia, Macedonia, Judea – as well as the more universal designation of 'the Church of God' in the context of the inclusive formula 'Jew and Greek' (1 Cor 10:32). Hospitality for strangers is a key Christian virtue (Rom 12,15) and this stipulation must be seen in relation to the 'letters of commendation', fragments of which have been identified within the Pauline corpus (2 Cor 8,1-34).

Most significant, perhaps, in view of the tensions that existed, is the insistence on the collection for the poor among the saints in Jerusalem.[16] Several suggestions have been made to explain this – for example, the obligation that Jews worldwide felt to send contributions to the Jerusalem temple, or to impress his detractors among the more conservative Jewish Christians. For the Gentile Christians it was a way of establishing their solidarity with an 'ancient and venerable city', and thereby confirming their own radical change of lifestyle. For Paul himself it was an expression of his unity and solidarity with his own religious past and the central role of Jewish election in the divine plan for all, despite the problems he had in the working out of that plan in practice (See Rom 14,25-33).[17]

For Paul the *oikymene* could be divided into two cultures, Jew first and then Greek. No philosopher or religious missionary known to us from antiquity had a greater or more urgent sense of the world-wide reality of the human family and its spiritual needs. His deep loyalty to his own cultural and religious history (both were inseparable) could never be in doubt and he is conscious of the privileges of being a Jew in religious terms (Rom 9,1-5). However, he can equally castigate his former co-religionists for their failures to live up to their own ideals (Rom 2,17-30). On the other hand he is thoroughly familiar with the Greek world, its religious aspirations, confusions and fears. The Gentiles have no hope, their gods are many (1 Thess 4,14; 1 Cor 9,4), they are guilty of all kinds of inhuman and unnatural behaviour (Rom 1:18-31), and yet he can admit that in following their conscience they too can attain the righteousness of God that is the very centre of his own Gospel. Paul, then, as a missionary of Jesus Christ, stands in the critical prophetic tradition that recognises the need to challenge cultural assumptions and values, whether Jewish or Greek. Underlying what at times might appear to be a very pragmatic approach in terms of missionary praxis was a genuine theological vision. It is to this we must now turn as a way of formulating an approach to mission in the context of the cultural challenges facing the Christian Church today.

Early Christian Missionary Theory: Paul's Theology of Mission

Paul's theology has been described as, in essence, missionary, a description that would seem to be particularly apt on a number of headings.[18] Leaving aside questions regarding stages of development of his thought in terms of early, middle and late, it certainly is true that the articulation of his thinking on the meaning of Jesus Christ took place in the hurly burly of an active missionary career and in response to the various issues that arose in the different churches. His theology can be styled missionary also in that the theme of the mission was a central issue that had to be worked out in the context of explaining his Gospel. As Ben Meyer puts it, 'the logic of proclaiming the universal Lordship of Jesus as good news necessarily entailed a world mission, and Paul's own role as well as that of his co-workers had to be articulated in terms of God's universal plan' (See Rom 10,14; 2 Cor 5,18-20).[19] Finally, we can say that Paul's theology was in essence missionary insofar as he provided the young Churches with a framework for understanding the character of their new life in Christ, their relations with other Churches in the light of the new situation and how to view their culture, be it Jewish or Greek, in terms of their past, their present and their future. As Ben Meyer again puts it: 'it was thought out and articulated in the service of a basic self-orientation in faith on the part of young missionary Churches'.[20]

Two issues were to prove central for this task – the meaning of Jesus' death and the nature and role of the Christian community gathered in his name. Paul inherited from the Hellenists an understanding of the death of Jesus in terms of its sacrificial character on behalf of sin, the wiping out of the accumulated debt that humans had incurred in the light of God's forbearance (Rom 3:25f. – a pre-Pauline formula). This inherited sense of God's positive acceptance of the death of Jesus was now given a proper context by Paul's searching, restless mind as he fused his apocalyptic Jewish faith with the universalist horizons that the urgent sense of mission to all had opened up for him. The result of this fusion was Paul's setting of the death and resurrection of Jesus at the decisive turning point in the cosmic struggle between the forces of good and evil, which was part of

TEXTS, CONTEXTS AND CULTURES: ESSAYS ON BIBLICAL TOPICS

the universal human experience and which Jewish apocalyptic had articulated in terms of the present evil and the future good age. For Paul the cross became not just something to be included in his system but pivotal to his explanation of how God's universal justice, his will to save, had finally and paradoxically resolved a universal human dilemma. In Romans in particular Paul expressed this conviction in a number of different contrasts: death/life, old/new, condemnation/justification, slavery/freedom – images that were drawn from the Hebrew scriptures, but which also resonated within his particular social setting. By universalising the problem and the solution through the use of the ancient divine combat myth as this was mediated into the Jewish world through the apocalyptists, Paul might appear to be using metaphors that were foreign to his Greek converts. But before we pass such a judgment we should reflect on the central role that apocalyptic language played in his early letters to Greek converts at Thessalonica and Corinth, where he refuses to speak the rhetoric of human wisdom and sophistry. Certain topics call for bold and vigorous language and the rhetoric of millennial victory can strike a chord deep in human hearts of whatever cultural background, precisely because of its shared mythic imagery in terms of the victory of good over evil. Indeed in his famous *Fourth Eclogue*, the Roman poet Virgil had also spoken of the new age of Augustus in terms not dissimilar to those of Paul and other Christian apologists.

What of the communities that emerged in response to this good news and how were they to live in the world with their new-found belief? Earlier we said that an apocalyptic view of history had provided Jews in the homeland with the power to resist Rome in the two great revolts. Noble as such resistance was, it proved in the end to be damaging to Jewish self-identity, which had to be refashioned in the wake of the destruction of the temple and the banishment of the Jews from Judea. In Paul's case an apocalyptic imagery and worldview fuelled his zeal in a way that was to prove in the long run more threatening to the tyranny of Rome, in that it produced communities of believers in every city who shared a common conviction that the Lordship of Jesus Christ rather than that of the Emperor was the decisive power at work in the world, and that they must obey the one rather than the other. If this conviction was to make them not 'at home' in either culture – Jewish or Greek – then so be it. In the description of Edward Schillebeeckx they were Exodus communities, that is, communities who were convinced that they had already tasted something of the better world that was coming.[21] The 'critical variant' of the Christian vision, in contrast to the pessimism of the age, did not summon them to flee the world nor to attempt to change it, but rather to create their own culture, waiting in hope and joy for the fulfilment of their beliefs that death and evil had indeed been conquered. Together with Paul they could sing that, since God was with them nothing could harm them or separate them from the love of the one through whom they had conquered beyond measure (*hupernikomen*, Rom 8, 31-39). And when the might of Rome would be brought to bear on them they could once again revision the triumph in the most unrestrained set of images of victory that any religious movement has produced (The Revelation of John), even sparing a mildly sympathetic thought in the process for the fall of 'Babylon the great' with all her very worthwhile human achievements! (Rev ch 18).

Conclusion

This discussion of the early Christian mission experience has shown that in responding to its missionary urge, the early Christians were indeed open to the various cultures they had encountered and were able to translate their distinctive beliefs and practices into a number of cultural variants. In doing so, however, they never lost their deep rooted identity with its alternative vision and memory, which, they believed, was 'good news' for others also. This could take an ethical form of solidarity with the poor after the manner and teaching of the earthly Jesus, or alternatively, it could express the conviction that in the death/resurrection of Jesus the great human dilemma had at last been resolved in favour of the whole of humanity, despite its history of waywardness. This distinctive identity meant that they were able to resist the pressures of becoming so grounded in a particular culture – Jewish or Greek – that they would lose both the sense of their good news and their mission to humanity as such – since the one was the correlative of the other.

The success of both the Jewish and Christian inculturation processes should be measured against the backdrop of imperial propaganda of the Augustan Age and the glory that had been achieved by Rome. This propaganda had been expressed throughout the Mediterranean world in architecture, military and administrative presence as well as in literature – a fact that was not lost on either Jewish or Christian commentators. Both in their different ways chose to challenge the hegemony of Rome, and both refused to succumb to imperial power even when the price of such resistance was national destruction or martyrdom.

After the failure of the two Jewish revolts in the homeland (66-70 and

132-135 c.e.), Rabbinic Judaism was still able to draw on the deep-seated conviction of God's protective care for his chosen people. While recognising the reality of Rome and accepting the continuing legal status granted to them, the Rabbis were not about to succumb to its charms or be deluded by its power and propaganda. Its value system was different to that of the Jews, and Rome would always remain 'other' for them. The Christians, for their part, did not enjoy official recognition under Roman law, but their approach to Roman power was shaped not only by their faith in the one God of their Jewish inheritance, but also by the memory of Jesus who was unjustly put to death by the Romans as a criminal only to be vindicated by God. This memory was to encourage others of later generations to accept martyrdom rather than recognise Rome's authority over them.

The sense of independence with regard to the might of Rome of both Jews and Christians should not disguise the very different trajectories they represent, in terms of the relationship of faith and culture. Judaism was to continue its distinctive way of life within the empire, refashioning itself not on a rebuilt temple but on the teaching of the Rabbis and the worship of the synagogue. As such it survived, even with the increased marginalisation it suffered within a Christian empire from the early fifth century onwards. For the most part it was able to maintain its own distinctive culture, which, with some minor variations, was to remain intact and largely homogenous down to the modern period. By contrast, the early Christians strike a defiant note that could not be silenced by the persecutions. Yet, so successful was the appeal of this 'hated superstition' with the masses that, by the early fourth century, already it was the best religious option open to Constantine in terms of giving a unified worldview to his empire, east and west. But that symbiosis of Church and Empire, faith and culture, was to change dramatically, and many would say drastically, the character of Christian faith itself as this had first found expression in the hostile world we have been exploring.

Notes

1. 'The New Voice', in Amos N. Wilder, *Jesus' Parables and the War of Myths. Essays on Imagination in the Scriptures*, (London: SPCK, 1982), 121-132.
2. See John J. Collins, *Between Athens and Jerusalem. Jewish Identity in the Hellenistic Diaspora*, New York: Crossroad, 1983; John R. Bartlett, ed. *Jews in the Hellenistic and Roman Cities*, (London: Routledge, 2002).
3. See Paul Zanker, *The Power of Images in the Age of Augustus*, (English trans. Alan Shapiro), (Ann Arbor: The University of Michigan Press, 1990).

4.   'Between Jesus and Paul: The Hellenists, the Seven and Stephen', in Martin Hengel, *Between Jesus and Paul. Studies in the Earliest History of Christianity*, English trans. (London: SCM Press, 1983), pp. 1-29; see also Craig C. Hill, *Hellenists and Hebrews. Reappraising Division within the Earliest Church*, (Minneapolis: Fortress Press, 1992).

5.   *Between Jesus and Paul*, 'Hymns and Christology' 78-96.

6.   Sean Freyne, 'Reading Hebrews and Revelation Intertextually' in S. Draisma ed., *Intertextuality in Biblical Writings. Essays in honour of Bas van Iersel*, (Kampen: J.H. Kok, 1989), 83-94.

7.   John M. Barclay, *Jews in the Mediterranean Diaspora from Alexander to Trajan* (323 BCE-117 CE), Edinburgh: T. and T. Clark, 1996.

8.   See Robert Murray, 'The Exhortation to Candidates for Ascetical Vows at Baptism in the ancient Syriac Church', *NTS 21*(1974) 59-80. For later Syriac Christianity see also Peter Brown, 'Town, Village and the Holy Man: the Case of Syria', in Peter Brown, *Society and the Holy in Late Antiquity*, (London: Faber and Faber, 1982, 153-165).

9.   See David Hutchinson-Edgar, '*Has God not Chosen the Poor? The Social Setting of the Epistle of James*', *JSNT Suppl. Series 206* (Sheffield: Sheffield Academic Press, 2001).

10.   See Jerome Neyrey, ed. *The Social World of Luke-Acts*, (Peabody, Mass: Hendrikson, 1991).

11.   Wayne A. Meeks, *The First Urban Christians. The Social World of the Apostle Paul*, (New Haven and London: Yale University Press, 1983).

12.   Gerd Theissen, *The Social Setting of Pauline Christianity*, English Trans. (Edinburgh: T. and T. Clark, 1982).

13.   See in particular, Abraham Malherbe's discussion of Paul's self-presentation to the Thessalonians: *Paul and the Thessalonians* (Philadelphia: Fortress Press, 1987) and in more detail *Paul and the Popular Philosophers* (Minneapolis: Fortress Press, 1989).

14.   See Abraham J. Malherbe, *Social Aspects of Early Christianity*, (Baton Rouge, La.: Louisiana State University Press, 1977), especially 29-59.

15.   Theissen, *The Social Setting of Pauline Christianity*, 145-174.

16.   Nils Dahl, 'Paul and Possessions', in his *Studies in Paul*, Minneapolis: Augsburg, 1987, 22-40, especially 31f

17.   For a recent stimulating discussion of the issue see Sze-kar Wan, 'Collection for the Saints as Anti-Colonial Act. Implications of Paul's Ethnic Reconstruction,' in R. Horsley ed. *Paul and Politics*, (Harrisburg, Pa: Trinity Press International, 2000), 191- 216.

18.   See in particular the outstanding study of Ben F. Meyer, *The Early Christians. Their World Mission and Self-Discovery*, Wilmington, Del.: Michael Glazier, 1986; Nils Dahl, 'The Missionary Theology in the Epistle to the Romans' in *Studies in Paul*, 70-94.

19.   *The Early Christians*, 111.

20.   *The Early Christians*, 123.

21.   Edward Schillebeeckx, *Christ. The Experience of Jesus as Lord*, (New York: The Seabury Press, 1980), 544-561.

13

JESUS CHRIST: THE ANCHOR OF HOPE

'And now faith, hope and love abide, these three, but the greatest of these is love' (1 Cor 13, 13). Of the three so-called 'theological' virtues hope is the one that is least spoken about. It is difficult enough to be hopeful in our world without having to justify such beliefs. Yet the image of Jesus as 'the anchor of hope' (Heb 6, 18) was particularly beloved to the early Christians, suggesting, as it does, the security and stability in the midst of turbulent seas. Christian imagination is today summoned to retrieve this symbol in the midst of the prevailing, post-modern worldview, which threatens to undermine our civilisation by denying the basis for all stable meaning, not just in our texts, but in our lives.

Human Hope

What is hope? I felt the need to get some preliminary handle on that question before addressing the distinctively Christian perspective on this most basic, yet elusive dimension of our conscious life. When in doubt one should always turn to the plain person's understanding of the matter. It is surprising how frequently the language of hope crops up in our everyday speech, almost unnoticed, it would seem. 'While there is life there is hope' is as old as Plato and as recent as the last time somebody tried to console another faced with some disappointment or failure. 'Hope springs eternal' and 'hoping against hope' are variations on the theme of the human capacity to strive and strive again to achieve certain goals irrespective of the obstacles to be encountered. We preface many of our wishes with the adverb 'hopefully', indicating our caution, our determination and yet our sense of insecurity with regard to our objectives. 'Hopes are high' is a description of communal anticipation that some desired end can be achieved. Our language of hope tells us that there is a sense of the unfinished agenda about life, an absence of completeness. Yet our hoping shows an awareness that we can successfully direct our energies and our wills to struggle for a greater sense of meaning to life, despite all the evidence to the contrary.

To be human is to hope and to hope is to be human. Hope at once expresses a hunger within the human spirit for what is not, or at least for what is not yet, and at the same time is based not on an empty illusion, but on the future as objective possibility now. Hope springs from our consciousness of time and our ability to distinguish past, present and future, while at the same time holding these three aspects together in a meaningful whole. Ultimately, hope seems to be about our ability to create meaningful symbols that make it possible for us to identify in some inchoate way with what is really real for ourselves and for those with whom we are related, and to strive to make that really real still more real, more actual, despite all the obstacles. Hope is faith and trust in the possibility of the not-yet, which makes it worthwhile to live and be in the present. Hope is what you make it, or better, what you make of life.

The Greeks had their own version of the Garden of Eden story. According to an old fable Zeus gave mortals a vessel full of good things, but when in curiosity the lid was lifted all the good things escaped to the gods and hope alone was trapped when the lid was restored, making it the only comfort left to humans. In truth, however, it proved to be a fairly limited comfort. The future had an uncertain, if not downright malevolent aspect to it. Fate controlled the destiny of mortals, and in the Hellenistic age religion, magic and philosophy were concentrated on the need to deal with her foibles – not to overcome them, but simply to negotiate one's way through the many pitfalls that lay in store for mortals. Despite the centuries of both the Jewish and Christian religions in the west, both of them eschatological religions grounded in hope, a lot of the Greek scepticism still prevails in our culture. Hope is still at a premium, whereas cheap optimism or crippling fatalism are all too prevalent.

Israel – A People of Hope

By contrast, the Israelite experience was one of hope from its very inception. A common description of the distinctiveness of Israelite religious belief is the claim that their God was a God of history. Yahweh who brought Israel out of Egypt would eventually lead it to its ultimate destiny. Unlike its neighbours who believed in the endless and repetitive cycle of nature and understood God in terms of the recurring rhythms of the seasons, Israel had a linear, rather than a cyclical, trajectory to its self-understanding. This, at least has been the standard account, very often by Christian scholars anxious to find a linear progression from Old to New Testament, of what made Israel different from her neighbours. Like all such generalisations there is an element of truth here, but it is by no means the whole story, with regard to either Israel or her neighbours.

It is true that the memory of the Exodus experience and the naming of their God in relation to that event was foundational for Israel: 'I will be with you' is the answer to the query of Moses : 'What is your name?' To this foundational moment were added other events – the giving of the covenant at Sinai, the wandering in the desert and the entry into the Promised Land. On to this historical credo, which was recalled in solemn cultic assembly (Joshua 24), were grafted other moments both from the prehistory (creation, flood, tower of Babel, e.g.) and from various other local traditions dealing with the Patriarchs, Abraham, Isaac and Jacob. It was around this historical axis that Israel, quite late in its history, constructed a complex but continuous narrative account of its origins as a way of stating its own self-understanding. When one considers that this account was produced at a moment in its history when Israel's position was quite precarious (either during or immediately after the Babylonian exile in the sixth century b.c.e.) then it becomes obvious that this exercise of 'history writing' was not a nostalgic recalling of the past, but a defiant statement of hope, based on the belief that the same God who had initiated their communal experience in the Exodus was still with them, as prepared now as then to make a people from a non-people. Slavery in Egypt or captivity in Babylon were equally good circumstances for God to show God's true self.

This concentration on historical moments as constitutive did not mean an abandoning of nature, something that is always close at hand for pastoralists, peasants and nomads. The ongoing attraction of what is called in the Bible 'the cult of Baal' at local sanctuaries shows that despite the best efforts of the ruling elite to centralise all worship in Jerusalem for political as much as religious reasons, the ordinary people never abandoned nature for history as the place of encounter with the divine. Despite the railing against the Baal worship the priests and scribes who were responsible for the official version of Israel's history were not unaware of the sacral character of nature either. Yahweh was, after all, the creator God, lord of the storm, present in thunder, lightning, wind and rain; the summer sun and the seasonal rains were Yahweh's doings; ice and snow were in Yahweh's keeping; land and sea, desert and forest could all speak of Yahweh. Israel's cult was decisively shaped by the gift of the land, both in terms of its festivals and the offerings, even when feasts like Passover and Tabernacles were also given an historical dimension in terms of the events of the Exodus. The Book of the Psalms is replete with reminders of the blessings of the land based on the daily necessities of life. Hope and trust are virtually indistinguishable as past experience and future expectations blend together in the constant praise of the God who is with Israel in its wanderings. Unlike the Greek world where hopes can be uncertain, good or bad, in Israel God alone is the hope and trust of the righteous (Pss 60,4; 70,5). True hope can never be confused with mere human longings or aspirations. It is for God to decide what is to be hoped for since God alone is the fulfillment of all hope. The divine will has been revealed to Israel and the wise know what can and should be hoped for. The fool, on the other hand is caught up in his own longings and self-indulgence and will never experience the blessings that are at the centre of Israel's hopes.

The prophets stand out as the ones who most clearly articulated the hopes of Israel and how these impinged on ethical concerns in Israel present life. The fact that the hopes for the future inherent in the covenant blessings became associated with the king, the son of David, gave the prophets a focal point with which to express their dissatisfaction with the present and express the contours of a future that was more in keeping with the nature of Israel's God. They were able to tap into the rich reservoir of hope, expectation and longing associated with the covenant, showing how these could never be realised as long as Israel did not conform its will to that which its God had revealed. They were able to point to the narrowing of the hopes and expectations to those of sectional interests of the ruling classes, while the poor, the orphan and the widow went needy. Such conduct could not conform to the will of a God who had been revealed in the liberation of slaves from oppression. The various collections of oracles attributed to the great prophets of Israel all combine condemnation of Israel's unfaithfulness with images of hope for a better way. What is interesting is that these images are all drawn from past experience, but call for a realisation that transcends the past. New creation, new exodus, new covenant, new temple, new king are brought together in various combinations to express at once the hope that is central to Israel's beliefs and to present a challenge to those who are contented with the present and are not interested in a future that would be more in conformity with the divine self-revelation. The prophets are therefore witnesses to hope, a hope that need not, nor should be, deferred, but can be realised now in communities of hope and justice, if only the God of hope is listened to.

Israel's trust, and therefore Israel's hope, found expression in two other literary forms in the later Jewish period, namely in the wisdom and apocalyptic writings. These two apparently divergent expressions, the one focused totally on the present, the other directed wholly to the future, can be seen to maintain the tension inherent in Israel's religious experience and the historical realisation of that experience. Traditional wisdom, whether in proverbs that seek to discern broader patterns in daily life, or longer reflections about everyday issues, are both based on the understanding that the world is good, if enigmatic, and that the human will can through wise discernment and appropriate action be brought into harmony with the deeper forces that shape the universe. Apocalyptic, on the other hand, continues and intensifies the disruptive speech of the prophets, expressing not just discontent with but abhorrence of the present as evil. Instead, a totally other vision of how life might be organised and lived is presented which subverts the present structures and replaces them with their opposite. Yet even then pessimism about the human enterprise never has the last word, despite the judgment of the present as pervasively evil. The religious imagination of the apocalyptists can paint startling, even bizarre, pictures in which there is an intensification and distortion of familiar images in order to arrest the readers/hearers and shock them/us into seeing the world in a manner that is very different from our present experience. Such literary artistry is not the product of despair, but is rather the fruit of hope, struggling to find new ways of hoping that would conform to the divine will, so that God's rule might prevail. The present can be radically different because a future that is both possible and plausible can be imagined, based on what is known of the God of hope from the past.

This very rapid sketch of the main literary expressions of Israel's self-understanding shows how central to its life the theme of hope was. Hopefully it also shows how this theme was decisively determined by the understanding of God that Israel espoused from the start – a God who was totally trustworthy, a God who sought justice for all, especially the powerless, and who could not therefore be expected to sanction any expression of hopes that was not totally inclusive of all legitimate human longings. Throughout its history there was a waxing and a waning of Israel's hopes at various periods, but hope itself was never abandoned, because God's care not just for Israel, but for the whole creation was assured. Complaint, frustration, disappointment, anger – all the human emotions are to be found in the pages of the Bible, but despair never. The nearest one comes to that is in the book of Job, that classic dramatisation of the human dilemma when all the certainties about God, and therefore about life, are called into question by Job's unjust treatment and suffering. So intense is the suffering and so baffling is the experience that only the power of the author's poetic imagination and expression is able to ease what would otherwise be black despair. In the end, however, faith and hope triumph, but not before their horizons have been enlarged to include the mystery of suffering and evil, while still affirming the goodness of God who transcends human expectations because God is greater than all human estimations.

Jesus, A Witness of Hope

When one turns to the recorded sayings of Jesus there is a singular and surprising absence of words for hope and hoping, even though Jesus was heir to the tradition of hope of his people. He draws freely on many of the symbols and images of hope found in the Scriptures which were read in the synagogue. Contrary to some recent lives of Jesus that seek to present him as a Greek, Cynic-style philosopher who propounded ways of coping with life's difficulties, I am firmly of the opinion that Jesus' inspiration and understanding of his life's mission were grounded in Jewish restoration eschatology which expressed the hopes and longings of Israel in a variety of different literary forms in the centuries prior to Jesus' coming, and were particularly intense since Rome's entry into Palestinian politics in 67 b.c.e. However, it will come as a surprise to many to find that the figure of an 'anointed' one or a messiah does not play such a central role in these expectations as we might be led to believe from reading the Gospels. Whether or not Jesus ever thought of himself as such a figure, and if so how precisely he conceived that role, must remain problematic, despite the Gospel evidence. The expectations associated with the Messiah in the highly politicised atmosphere of the first century were such that if Jesus were tempted to think of himself in that role he would have had to abandon his own more inclusive understanding of the hopes of Israel, or be rejected as an impostor, since his agenda was not that of a political liberator as conceived by many of his co-religionists in the first century. In their differing ways all the

Gospels give expression to a reluctance on the part of Jesus to be thought of simply in the messianic role, when other people typecast him in that way, whether disciples or his religious and political opponents.

If Jesus did not claim to be *the* Messiah he certainly sought to bear witness to many of the values that were associated with not just the messianic age, but with Jewish hopes for the future generally. All are agreed that the apocalyptic symbol of kingdom of God was central to his self-understanding. This notion was grounded in Ancient Near East mythological thinking about the forces of good and evil with which humans had to deal, understood as a cosmic struggle in which the forces of good ultimately triumphed. As we have seen it was taken up in Jewish apocalyptic literature in which Yahweh, the good God, was seen as the ultimate victor over evil. Thus it was a master symbol or root metaphor for all of Israel's hopes and expectations for the future within those circles. By making this notion central to his own ministry Jesus was aligning himself with this aspect of his own religious tradition, but characteristically there is a subtle, but highly significant, transposition of the ideas associated with the symbol in other branches of Judaism, in line with his own conduct and lifestyle. Aspects such as domination, majesty, power, conquest, destruction of enemies were shed in favour of different values – peace, justice, meekness, single-mindedness – so succinctly summarised in the beatitudes that form the introduction to the Sermon on the Mount. Thus, another way of establishing God's kingdom was being proposed, not as a distant hope for the future, but as a way of life for the present, a way that was in stunning contrast to the often violent pursuit of particular aims by various other groups among Jesus' contemporaries, groups who also claimed the hopes of Israel as the legitimation for their activity.

Jesus was no starry-eyed mystic, however. His hoping had universal possibilities, but his focus was local to the point of being almost parochial. Yet, despite the modern tendency to want to make Jesus relevant by making him the purveyor of universal truths, it is this localisation and concentration of hope that makes his witness so enduring, as many liberation theologians are teaching us today. Jesus did not believe in dealing in abstractions, but with people. Hope for him is hope in people's capacity to be empowered to change their world, thereby, hopefully changing the world.

The immediate context for his ministry of kingdom-praxis was the rural culture of Galilee, and it was in relation to the tensions inherent in that situation that the hopes witnessed to by Jesus are best profiled. That village culture was itself situated on the margins, both geographically (Galilee) and religiously (away from the Jerusalem cult-centre). In the first century two competing and oppressive systems, though in principle natural rivals, had tacitly collaborated, so that the ordinary peasant people of the region were sorely harassed. On the one hand, those who controlled the Jerusalem temple and its worship and their agents (high priests, Sadducees and Pharisees) were able to make claims on the loyalty of the peasants so that they themselves profited from the tithes, the pilgrimages and the offerings which were stipulated by Jewish religious observance, but without allowing the peasants to participate equally within a thoroughly hierarchical and patriarchal system. 'Search and see if the Messiah could come from Galilee' and 'Are you too a Galilean' are examples of disparaging remarks made by Jerusalemites about their country bumpkin co-religionist that are recorded in the Gospels (Jn 7, 40-44).

On the other side was the Herodian nobility who had come to prominence with the arrival of Herod Antipas as Tetrarch in the region, and who, with his patronage, were able to challenge the ascendancy of the older priestly aristocracy. Antipas, frustrated in his ambition to succeed his father, Herod the Great, as king of the Jews, was highly motivated to bring about rapid social change within the region assigned to him by the emperor Augustus. The building of two hellenistic style cities in the heartland of lower Galilee, Sepphoris (six km from Nazareth) and Tiberias on the lake shore, during the actual life of Jesus were immediate and obvious signs of the rapid social change occurring. No prophetic figure who treasured the value system of Israel could ignore such developments by which the market economy was being intensified at the expense of the peasantry and giving rise to a new wealthy, retainer class, known to us in the Gospels as the Herodians. Mark tells us that they joined forces with the Pharisees in order to plot the destruction of Jesus (Mk 3, 6; 12, 13). With the rise of this class the values that were built into the Jewish system, whereby – in theory at least – all could share in the covenant blessings, by sharing in the fruits of the land, were rapidly being eroded. The pressure was on the country people, and the slide was rapid – from land-owner to tenant to dispossessed to banditry – all of these stages of social disintegration being clearly echoed in the parables and other sayings of Jesus.

This unfinished sketch of Galilean social relations in the first century provides us with enough background to be able to highlight how hope functioned for Jesus within that situation. His own life-style and that of his immediate followers, deliberately abandoning the security of home, family and possessions, to the point that 'the Son of Man had nowhere to lay his head', must be seen as a revolutionary statement of protest against the prevailing value-systems, whether one considers the naked greed and opulence of the Herodians or the judgment of material possessions as signs of divine blessing by the temple-based religious aristocracy. In terms of the prevailing norms this was dangerous and deluded behaviour, but from the perspective of Jesus' apocalyptically motivated kingdom values such conduct was a statement of profound hope. Jesus did not undertake such a daring experiment on his own as an isolated figure, but actively propagated such an ideal among the hard-pressed village people of Galilee and its hinterlands, in the process transgressing all the religious and cultural barriers that had been erected on the basis of a narrow, purity-based interpretation of Israel's hopes. Not merely did he propagate such an ideal, but he actually dared to call this the kingdom of God occurring now in the present.

This reckless hopefulness was grounded in his Jewish faith in the God of hope. This God, Jesus reminded his followers, took care of the smallest and most insignificant creatures, and could be trusted to take care of humans too, making their fretful anxiety about life needless and absurd (Mt 6, 25-35). Greed and acquisitiveness were inappropriate in the light of such considerations, their true character unmasked in their refusal to trust and refusal to hope. Jesus may not have spoken directly about hope, but his and his followers' kingdom-praxis was a powerful and provocative statement of hope in action that challenged others to do likewise. As such his movement was a direct challenge to the two prevailing power systems, the one with its narrow, constraining and controlling view of the God of hope and the other with its need for self-gratification in the name of progress, irrespective of the consequences for others outside the elite. Jesus' presence offered hope to ordinary people by offering them an alternative vision where previously they were trapped; his call to hope cut across national, cultural and social boundaries; for him hope is a summons to think beyond the narrow limits of greed and fear; for him hope is about authentic human community now in the light of God's ultimate rule of the universe.

'Could Jesus have faith?' used to be an old theological conundrum, since scholastic theology claimed that he already enjoyed the beatific vision. Nowadays we are happy to allow Jesus to be fully human, and so we might reframe the question thus: 'Did Jesus doubt?', since to hope is to be human as we have seen and to doubt is to be all too human, as we know. Perhaps an answer to this question is yielded by the so called 'growth' parables, which may be read as Jesus' answer to his disciples and perhaps, his own doubts, faced with the reluctance of his Galilean audiences to share his audacious hopes (Mk 4). This may also indicate the real meaning of the temptation stories which form the prelude to his public ministry in the Synoptic Gospels, namely, Jesus' readiness to allow God be God and still go on hoping despite the apparent evidence to the contrary. In the first of the growth parables (the sower) a threefold pattern of failure is established only to be suddenly and surprisingly broken beyond all measure of expectation in terms of the final harvest yield. The mustard seed playfully suggests that from tiny and insignificant beginnings great and unexpected blessings accrue. In the seed growing secretly the mysterious and independent ways of the earth, which humans cannot control or hasten, speak of God's kingdom coming in God's time; humans must go about their daily routines and wait to be surprised. All three parables draw on nature and its processes rather than on history and it happenings. All talk about ultimate success and abundance achieved only through the pain of disappointment, disbelief and discomfort at not being in charge. This is the stuff of hope as witnessed to by Jesus, whose life is the living testimony to that moving assertion of the Epistle to the Hebrews: 'Faith is the substance of things hoped for, the proof of things unseen' (Heb 11, 1).

Jesus Christ, Embodiment of Israel's Hope

Jesus' social revolution in Galilee, based on hope, failed, to be replaced thirty years after his death by a bloody political rebellion against Rome that led to the destruction of the Jerusalem temple. Those who had embarked on such a course in the name of Israel's hopes had entered a blind alley. Yet immediately after Jesus' death his witness to hope in a different key appeared to have been shallow and an illusion, finally exposed in the failure that was the crucifixion. Except that the God of hope had other ideas about what constitutes failure. It was Jesus' witness to hope that was to prevail, as in and through the Resurrection experience his witness was recalled, reshaped and remembered in order to address other people in other contexts who were desperately in need of a word of hope also within the oppressive social conditions of the Mediterranean world, conditions that were euphemistically named by the elite as the *pax Romana*.

It was in this context, rather than in the Galilean homeland of Jesus, that Christian hope began to sprout and find its first concrete expression.

The hopes to which Jesus witnessed in rural Galilee now found a new setting, but with one very important change: Jesus himself was to become the embodiment of, as well as the witness to, Israel's hopes: 'this Jesus whom you crucified, God has made both Lord and Christ' (Acts 2, 36). This is the confident statement of Peter at Pentecost, according to Luke. Having borne witness to the messianic hopes of Israel in life it was appropriate for Jesus to be proclaimed the universal Messiah in his death and Resurrection. The hopes of Israel were now to find new expressions and new configurations in communities of faith, hope and love both inside and outside Israel. A new force and energy which were identified in faith as the Risen Christ, generated Christian communities that described themselves as the body of Christ, and whose lives were modeled on the witness to the hope to which Jesus' earthly life attested.

It is interesting to observe that when one turns from the Gospels to the epistles, primarily, but not exclusively, the Pauline ones, addressed to early Christian communities outside Palestine, words for hope occur much more frequently. Thus the verb *elpizein*, 'to hope' occurs thirty-one times in all, of which only four references are found in the Gospels, three in Acts and the rest (twenty-five) in the letters. Similarly the noun *elpis* (hope), which occurs fifty-three times in all does not appear at all in the Gospels, there are eight occurrences in Acts and forty-three in the letters. This preponderance of words for hope in the letters suggests that they addressed a milieu in which the concept of hope was widely discussed and had great significance. Paul and other early Christian missionaries expressed their message in a way that was not merely intelligible, but also appealing to their hearers.

Earlier we touched briefly on Greek ideas about hope, noting the sense of precariousness, almost arbitrariness about life with which people had to contend. Paul contrasts Christian hope about death with that of pagans in Thessalonica 'who have no hope', as he puts it. This can scarcely mean that pagans did not have any belief in an afterlife, but that it was vague and uncertain by comparison with the 'sure hope' that Christians experienced (1 Thess 4, 13). This makes Christians 'joyful in hope' (Rm 12,15) and gives a special quality to their lives, which was not lost on their pagan neighbours. In designating the Christian life in terms of hope, Paul and others were deeply conscious of the fact that in terms of both the grounds for hope (God) and the object of hope (Christ) Christian hope differed radically from the contemporary understanding in the Greek world. There hopes could be either good or bad, they were uncertain and only the gods could hope with security. Humans should be concerned with what was before their feet rather than what is distant, as Plato puts it. In contrast, what Edward Schillebeeckx calls the 'critical variant' of Christian hope was the removal of uncertainty and the confidence with which the present could be dealt with, because fear of the unknown had been removed definitively, even the great unknown of death itself. Hope dealt with what could not be seen, but far from generating insecurity, the lack of vision is the very condition for hope. As Paul puts it, paradoxically but confidently: 'Hope that is seen is not hope; for how does one hope for that which one sees?' (Rm 8,24). The very unseen character of the object of hope only makes it more certain that it truly can fulfil our deepest needs and wishes (Rm 8,25). Or, as the author of the Epistle to the Hebrews puts it, 'hope is the test/proof of things not seen' (Heb 11,1).

This contrast with other forms of hoping in the world of early Christianity in terms of a sense of certainty of fulfillment and a clearly defined object, gave rise to a distinctive Christian anthropology, or awareness of what it means to be human. 'If anyone is in Christ there is a new creation,' as Paul declares with a certain note of exhilaration (2 Cor 5, 17). To be a Christian was to think of oneself very differently from others who did not share membership of the household of God. Hope was a decidedly important dimension of this new self-understanding. In a singular passage Paul develops a veritable psychology of hope: the Christian is at peace; the Christian has access to God experienced as *charis*, that is, pure gift; the Christian can boast of their hope of glory, that is their sense of self-worth is determined by the defining object of their hope, namely sharing in God's way of being (glory); because of this assurance and self-assurance the Christian can accept the tribulations of life not just as obstacles to be coped with, but as aspects of the process of transformation to which the new life in Christ summons them. Thus, tribulation leads to endurance (patience), which in turn leads to perseverance, which then leads to hope, which will not be confounded since it is grounded in God's unconditional love, which has already been experienced. Hope may come at the end of this list of stages in the Christian life, but for Paul it informs the whole process backwards (Rm 5,1-5). Repeatedly, Paul brings together faith, patience and hope, recognising the intimate connection between them as three intimate facets of the unique orientation of the Christian life – to trust, to hope, to be patient, – since 'Love excuses all, trusts all, hopes all, endures all' (1 Cor 13,6).

There is one final aspect of Paul's psychology of hope that needs to be adverted to in terms of contemporary discussions of hope. Since

Paul's theological expressions are fashioned in an almost autobiographical manner, the temptation has been strong to read him in an individualistic way, making him a twentieth-century existentialist rather than a first-century Jew. This is particularly true in the case of his treatment of hope, forgetting all too easily that for Paul, and indeed for all early Christians, the communal self-understanding in terms of the body of Christ is the primary experience, so that the Christian community is the present anticipation of the total restoration when 'God would be all in all'. This perspective does not exclude a reading of Paul whereby the individual who is in Christ overcomes the anxiety about existence that is part of the human condition according to Martin Heidegger's existentialist philosophy. The identity of the self is so totally bound up with the identity of the whole, however, that no separation of the two is possible in Paul's perspective in contrast to a modern individualism that is concerned only with the self. This dimension of Christian communal existence found its most complete expression in Christian worship with its intense longing for the actual return of Christ – Maranatha, Come Lord Jesus. However, such community worship was only possible because of the shared life of caring that operated, based on the radical example of Jesus' witness to hope as this was remembered and re-enacted. Not that the ideal was always attained, as the example of the divisions, even in the Eucharistic celebrations at Corinth illustrated all too painfully. Yet such failure only made Paul's prayer of hope at the end of his *Magnum Opus*, the Epistle to the Romans, all the more poignant and pregnant: 'May the God of hope bring you such joy and peace in your faith that the power of the Holy Spirit will remove all the bounds to hope' (Rm 15,15). It is a prayer that is as relevant for our fractured Church life today as when it was first uttered.

Concluding Reflections

I have been attempting to highlight the distinctive features of Christian hope by first seeing how it was grounded in the Israelite/Jewish experience of a God who is utterly trustworthy, whose promises are inclusive for the whole creation and who is the fulfillment of its deepest yearnings as the as yet unfinished project of the whole of creation; secondly, by showing how in Jesus' witness to the hope engendered by this God, transformative action of the most radical and subversive nature could be undertaken in a very specific social situation. Thus a new paradigm of human togetherness was proposed to counteract narrow, sectional interests that lacked the full vigour of radical hope and trust in a faithful God; and thirdly that the memory of that radical model, illumined by the experience of ultimacy in terms of the hopes of Israel that the followers of Jesus claimed, gave rise to communities of faith, hope and love, which, because of their firmly grounded hopes, fostered a new sense of human self-understanding that was essentially communal in character, and which made Christian self-identity quite unique in the ancient world. This understanding of hope is, in my opinion, as relevant today as when it was first experienced and expressed.

There is an urgent need today to rediscover a sense of the presence of God as the faithful sustainer of life and fulfiller of all human yearnings if Christian hope is to be grounded in a way that will sustain it in the face of the many troubling aspects of our contemporary global culture. For many honest enquirers, unfortunately, such a sense of God is no longer possible in the wake of the secularisation process that followed the Enlightenment. A simple recounting of the biblical witness will not of itself remedy the situation in which not merely is God dead for many, but the human subject itself is under severe threat in the wake of the scientific revolution. For those interested in the ongoing quest for an adequate theology to underpin Christian hope the Bible can certainly help in showing how Israel continued to grapple with the notion of the God of hope, even when circumstances put that very belief into serious jeopardy. The dangers of reducing God to either history or nature are all too obvious from the pages of the Bible. Yet the continuing search for adequate ways to name God in our times can receive a powerful stimulus and inspiration, as well as not a little illumination, from Israel's iconoclastic approach. On the one hand this theology did not allow any image of God, even when God was deemed to be very near, but yet it continued to probe the manifold experiences in both history and nature in order to capture, however provisionally, some fleeting glimpse of the mystery that was their God.

The memory of Jesus' radical expression of faith and hope in his daring experiment is today a powerful summons to hope, especially for those who are left without hope because of oppressive and alienating structures controlling their lives. In Jesus' witness we encounter hope, not as some deferred expectation or vague wish for the future, but as a possibility for transformation within the present that can empower and support movements for change. The 'failure' of Jesus' radical experiment in his lifetime, only for its memory to engender new communities of hope throughout the Mediterranean world after his death, should at least alert Christians everywhere to the ways in which 'hope springs eternal', and in the most unexpected ways! If we wish to be true to the vision of Jesus we are not expected to be successful, but to be faithful, that is to be ready to challenge in communities of faith and love the injustices that are in our midst, whether they be of the Jerusalem or Herodian variety. Many of the women from past centuries whose struggles for justice are today being retrieved in the feminist movement could scarcely have anticipated how their 'unsuccessful' and lonely struggles are now empowering others to succeed where they must have surely felt no success was ever possible.

To recall the memory of the first Christian communities of hope, their sense of joy and self-assurance, their new found communal identity based on the experience of connectedness with one another and with the God of hope by being 'in Christ', and their liturgies of joy and celebration of the hope that shaped their lives, to recall and remember all that is to make one a little envious when one thinks of our faded Church life and the pallid liturgies that are the experience of most contemporary Christians, irrespective of denominational allegiance. We cannot turn the clock back and pretend that we are in the first glow of Christian self-expression, however. As Christian Churches we bear the marks of our abandoning of Christian hope for some more ephemeral fulfillment. If our Churches were truly communities of hope, however, not just in word, but in deed, we would most certainly receive a hearing from those who have pinned their hopes in secular Utopias, only to see them crumble like a pack of cards. If Christians cannot any longer be hopeful then there is little hope for our universe despite all our achievements. May the God of hope bring such joy and peace in our faith that the power of the Holy Spirit will remove all bounds to our hoping.

14

GOD AS EXPERIENCE AND MYSTERY: THE EARLY CHRISTIAN UNDERSTANDING

Early Christian *theo*logical speculation occurs at the intersection of Jewish belief in one God and Greco-Roman speculation about the nature of the divine and its interaction with the world of humans. Indeed, this encounter between Jewish monotheism and Greco-Roman paganism had already taken place among Hellenistic Jewish writers, and is represented best in the writings of Philo of Alexandria, and to a lesser extent Josephus, both of whom are first-century c.e. figures, contemporaneous with the rise and spread of Christianity. These Greco-Jewish writers had sought to explain their faith in 'one God' in ways that met the exigencies of Greek philosophy and apologetic discussion without dissolving it into the tolerant monotheism of the times represented by the slogan 'God is both one and many'.

Two aspects emerge as highly significant, aspects that are in some tension with each other. On the one hand the mysterious nature of God was central to Jewish thought from the episode at the burning bush: God refuses to give his name but assures Moses that he would be with Israel in its desert wanderings. Thus the second command of the decalogue prohibits any graven images of God, who is deemed to be beyond any form of human representation. Yet, this God can equally be described anthropomorphically as having walked with Adam and Eve in Paradise 'in the cool of the evening' (Gn 3,8). This sense of God's nearness never deserted Israel: God was the God of history, present to Israel in the desert wanderings, the conquest of the land, the Babylonian exile, or the return to Zion.

The Jewish tradition, be it in the homeland or the Diaspora, was always concerned therefore with the tension between the immanence and the transcendence of God, so central to its scriptural heritage, but without compromising the principle of only one God, enshrined in the daily prayer of all Jews: 'Hear O Israel, the Lord your God is one.' Greco-Roman paganism, on the other hand, has traditionally been described as polytheistic, since the traditional pantheon consisted of various identifications of the divine in terms of natural forces, such as sea, wind, sky, water, fire etc. The various myths or stories about the origins and exploits of these gods had continued to be commented on and interpreted throughout the centuries prior to the emergence of Christianity. Increasingly, philosophers were critical of the myths, and tended to develop ideas about the divine as both 'one and many'. Thus the stereotype of paganism as essentially polytheistic is coming to be revised. The various images of the gods are merely different ways of representing the one divine reality that controls the universe and is at its very heart. Philo, the Jewish Alexandrian philosopher is to be understood in this context, drawing on ideas that were current in middle Platonism. According to this tradition the Supreme God can only be known through philosophical speculation and was not, therefore, accessible to the masses. According to Philo, this is the unnamed God of the Israelite tradition. The various anthropomorphisms for God in the Hebrew Bible on the other hand referred to the demiurge or creator God whom the philosophers regarded as distinct from the Supreme God, whose nature it was 'not to be named, but to be'. (Philo, *On Dreams* 1, 230-33).

The Rabbinic scholars were less concerned with the philosophical tradition than with interpreting the scriptural witness within the emerging system of orthodoxy that they sought to establish. The tradition of speaking about God in such images as king, shepherd, teacher, judge, warrior and the like was extended in the later books of the Bible, particularly through the figure of personified wisdom who was deemed to be separate from God but that still acted as a partner in creation (Proverbs 8, 22-31). Other personifications of God of a more impersonal kind were also developed in terms of God's name (*memra*), God's glory (*chabod*) and God's presence (*shekinah*), in order to avoid any dissolution of God's transcendence, but also to avert the dangers of more crass anthropomorphism.

Both the philosophical and exegetical efforts to preserve the distinctive Hebraic notion of 'one God alone' were not without their difficulties, however. Philo's acceptance of the distinction between the

Supreme God and the Demiurge, both fostered an elitism that was not part of the Israelite conception of election and also hinted at an oppositional dualism between pure spirit that is good and matter that is evil, as was fully developed in later Gnostic systems. Again this was a conception of God that was totally foreign to the Israelite tradition, no matter how mysterious God's true being might ultimately remain. Equally, the distinction between God and God's emanations (name, glory, presence, etc.) could easily give rise to speculation about two powers in heaven, a doctrine condemned by the Rabbis, because of the possible confusion with pagan mythological conceptions of the gods engaged in power struggles in heaven. A late Rabbinic treatise declares:

> Scripture could not give an opportunity to the nations of the world that there were two powers in heaven, but declares: I am Yahweh your God. I was in Egypt, I was at the sea, I was in the past, I will be in the future to come; I am in this world and in the world to come (Mekhilta de Rabbi Ishmael).

The reference to the nations of the world may well allude to the Christian understanding of God that had evolved from the New Testament Scriptures, giving rise to the formulations of the councils of Nicea (325) and Chalcedon (451) on the unity and trinity of God. In the earlier period, however, Christian ideas about God were still part of the ongoing Jewish debate, participating in both the philosophical and exegetical currents just mentioned. There was of course now a new factor that differentiated the early Christians from other branches of the parent religion, namely, the memory of Jesus and the present experience of him as the Risen One whose spirit was highly active in their community life. Thus it can be said that all early Christian *theology* should be described as *Christology*. This insight calls for further elucidation. In the Christian experience the transcendence of God was indeed maintained fully, but the more Jesus' status was conceived in divine terms and proclaimed, the more God's immanence came to be acknowledged in the history of one individual's life and death. It is this element of 'double exposure' that makes the Gospels such unique documents, at once faith-inspired records of Jesus' earthly life and witnesses to Christian understanding of his true identity with and in God.

We can trace the first stages of this development in the Pauline letters, which pre-date the Gospels by several decades. In some fragments of early Christian hymns, which are embedded in various letters, the process described slightly later by the pagan writer Pliny – 'singing hymns to Christ as to a God' – shows an acquaintance with the philosophical language of the time. Jesus is described as being in the 'likeness' (*morphe*) of God before his earthly appearance, and after his self-emptying obedience he is graced with a name that is 'above every name', so that all should bow in homage before it (Phil. 2, 6-11). This name is specified as 'Lord' (*kyrios*), the term that is invariably used in the Greek translation of the Bible (the LXX) for Yahweh. However, as is well known, Yahweh is not really a name for God, but is derived rather from the Hebrew version of God's promise to Moses at the burning bush: 'I will be with you' (Ex 3, 14). Thus in early Christian experience Jesus is endowed with the same quality as the Hebrew God who, despite his nearness to humans, is ultimately beyond naming or representation. This 'theology of the name' occurs in the post-Pauline Letter to the Hebrews also. Here the author seeks to counter speculation about Jesus that we know occurred in other contexts of Jewish thought of the period, especially at Qumran, dealing with the notion of angels representing the divine within the world. As befits the status of him who can be described as being the very expression of God's being, Jesus is said to have inherited a name far superior to that of the angels, heavenly beings though they may be (Heb 1, 1-4).

One can see traces of the exegetical trajectory also at work in the early Christian texts. The Markan Jesus responds to the address 'good master' by recalling the Jewish *Shema* : 'Why do you call me good? Nobody is good except God alone' (Mk 10, 18; Dt 6, 4). The apparent distancing of Jesus from God (cf. also Mk 13, 30) plays a role in Mark's theology as we shall presently discuss, but it is important to see how central the *Shema* was to early Christian thinking even prior to Mark. Writing to the Corinthinas Paul presumes that his converts were familiar with the Jewish prayer, and that it has played an important part in developing their thinking about Jesus and his relationship with God. The passage deserves to be cited in full:

> Hence, as to the eating of food offered to idols, we know that no idol in the world really exists and that 'there is no God but one'. Indeed, even though there may be so-called gods in heaven or on earth – as in fact there are many gods and many lords – yet for us there is one God, the Father, from whom are all things and for who we exist, and one Lord, Jesus Christ, through whom are all things and through whom we exist. (1 Cor 8, 4-6).

Thus the structure of the Jewish *Shema* is maintained but it is suitably adapted to include Jesus within its orbit. The epithet 'Father' (*Abba*) is now applied to God and the term Lord of the original is given to Jesus, corresponding to early Christian hymnic usage, as we have seen. Furthermore, the notion of creation is introduced, but in terms that reflect Hellenistic debates about the causes of things: God is the originating cause ('*from* whom all things exist') and Jesus is the instrumental cause ('*through* whom all things exist').

These examples must suffice to show how early Christian reflection on Jesus Christ was developed within the Jewish matrix of discussion about God's action in the world and God's transcendence of all created reality. The identification of Jesus with the many different expressions of God's expected emissary according to Jewish hopes – messiah, son of Man, son of God – helped to dilute to some extent the tension between God's total otherness and God's immanence. What was utterly new was that Jesus, the Galilean prophet, was identified as that expected one, thereby giving a very concrete response to the age-old question of God's agency and accessibility within the world. At the same time, early Christian experience, despite its faith claims about Jesus continued to maintain God's total otherness in line with its Jewish inheritance. The eschatological and apocalyptic milieu of early Christian experience provided one avenue of resolution to the dilemma caused to its theology by its belief in Jesus. The memory of Jesus' presence in the past, his words and actions, pointed forward towards their future fulfilment in the final stage of the eschatological drama, now unfolding when 'God would be all in all' (1 Cor 15, 28). However, another dimension was to reflect on the mysterious nature of Jesus' own earthly identity, as this came to narrative expression in the Gospels. The two modes of existence that Paul could describe in terms of flesh/spirit and earthly/heavenly dualities now provide the framework within which the narratives about Jesus become suffused with the presence of the Risen and Glorified One who shares in the mysterious reality of God. In this regard the Gospels of Mark and John provide and intriguing contrast *and* convergence in dealing with the mystery of God's revealed hiddeness, which is the paradox at the heart of the Jewish and Christian scriptures. Each work will be examined separately from this point of view.

Mark and the Mysterious Messiah

The author of Mark's Gospel has constructed a narrative that demands subtly from its readers. 'Let the reader understand' (Mk 13, 21) is directed not just to the reading of the 'little apocalypse' (ch 13), but to the whole work with the aura of mystery and paradox that pervades the narrative from start to finish. The author's strategy is to provoke the reader to explore beneath the surface of things, and discover for themselves the real story that is unfolding in the career of Jesus. It is not just Peter, but all would-be ideal readers/disciples who can be chided for 'thinking the thoughts of men, not the thoughts of God' (Mk 8, 33). To this end the reactions of all the characters to the narrated episodes – fear, bewilderment, misunderstanding, hostility – are intended to play on the reader's own emotions, and in the process hopefully lead them across the threshold of faith. 'Seeing' becomes the single most important metaphor for the understanding that it is hoped to generate, yet all too often the expected vision is lacking, most notably among the inner core circle of disciples who were specially chosen (3, 13-19; 8, 14-21).

The central, 'bread section' is particularly noteworthy in this regard, stitched together, as it is, with allusions to bread, granting of sight, hearing and understanding. After the first feeding miracle in the wilderness, an event full of resonances of Israel being accompanied by the divine presence in its desert wanderings, the disciples are sent away to the other side in the boat. In the midst of the ensuing storm Jesus appears to them but they do not recognise him, thinking that he was a ghost. At the end of the episode, when calm is restored to the sea and the troubled disciples, the Evangelist/author gives us the sharp, critical comment: 'They did not understand concerning the bread, their hearts were hardened' (Mk 6, 31). 'The bread' that should have been disclosive of Jesus' true identity points backwards to the manna of the desert wanderings, and forward to the Eucharistic bread of early Christian celebration. Both are signs of God's saving presence in the desert and in the life of the threatened Christian community, a presence that is concretised for ever in early Christian imagination and experience in the person of Jesus appearing to the stricken disciples on the sea of Galilee. Similarly, after the second feeding miracle (8, 1-10) a similar lack of understanding on the part of the disciples gives rise to a series of challenging questions from Jesus: 'Why do you debate that you have no bread? Do you not yet perceive nor understand? Having eyes do you not see and having ears do you not hear? And do you not remember? ... And he said to them do you not yet understand?'

Eyes to see clearly and ears to hear plainly are required by the disciples if they are to really understand the mystery unfolding among them. That such transformation is possible for those who seek it is illustrated by

Mark in the stories of healing deaf and blind individuals that bracket this encounter with the disciples (Mk 7, 31-37; 8, 22-26). Shortly after this artfully crafted section, Peter as spokesperson for the disciples proclaims Jesus to be the Christ. When, however, he objects to Jesus' acceptance of the consequences of this title by heading for opposition in Jerusalem, he is chided for 'thinking the thoughts of men, not the thoughts of God'. Obviously Peter's eyes have not been fully opened to understand the paradoxical nature of the events unfolding before him. In contrast to Peter's partial blindness there is the case of the blind Bar Timaeus outside Jericho, who on receiving the gift of sight from Jesus, follows him enthusiastically on the way that leads to Jerusalem. In addition to this 'outsider' there is also the Roman centurion who at the foot of the cross confesses Jesus as the Son of God, seeing that 'thus he breathed his last' (15, 39). Thus, 'seeing' for Mark means looking beyond the externals of events, and understanding their deeper significance in terms of God's expected intervention in the world of humans by discerning that that presence does not conform to everyday expectations and projections.

Mark's parable chapter, chapter 4, gives the clue to the source of his theological insights. Here he has collected three 'nature' parables, stories told by Jesus about growth in the natural world and its significance for understanding God's ways in the world. The different types of soil are illustrative of human success and failure in discerning the mysterious presence of God; the smallness of the seed that is sown is in stark contrast to the greatness of the end result, and the mysterious nature of the growth process indicates that humans can neither influence nor understand God's ways, yet must be reassured that those ways are gift-laden for humans. Around these stories Mark has built a framework illustrating his theory of understanding God's presence in the career of Jesus, and the difficulty of understanding this which the disciples (and we as readers) encounter as the narrative unfolds. Parables can so easily become riddles, blocking rather than disclosing its paradoxical meaning. Yet understanding *one* parable can lead to the insight that makes sense of the total drama. Disclosive moments are rare. Yet when they do occur it is often in and through the mundane that they are experienced and then they can suffice for a lifetime of meaning and commitment, despite all the counter signs that life brings.

John's Revelatory Signs

Mark's drama unfolds gradually because its starting point lies within the everyday world of people and nature, but from the outset John's meditative soliloquy addresses us 'from above'. The historical Jesus of the Markan narrative is identified with the *Logos* / Word who has had a prior history with God. The reader, like the disciples, is presented with an *epiphania* of the divine glory, which no longer resides in the Jerusalem temple, there to be accessed on the great feasts of the Jews, but in the encounter with Jesus, whose life symbolises the spiritual nourishment that those feasts represent (water, wine, bread, light). However, this encounter is like that of Moses, a veiled encounter, calling for seeing, perception, understanding, and believing, and above all loving, a disposition to see beyond the externals and to understand the deeds of Jesus for what they truly are, signs of his Father's glory that resides in him. Thus, despite its very different starting point that might appear to destroy the veil that hides the divinity from the very start, John is close to Mark in his thinking about the divine-human encounter. True to his Jewish roots, even when he might be accused of being anti-Jewish, God is both near and hidden in the Johannine scheme of things also.

Let us begin with the encounter from the divine side. The statement of 1, 14, 'the Word became flesh and pitched his tent in our midst' already strikes an exodus note of Yahweh's dwelling in the 'tent of meeting' in the desert wanderings of Israel. From this opening identification of Jesus' presence replicating the divine presence, the author's 'high' Christology serves to underpin the reality of the divine revelation manifested in the career of Jesus. Time and again the unique union between Jesus and the Father is stressed. 'My Father works until now and I work', Jesus declares in a reference to the creation story, as a way of justifying his own healings on the Sabbath. He shares the Father's name (5, 43; 17, 11), has power over all things (3, 35; 13, 3) and has life in himself as the Father has (5, 26), but without being open to the charge of being 'a second God'. His status is based on the complete union between Father and Son expressed in terms of mutual indwelling and mutual love (10, 38; 14, 10f; 17, 21-23). Hence Jesus' actions are really the actions of the Father who dwells in him 'who does the works' (14, 10). From the point of view of the author, Jesus' actions are an expression of God's creative power, which continues to be operative – his works – yet at another level they are not self-explanatory, but serve rather as signs that the truly discerning can identify as manifestations of the divine glory.

The implied author becomes the plural 'we', embracing both disciples then and later: 'we saw his glory, the glory of the only-begotten of the Father, full of grace and truth'. Unlike the Markan disciples, the

Johannine circle rarely waver from this stance expressed emphatically after the first Cana miracle: 'He revealed his glory and his disciples believed in him' (2, 11). Despite this blinding experience, there is no compulsion or inevitability about the disciples' or any other person's acceptance of the epiphany of divine glory that is the encounter with Jesus. After the Jewish crowds abandon him for his 'hard saying', Jesus himself puts the question to the disciples: 'Will you also go away?' To which Peter, as spokesperson for the group, replies: 'Lord to whom shall we go? You have the words of eternal life, and we have believed and have come to know that you are the holy one of God' (6, 67-69). At the very end of the Gospel the same structure of the Johannine epiphanic experience is acknowledged, though now extended beyond the immediate circle of his followers. Thomas requires physical evidence before confessing the Risen Christ as his Lord and God, and Jesus allows this, while proclaiming as blessed also those 'who have not seen but have believed' (20, 20).

This final statement looks beyond the immediate experience of eye-witnesses to a faith based on the word of others. Yet that proclamation is no mere human word in the Johannine perspective. Rather it is based on the Paraclete or Spirit of Truth, which comes as a gift from the Father, and is promised as a permanent presence to the disciples by the departing Jesus in his farewell meeting with them (14, 16f; 16, 13). The Johannine faith experience is, then, a gift received that transforms the receiver into the giver. God is defined as love as well as light, and those who accept the revelation are transformed by it. 'Love one another as I have loved you' (15, 12) and 'If we walk in the light as he is in the light, we have fellowship with one another' (1 John 1, 7). Thus, there is an ethical as well as a mystical aspect to the experience. Indeed it is only in the effort to replicate God's act of unconditional love that it is possible for the true union with God to occur (cf. 1 John 4, 13-21).

The various Johannine dialogues (for example, chapters 4 and 9) are excellent examples of how the faith experience occurs within the Johannine ethos. In both instances the dialogue is generated from an initial encounter that leads to a preliminary naming of Jesus, as messiah or healer. However, this is merely the first stage on the journey to full-blown Johannine faith. Misunderstandings can lead to further illumination through the statements of Jesus, which function as an in-depth commentary on the actions just performed. Alternatively, they can also lead to the blinding of those who refuse to take the initial step and cannot therefore be drawn into the deeper exploration of Jesus' true identity. It is this openness to the gift of the encounter that eventually generates the trusting acceptance of Jesus as the ultimate revelation of God. There is deep, if tragic, irony at work here, in that those who refuse the invitation (the Jews, the Pharisees, the world, as representative figures) think they know in advance who Jesus is, either because of his place of origin or their 'superior' knowledge of how God's plan is supposed to operate. Their religious elitism or their rootedness to 'below' blocks the possibility for a true encounter. There is a strong ethical note in describing the failure of some to accept the light that is in their midst. Their works are evil (3, 19), they have neither the word nor the love of God in them (5, 38-42), they judge according to the flesh (8, 15), they are of the world or from below (8, 23), they cannot bear to hear the words of Jesus because they are of their father, the devil (8, 43f), they do not know God (8, 55), they have preferred the praise (*doxa*) of men to the glory (*doxa*) of God (12, 43). By contrast 'everyone who is *of* (the pregnant *ek* of source and origin) the truth hears my voice' (18, 36).

Conclusion

Despite the fact that Mark and John represent two opposite poles of early Christian reflection on Jesus – the one from below, the other from above – both have a similar perspective on how the encounter with Jesus functioned in the life and faith of the first followers. Their conviction about the ultimate significance of Jesus' life did not come as a blinding flash that could not be ignored, but rather as a veiled revelation that demanded engagement, trust and commitment. Both the messianic secret of Mark and John's theology of signs are grounded in the Jewish experience of the hidden God who is very near. The more Christian reflection about Jesus' life was developed along the lines of transferring images for God from the Hebrew Scriptures to him and his actions, the more clearly we can see this theological reserve at work. The fact that those images are so many and varied, often rooted in the ecological, historical and social experiences of Israel, means that God's ultimately mysterious nature was maintained, despite the sense of intimacy and partnership between Yahweh and Israel that is expressed in the various writings. Familiarity and awe intertwined as the correct responses to God's favour to Israel. For John, knowing God is no mere intellectual experience, but rather being drawn into the mystery of God's life and love, as Jesus repeatedly emphasises in the farewell discourse that are meant to define Christian existence within the world after his departure (chapters 13-17).

Early Christian experience of Jesus as the ultimate expression of God's care would appear to have torn open the veil that kept the God of Israel from view (Mk 15, 38). Yet, even then, the historical particularity of Jesus' life and work raises other questions about God's presence and activity within the whole of creation. In Jesus Christians do indeed have a definite pointer to the nature of God, so profoundly articulated in the statement 'God is love' (1 John 4, 16). This conclusion was not arrived at by any abstract speculation but rather by the genuine experience and memory of one who was love and care personified within the limited contours of his life and times. Yet the paradox at the heart of the Christian experience of God is that such a one had to die to meet the demands of unconditional love. God indeed remains the ultimate mystery, but sufficient has been experienced to make possible the eschatological declaration that in the end 'God will be all in all,' (1 Cor 15, 28).

Further Reading

J. Ashton, *Understanding the Fourth Gospel,* Oxford: Clarendon Press, 1991.

P. Athanassiadi and M. Frede eds. *Pagan Monotheism in Late Antiquity,* Oxford: Clarendon Press, 2000.

J.M. Byrne, ed. *The Christian Understanding of God Today,* Dublin: Columba Press, 1993.

L. Hurtado, *One God, One Lord. Early Christian Devotion and Jewish Monotheism,* London: SCM Press, 1988.

B. F. Meyer, *The Early Christians. Their World Mission and Self Discovery,* Wilmington, Del: Michael Glazier, 1986.

J. Neusner, ed. *Judaic Perspectives on Ancient Israel,* Philadelphia: Fortress Press, 1987.

A. Segal, *Two Powers in Heaven. Early Rabbinic Reports about Christianity and Gnosticism,* Leiden: Brill, 1977.

W. Telford, ed. *The Interpretation of Mark,* Edinburgh: T. and T. Clark, second edition 1995.

15

FROM MESSIANISMS TO MESSIAHS: THE JEWISH SEARCH FOR REDEMPTION IN HISTORY

A totally different concept of redemption determines the attitude to Messianism in Judaism and in Christianity. What appears to the one as a proud indication of its understanding and a positive achievement of its message is most unequivocally belittled and disputed by the other. Judaism in all its forms and manifestations has always maintained a concept of redemption as an event that takes place publicly, on the stage of history and within the community. In contrast, Christianity conceives of redemption as an event in the spiritual and unseen realm, in the soul and in the private world of each individual and which effects an inner transformation that need not correspond to anything outside.[1]

This characterisation of messianic thinking in Judaism and Christianity, though coming from the pen of the most eminent Jewish scholar of the subject, Gersholm Scholem, has not gone uncriticised by both Jewish and Christian scholars. On the Jewish side, Scholem's own student, Moshe Idel, has called for a much broader taxonomy of Jewish understandings of the Messiah to Scholem's apocalyptic version.[2] From the Christian perspective, it is undoubtedly true that the doctrine of being 'in Christ' gave rise to what has been described as Pauline mysticism, that is, the internal experience of sharing a graced existence with all the baptised, and this understanding has dominated much of classical Christian theological reflection about the Christ. However, from time to time in

Christian history the public expression of Messianism that Scholem describes has also occurred, most notably in the so-called radical Reformation of Thomas Münser in the sixteenth century, and more recently still, in liberation theology with its call for a preferential option for the poor and the development of an inclusive community of love and justice to challenge the prevailing value systems of the free market economy.[3]

Of course Jewish and Christian forms of messianism will always differ. Within Jewish history there is room for individuals to claim for themselves the status of the expected Messiah, as, for example, in the movement associated with Shabbetai Zevi, in the seventeenth century, or more recently during the Gulf War in the figure of Lubavitcher Rebbe (R. Menachem Mendel Schneerson) of New York.[4] For Christians, on the other hand, messianic movements either take the form of a return to a radical way of Christian living based on the memory of Jesus and the first Christians, or alternatively, in the belief of the imminent return of Christ, as in the movement of David Koresh and his followers in the U.S. In this paper I do not plan to pursue these somewhat bizarre examples, interesting though that might be. Instead I want to explore the significance of messianic thinking for Jewish identity within a more secular context, contrasting that with the Second Temple period when expectation of a personal messiah was much more prominent than it is in modern Jewish consciousness. What has brought about the change and how significant has a rediscovery of the messianic thrust been for Jewish and for world history today? In attempting to answer these questions I intend in the first part of the paper to explore the thinking of two influential Jewish scholars who have played an important role in twentieth century discussions about history and its outcome, namely the aforementioned Gersholm Scholem and Walter Benjamin. In the second section I will discuss the different forms of messianic expression in its originating period of the Second Temple, including the Jewish messianic sect of the Christians. By way of conclusion, I will offer some suggestions on the lessons that messianism has to offer to our post-modern world, when the very notion of meaning is itself under threat.

Scholem, Benjamin and the Messianic Idea of Judaism

'To the Jew as individual, everything, to the Jew as a nation, nothing.' With that chilling statement of *liberté, fraternité,* and *egalité* the post-revolutionary French assembly of 1791 declared that European Jews would no longer be condemned to the ghettoes, even if it took almost a hundred years before the liberation was completed in Italy. The emancipation presented the Jews with a dilemma that had not been theirs since first century b.c.e. Alexandria, when the possibility of assimilation to the larger cultural ethos beckoned as both a challenge and a threat.

In the Diaspora Jewish life was built around the observance of the *halakah*, which included dietary and marriage laws, celebration of Shabbat, the annual festivals and the synagogue service for males. This was Judaism as defined by the Rabbis from the second to the sixth century and was based on the Talmud. The *haskalah* or Enlightenment that was sweeping through the European continent from the eighteenth century onwards posed a particular threat, now that Jews were free to participate fully in the intellectual life of Europe. As economic and social opportunities opened up choices had to be made with regard to the traditional and distinctive way of life that was deemed canonical throughout the middle ages and into the early modern period. The separatism that marked the Jewish way of life ran totally counter to the spirit of universalism of the age of reason. Some, like the earlier Karl Marx, opted to convert to Christianity as a way of openly abandoning their Jewish heritage; others chose to redefine Jewishness as a private religious affiliation independent of nationality or ethnicity, and others still accepted a nationalism without religion, as in the early Zionist movement with its dream of a separate homeland for Jews and the establishment of a socialist Jewish state. As Jews began to climb the social ladder, the latent anti-semitism that had kept them in the ghetto once again manifested itself, especially in Germany, as eugenic race theories were combined with the other strands of anti-Jewish propaganda. In the Weimar Republic that emerged from the ashes of first world war, left-wing socialism or communism were other options for young German Jews, dissatisfied with the shattered dreams of the liberal agenda and its promises of progress.

This was the climate within which two significant thinkers for the topic of Jewish messianism emerged, each developing a distinctive approach to the dilemmas that modernity, with its illusory promises of progress posed for them as Jews. Gersholm Scholem (1897-1982) and Walter Benjamin (1892-1940) were the children of middle-class, bourgeois families, both of whom refused to follow the assimilationist route of their parents. For both of them messianism was to make an important contribution to their search for an alternative to either assimilation or acceptance of the received orthodoxy that continued to be propagated by the Rabbis. As we shall see, the particular circumstances in which each lived their life was to be decisive in their particular appropriation of the messianic hope.[5]

Scholem

In refusing both the assimilationist and orthodox options Scholem had to search for an alternative version of Jewish identity. For him, this other way was the Jewish mystical tradition that had been deemed heretical by the Rabbis, but that, according to Scholem, had always been a part of the tradition and had preserved the messianic impulse within Judaism. As noted at the outset, Scholem claimed that an apocalyptic understanding of the messianic idea was central to the Jewish experience throughout the centuries. This involved a catastrophic understanding of history: every incident of messianic outpouring was, he claimed, the result of some disastrous event that threatened the very continuation of the Jewish tradition. The footsteps of the Messiah are preceded by presumption and destruction, as the *Mishnah* declared. Scholem writes: 'Jewish messianism is in its origins and by its nature – this cannot be sufficiently emphasised – a theory of catastrophe. This theory stresses the revolutionary, cataclysmic element in the transition from every historical present to the Messianic future.'[6]

At the same time the catastrophic understanding of history was only one side of the equation, to be balanced by a combination of the restorative and utopian elements, which combined to present a future that was totally other than the present, and which made the present bearable. Thus, while Jewish life was always 'a life lived in deferment, in which nothing can be done definitively,' it was always also a life lived in hope. The restorative dimension recalls an idyllic past for the nation whereas the utopian looks to a future state that has not yet existed, and the messianic idea crystalises out of a combination of both impulses. The balance between the two has varied at different times and among different groups, but they are both always present and active in articulating the Jewish belief that history can be redeemed.

Scholem eventually emigrated to Israel in 1923, as a cultural rather than a political Zionist. He refused to identify the realisation of a Jewish state with the messianic hope. His life was lived in scholarly research into Jewish mysticism, promoting through his scholarship the messianic impulses he had uncovered in this forgotten legacy of his people. He was always particularly insistent that the messianic idea should not be confused with the idea of human progress. It bore witness rather to the belief that history could not redeem itself, but must await redemption from outside. He writes:

> The redemption is not the product of immanent developments, such as we find in modern Western re-interpretations of Messianism, where secularised as the belief in progress, Messianism displayed unbroken and immense vigour. It is rather transcendence breaking in upon history, an intrusion in which history itself perishes, transformed because it is struck by a beam of light. The construction of history in which the apocalyptists (as opposed to the prophets of the Bible) revel has nothing to do with modern conceptions of development or progress, and if there is anything that in the view of these seers history deserves, it can only be to perish…Their optimism is not directed to what history will bring forth but what will arise in its ruin, free at last and undisguised (*Messianic Idea*, p.10).

Because of this 'anarchic breeze,' as he describes the messianic impulse, Scholem is suspicious of any attempt to rationalise the idea as had happened in secular Messianism of his own day. Already in the twelfth century the Spanish Jewish philosopher, Maimonides, had sought to downplay the apocalyptic element in messianism, insisting on the restorative dimension only, which would allow for the life of proper study and observance of the Torah. The only difference between the present age and the age of the Messiah, according to Maimonides, is that Israel will have the opportunity to fulfil all the demands of the law. He shows no interest in any idea of future cosmic upheavals or the like, nor is it possible to calculate when the Messiah will come. 'The sages and prophets longed for the days of the Messiah not in order to rule over the world and not to bring the heathens under their control, not to be exalted by the nations, or even to eat, drink, and rejoice. All they wanted was to have time for the Torah and its wisdom, with no one to oppress or disturb them.'[7]

Scholem understands this 'rationalistic' approach of Maimonides in the context of the intense speculation about the date of the Messiah's coming among Jews of the day, and the disturbances caused by the emergence of a messianic movement among the Yemenite Jews. At the same time he insists that the great Spanish master never made any connection between human achievement and the advent of the Messiah. That event remains a mystery and a miracle in his thought, even if it is stripped of its apocalyptic colouring. According to Scholem, this deapocalypticisation of the messianic idea differed from the racist tendencies of the modern period. Whereas Maimonides had insisted on the restorative dimension of the idea, the rationalism of the Jewish and European Enlightenment had abandoned this aspect entirely. Instead they had interpreted the utopian dimension in a wholly new way that tied messianism to human progress. Thus, the nationalist and historical elements were superseded by a purely universalistic interpretation that was in danger of losing all connection with the Jewish experience and heritage.

The insistence of the centrality of the apocalyptic dimension in Jewish messianic thought arose from Scholem's resistance to the contemporary *Zeitgeist* of human progress and the denial of any sense of transcendence even among Jewish thinkers. He was highly suspicious of what later came to be known as 'the non-Jewish Jew,' a long list of highly influential thinkers from Spinoza to Marx and Freud, who have been described as having 'gone beyond the boundaries of Judaism, which they all found too narrow, too archaic and too constricting.' It was this perceived threat to the Jewish heritage from modern European thought that gave rise to his life-long intellectual struggle with his friend Walter Benjamin, who has been described as 'the Marxist Rabbi.'

Benjamin

Benjamin, like Scholem, was born into a comfortable bourgeois family, but he shared his younger friend's unease with the erosion of Jewish identity that he experienced everywhere. They had both vehemently opposed the First World War, and spent time together in Switzerland where Benjamin was working, unsuccessfully as it transpired, on his doctoral dissertation. He subsequently became a writer and literary critic, with much of his writing concerned with the philosophy of language. He and Scholem remained life-long friends, even though after the latter's departure to Israel he came increasingly under the influence of such Marxist theoreticians such as Lukaks and Brecht. Scholem was dismayed by this turn of events in his friend's search for an authentic Jewish identity. Throughout the 1930s a long correspondence ensued between them in which Scholem chided his friend for his attempts to wed his philosophical insights about the metaphysical status of language with economic materialism. 'You would certainly not be the last, but perhaps the most incomprehensible victim of the very confusion between religion and politics, the true relation of which you could have been expected to bring out more clearly than anyone else,' he writes.[8]

Benjamin replied by admitting the ambiguity of his position: 'I am going to extremes,' he responds, 'a castaway who drifts on a wreck by climbing to the top of an already crumbling mast. But from there he has at least a chance to give a signal leading to his rescue.'

In this exchange one catches a glimpse of the confusion that beset a German-Jewish intellectual in the Weimar Republic, as the storms of Nazism had begun to gather. In fact Benjamin's brother, Georg, as well as Scholem's brother, had joined the Communist party, both to die in concentration camps. Benjamin himself never joined any left-wing political alignment, and he died, taking his own life, as he attempted to cross from France to Spain in 1940, fleeing from the Nazis. The following year Scholem dedicated his now famous *Major Trends in Jewish Mysticism* as follows: 'To the memory of Walter Benjamin (1892-1940). The friend of a life-time whose genius united the insights of the metaphysician, the interpretative power of the critic and the erudition of the scholar. Died at Port Bou (Spain) on his way into freedom.'

The dedication shows how much Scholem treasured his friend's struggle to integrate his Jewish messianic faith (the metaphysician) with the pressing social demands of the left-wing critic of the Weimar establishment, with its growing anti-semitism and the reactionary forces of Nazism. Benjamin's intellectual enterprise of attempting to develop a creative dialectic between messianism and materialism has been variously described as 'secular messianism' or as the 'the fusion of "left wing" ethics and "right wing" epistemology.' The former label is derived from revolutionary socialism, and the latter refers to the emancipatory thrust of the Jewish messianic idea. For Benjamin the legacy of this Jewish heritage that was of most importance was the notion of memory, not in the active sense of the human capacity to recall, but as a given that can transform time and history through the insight that it gives to the 'unattained and an inexpressible meaning of life.' The notion that time is continuous, that 'things just keep going on' *is* the catastrophe. It is not something that is impending at any given moment 'but is something that is always given.' Time as continuous progress is abhorrent, 'redeemable only through Memory which can make the incomplete (happiness) into the complete, and the complete (suffering) into the incomplete.'[9] Memory allows Now-time – for Benjamin a trans-temporal moment that is the prototype of Messianic time – to enter the finite world as both a 'utopian hope and a revolutionary chance for the oppressed.' As Benjamin graphically puts it: 'Every second of time is the strait-jacket through which the Messiah may enter.'

Benjamin did not see human progress as reflective of the messianic moment, and on this he and Scholem could agree. 'Nothing historical can of its own account strive to relate itself to anything messianic. ... Only the messiah himself completes all historical happening by himself redeeming, completing and creating its relationship to its messianic future.' The so-called arrow of time, which determines the human search for progress, points directly opposite to the messianic direction. 'But just as a force, can through acting increase another that is acting in the opposite direction, so the order of the profane (i.e. human progress) assists through being profane the coming of the messianic kingdom.' This seeming paradox in Benjamin's thought has been explained by one commentator as reflecting his tolerance for progress only insofar as it accelerates the rate of decline. The idea finds a particularly moving expression in Benjamin's image of the angel of history, which he developed from a painting by Paul Klee, showing an angel about to depart from something he is fixedly contemplating. Its eyes are staring, its mouth is open, its wings are spread. Scholem wrote a poem about the significance of this image for Benjamin, entitled 'Greetings from Angelus.' The angel's face combines horror and blessing, melancholy and hope at one and the same time, he explains. But the angel is only a messenger, not a redeemer, and its presence is merely a reminder. The angel would like to stay and redeem but it is being propelled backwards to Paradise by a storm that originated there and so one can only hope that the redeemer will one day come.[10]

Benjamin's philosophy of history could be summed up as an attempt to allow the messianic 'Now' that could redeem, break through the crevices of history as progress. In moments of real threat Memory comes to the fore, and as the catastrophe looms, the power of Memory can take over, a power that is involuntary, arising from a realm other than personal knowledge or the chronological narration of things past. It is a compression of things past that gives meaning to the totality, thereby unleashing an otherwise unavailable sense of the whole. In that moment time itself stands still so that all of the past is present as a single whole. Thus, it is in the wreckage of history that sparks of messianic light can appear. Redemption is possible, especially for the poor, when the continuum of progress is interrupted. Thus, Benjamin's notion of the redeeming power of the catastrophic brings him close to Scholem's apocalyptic understanding of the messiah. It is on the stage of human history that intimations of messianic history can be sensed, though the two can never be fused. Memory and hope are joined together, so that the future is no longer just utopia, but is shaped by a lost past, whose restoration is also desired.

Differing Roles, Differing Messiahs

The second stage of our discussion brings us back to the Second Temple period, when messianism, in the sense of an end-time redeemer figure, emerges clearly for the first time. Our discussion of both Scholem and Benjamin has shown how central messianic thinking and belief were to them in their struggle for an adequate sense of identity, yet how nebulous the figure of *the,* or *a* Messiah was for them. There had been too many messiahs, perhaps, in Jewish history for them to focus on the notion of a single individual whose task it would be to redeem Israel, or more cosmically still, to right the wrongs of world history. This reserve about the figure of the Messiah had already been a feature of Rabbinic literature: the Messiah is somewhere, but he is hidden and his appearance or identity cannot be disclosed. Or as Franz Kafka, that most Jewish of the European 'non-Jews' puts it: 'There is plenty of hope, but not for us.' The thing about the messiah is that he is always coming, as a Yiddish tale about the Rabbi who refused to increase the meagre pay of the watchman, sent to look out for the messiah's coming, acknowledges: Yes, the pay is meagre. But one must take into account that this is a permanent job!

Contrary to general perceptions the idea of a messiah is not a given in the Hebrew Scriptures. There is, of course, a prophetic eschatology that looks for an ideal king, or a restoration of Israel, but as yet these hopes are very much within the realm of this world continuities. As William Scott Green notes, the notion of the messianic idea being the generative force of Hebrew and Jewish religious perceptions is a construct that depends largely on a Christian reading of the texts in the light of the New Testament pattern of promise and fulfilment. This in turn gives rise to the understanding of a chronic and endemic problem within Judaism to which the messiah alone is the answer.[11] This impression would do less than justice to many other strands within the Jewish tradition, most notably the *halachic* and wisdom strands on which so much of Rabbinic Judaism is based, and which concern themselves with the present moment and how to understand and relate to it. Thus, scholars today speak of pre- or proto-messianic conceptions in the earlier biblical traditions. Even when one turns to the Second Temple period itself it is noteworthy that messianic speculation does not feature as prominently as one might anticipate on reading the Fourth Gospel, for example, with its scenarios of ordinary Jews, Samaritan schismatics and scribal elites engaged in endless debates about the coming of the Messiah.

After a brief appearance in the Persian period when, significantly, there is talk of two messiahs – one royal and the other priestly – one has to await the late first century b.c.e. collection known as The Psalms of Solomon before messianic speculation recurs. Neither the struggles of the Maccabees against the Greek 'Hellenisers', nor the conquests of their successors, the Hasmoneans, in the intervening centuries were interpreted messianically, to judge from the literature of the period. The Psalms of Solomon are attributed to Pharisaic circles who were deeply critical of the new Jewish ruling elite, the Hasmoneans. The Hasmoneans were said to have behaved arrogantly, giving rise to the Roman intervention and the pollution of Jerusalem by foreigners. Psalm 17 looks for a true son of David who will restore justice, defeat the enemy and renew Israel, and Psalm 18 aspires for a wise teacher who will not merely instruct Israel in the ways of Torah, but will, himself, observe it. In other words, messianism emerges not as an ideology of power, but as a critique of its misuse, among dissident circles that are disillusioned by the way in which a native aristocracy has succumbed to the value systems of the larger ethos.[12]

A similar pattern can be detected in the first century c.e. when the Idumean, Herod the Great, was the client king of the Jews on behalf of Roman power in the east. Herod's policies of both honouring his Roman overlords and presenting himself as a patron of Hellenistic culture offended at once the political and religious sensibilities of many Jews. Popular disturbances of a 'messianic' nature are reported by Josephus, and among various dissident groups, especially the Essenes and the Jesus-followers, intense messianic speculation seems to have been prevalent. A new feature of this speculation was its apocalyptic colouring, reflecting perhaps the repressive nature of the Herodian administration, which drove much of the opposition underground. Apocalyptic thinking also had the effect of distancing its proponents from immediate political action against the oppressor, since it was God, not humans, who was understood to right the wrongs of history in this scenario.[13] Of course that did not prevent elements of an active messianism being combined with apocalyptic end-time speculation, as in the case of the Zealots who were central in initiating the first revolt against Rome in 66 c.e. However, it does help to understand how both the Essenes (it would seem) and the Christians could adopt a pacifist attitude to the revolt. Insofar as Jesus and his followers found messianic symbolism and language appropriate for interpreting his career and its aims, it is noteworthy that in the earliest strands of that thinking he is seen as a prophetic/teacher figure rather than a royal leader.[14] It is only when the heat of political action had been removed that titles like 'son of David' could be aggressively appropriated in a more academic setting of disputes with the synagogue, as in Matthew's Gospel towards the end of the first century. Even then the political and militaristic associations of this title are attenuated considerably by its combination with others such as 'Son of Man' and 'prophet'.[15]

That strand of Jewish messianic thinking, which fed into the upsurge of Jewish nationalism of the first revolt, was still to the fore some seventy years later in the equally unsuccessful Bar Cochba revolt. Not merely was the ruined temple not rebuilt, but the holy city, Jerusalem, was turned into the pagan Aelia Capitolina and Jews were no longer allowed even to visit. It was in Galilee, and later in Babylonia, that the sages who fashioned the Rabbinic corpus could contemplate the role of the messiah in Jewish history for the future. The earliest document, the Mishnah, sees redemption not in the arrival of the Messiah but in the observance of the *halakah* as this applies to the everyday routines of life in the home and village. Several centuries later the Christians had seemingly triumphed with the conversion of Constantine and the privileged role now granted to the once outlawed sect within the empire. Perhaps the sight of Christian churches and monasteries everywhere in the Holy Land prompted the return to messianic thinking as this is reflected in the Palestinian Talmud. Here the Messiah is a faithful teacher of Torah, no longer king David, but Rabbi David, however.[16] The Babylonian sages developed a view of the Diaspora that challenged the centrality of Jerusalem and the land as the primary symbols of Jewish identity. No doubt it was this shift in Jewish consciousness that gave rise to the kind of thinking about the messiah that one finds in the Babylonian Talmud. In the tractate Sanhedrin, in particular, a variety of points of view are put forward by different Rabbis. There is no definitive position and no one perspective. The coming of the Messiah is both a set of political expectations and also a demand for ethical responses on the part of Israel. And the emphasis can oscillate between these two perspectives.[17]

What is noteworthy from this rapid survey of earlier trends in messianic thinking is that the figure of the Messiah and his specific role in history was initially more prominent, only to fade somewhat into the background as political failure gave way to the needs of describing a

Jewish way of life in exile that could be deemed authentically Jewish. This trend continued in the rational messianism of Maimonides, as we have seen, but also in the more mystical tradition of the middle ages. Thus, a near contemporary of Maimonides and also a product of the Spanish-Jewish community, Abraham Abulafia, could speak of the Messiah under three separate guises, combining elements of medieval philosophical speculation about human knowing with more traditional understanding of the Messiah as a redeemer figure. The term *'massiah'* is equivocal, he writes. It refers to the *Agens Intellectus*, or source of all human knowledge as defined by Aristotle; it applies also to the one who through his special contact with this supernatural principle of knowledge 'will lead us out of exile from under the rule of the nations; and it describes the human intellect that controls 'the lowly bodily desires that seek to rule our lives.'[18]

Some Concluding Reflections

An interesting contrast emerges between the modern and ancient expressions of the messiah and messianism that we have so far discussed. In the Second Temple period the emphasis was on a personal messiah, even when there was a variety of names and roles associated with the figure – son of David, son of God, *mashiah/christos*, the prophet, Elijah, the priest, Melchisedek. In the modern discussions, on the other hand, the figure of a personal messiah is distinctly vague and the discussion is rather on messianism or messianic thinking. This contrast is probably due to changing cultural and social perceptions between the ancient and the modern world. In the world of ancient empires individuals of status stood for and were representative of the hopes and aspirations of the group as a whole. In our modern, highly individualistic world, by contrast, each individual stands separate and alone. The notion of group identity has weakened as the awareness of personal freedom has developed. Could it be then that the Messiah as an individual is one of those childish illusions that humankind come-of-age has outgrown, a Freudian dream projection that can never be realised? Is modern messianism a mere remnant of a past world, devoid of any relevance for our time?

> The Jewish heretic who transcends Jewry belongs to a Jewish tradition. He is the prototype of these great revolutionaries of modern thought: Spinoza, Heine, Marx, Rosa Luxembourg, Trotsky and Freud. … They all went beyond the boundaries of Jewry. They all

found Jewry too narrow, too archaic, too constricting. They all looked for ideals and fulfilment beyond it, and they represent the sum and substance of much that is greatest in modern thought ... in philosophy, sociology, economics and politics of the last three centuries.[19]

This citation dealing with the contribution of Jewish thinkers to the Enlightenment project represents one view of the dilemma facing Jewish intellectuals, in particular, in dealing with messianism. Despite Scholem's claim that of the three central doctrines of Judaism – creation, revelation and messianism – it is only the last that has continued to have a genuine vitality in the modern age, has the time come again for Jews to opt for the Rabbinic solution, namely to ignore the ideas that are encapsulated in the myth and person of the Messiah and fashion a non-messianic Judaism based on the everyday?

Yet the fact that something akin to the messianic idea has continued to surface in the work of several of those thinkers listed above, most notably Marx and Freud, despite their subsequent disavowal of their own religious heritage, suggests that there may be something of perduring value in the messianic idea, not just for the Jews, but for humankind. The prevalence among modern Jewish thinkers of deep dissatisfaction with the present state of things *and* a longing for a future world that would be radically different from the present, indicates that we are not just dealing with a universal human longing, but with a distinctive Jewish contribution to the human search for meaning, arising from that people's experience of history.

Inherent in the messianic idea, especially the apocalyptic version espoused by Scholem, is the sense that there is something radically wrong with the world, something that, according to both Scholem and Benjamin, cannot be put right by human achievement. Scholem's insistence that there is no easy transition from history to redemption makes a genuine contribution within a modern perspecive. It reaffirms the centrality of the Transcendent breaking into history, 'in which history itself perishes,' as a key insight in terms of the modern search for an adequate understanding of the concept of God. It is a ringing statement that the messianic idea is at root a theological conception, not just a human projection, in an age when the very notion of transcendence is deemed incomprehensible, if not downright naive. The metaphysicians have a point, even if today we are rightly suspicious of those who seek to build unchanging systems on shaking foundations.

What is significant about the Jewish notion of transcendence is that God is both transcendent and immanent, the one who refuses to be named or represented *and* the one who wanders in the wilderness with Israel and walks in the garden with Adam and Eve. God is an absent Presence and a present Absence. Only such an understanding of the divine could have made the messianic idea possible in the first instance. This renewal of messianic thinking in Judaism has prompted Christian theologians such as Jürgen Moltmann to move away from the static theism of the Scholastics to a more dynamic understanding.[20]

Yet, as Scholem acknowledges, apocalyptic does adopt a very negative view of the world and of human nature. A life lived in constant deferment can easily become no life at all. Indeed Martin Buber rejected apocalyptic entirely as being an alien import to Jewish thought from Babylonia, which distorted the demand for inner personal conversion by the prophets. Benjamin's uneasy fascination with Marxist materialism was a reminder that even if the present cannot be identified with the messianic moment, 'Now-time' in which the meaning of the whole is disclosed, can, nevertheless, send its sparks into the present and transform it, most of all for the oppressed. Ernst Bloch, whose influential *Prinzip der Hoffnung* (1919) was a defiant refusal to accept the misery of human existence as this expressed itself in his immediate setting, does not hesitate to describe his revolutionary politics as messianic, but in a way that would not have pleased Scholem. 'The world is not true,' writes Block, 'but it will successfully return home through human beings and through truth.' This combination – human beings and truth – points to an ethical response to the demands of the present if the world is 'to return home,' to use Block's phrase.

The human struggle for justice may not be intended to hasten the coming of the messiah, but it allows for 'truth' to have a role. Humans are not reduced to the paralysing negative waiting of Kafka's messianic nihilism. Truth can guide action, 'as if' the messianic age was upon us. This idea of the messianic longing generating a genuine ethical stance in terms of present society was to prove influential in the writings of the Frankfurt School of Critical Theory, with its indebtedness to a secular messianism. Theodore Adorno expresses it as follows: 'The only philosophy which can be responsibly practised in the face of despair is the attempt to contemplate all things as they would present themselves from the standpoint of Redemption. Knowledge has no light but that shed on the world by Redemption: all else is reconstruction, mere technique. Perspectives must be fashioned that displace and estrange the world, reveal it to be, with its rifts and crevices, as indigent and distorted as it will appear one day in the messianic light.'[21]

I have already mentioned the way in which Christian theologians like Moltmann have profited through dialogue with Jewish messianism in terms of God-talk. The issue of Christology would seem to pose an altogether different problem in terms of Jewish-Christian dialogue. How can the idea of the messiah as the 'coming one' of Jewish hopes be related to Christian claims that the messiah has already come in the person of Jesus of Nazareth? Yet a little reflection will indicate how superficial such a view in fact is. Christian existence is lived in the tension between the first and second coming of Jesus. While the early Christians did indeed develop biographies of Jesus that reflect his claims to living a messianic lifestyle, they show a certain reserve also. In Mark's Gospel Jesus is the mysterious or hidden messiah, who can easily be misconstrued as a 'false messiah,' and in John's Gospel his true identity is also veiled, revealed only in signs that call for proper understanding. This messianic 'reserve' of the Gospel narratives with regard to the messianic status of Jesus was quickly bypassed in favour of the developing Christology of the Hellenistic Christians that articulates his divine status in line with Greek thinking about the presence of he divine in the world. Nevertheless, Christian Christology, like Jewish messiology, presupposes a transcendent God active in the world. It would not be inappropriate for Christian theology to recapture something of the hesitation of its earliest documents, while at the same time engaging in the imitation of the one whose messianic lifestyle is indeed hope for the oppressed. This is the approach that has given rise to liberation theology, with its concern for praxis over theory, and its readiness to defer until later the confirmation of Jesus' messianic status in the belief that a life lived in solidarity with the poor cannot be too far removed from the kingdom of God.

It seems appropriate to end this paper with a citation from another Jewish theologian of the modern period, Franz Rosenzweig:

> The false messiah is as old as the hope for the true messiah. He is the changing form of the changeless hope. He separates every Jewish generation into those whose faith is strong enough to give themselves up to an illusion, and those whose faith is so strong they do not allow themselves to be deluded. The former are the better, the latter the stronger.[22]

Perhaps we need both kinds of Jews and Christians today.

Notes

1. Gersholm Scholem, *The Messianic Idea in Judaism and Other Essays on Jewish Spirituality,* (New York: Schocken Books, 1971), 1- 37.
2. Moshe Idel, *Messianic Mystics,* (New Haven: Yale University Press, 1997) 30-37.
3. Helga Hammerstein-Robinson, 'Messianic Ideals in the German Reformation,' in Sean Freyne and Wim Beuken eds. *Messianism through History,* Concilium (1993) 82-98.
4. Idel, *Messianic Mystics,* 182-211; Joel Markus, 'The Once and Future Messiah in Early Christianity and Chabad,' *New Testament Studies* 47(2001) 381-401.
5. I am indebted to the masterful study of Susan A. Handelman, *Fragments of Redemption. Jewish Thought and Literary Theory in Benjamin, Scholem & Levinas,* (Bloomington: Indiana University Press, 1991) for this account of this dramatic relationship between the two Jewish scholars and their background.
6. *The Messianic Idea* 7.
7. Moses Maimonides 'Laws concerning the Installation of Kings,' cited in Scholem *Messianic Idea,* 28f.
8. G. Scholem ed. *The Correspondence of Gersholm Scholem and Walter Benjamin,1932-1940,* (English trans. New York: Shocken Books, 1989).
9. Handelman, *Fragments of Redemption,* 160f.
10. Ibid. 167ff.
11. William Scott Green, 'Messiah in Judaism: Rethinking the Question,' in Jacob Neusner, William S. Green and Ernest Frerichs eds. *Judaisms and their Messiahs at the Turn of the Christian Era,* (New York: Cambridge University Press, 1987) 1-16, especially 6f.
12. In addition to several articles in *Judaisms and their Messiahs,* see John J. Collins, *The Scepter and the Star. The Messiahs of the Dead Sea Scrolls and other Ancient Writings,* (New York: Doubleday, 1995); Gerber Oegma, *The Anointed and his People. Messianic Expectation from the Maccabees to bar Kochba,* (Sheffield: Sheffield Academic Press, 1997).
13. In addition to Collins and Oegma (previous note) see J. Charlesworth, H. Lichtenberger and G. Oegma, eds. *Qumran Messianism. Studies in the Messianic Expectation of the Dead Sea Scrolls,* Tübingen: (J.C.B. Mohr, 1999)
14. Sean Freyne, 'A Galilean Messiah?' in *Studia Theologica* (Lund) 55 (2001) 198-218; Martin Hengel and Anna Maria Schwemer, *Der Messianische Anspruch Jesu und der Anfänge der Christologie,* WUNT 138 (Tübingen: J.C.B. Mohr, 2002).
15. Sean Freyne, 'The Early Christians and Jewish Messianic Ideas,' in *Messianism through History,* 30-42; Christopher Rowland 'Christ in the New Testament,' in John Day ed. *King and Messiah in Israel and the Ancient Near East,* (Sheffield: Sheffield Academic Press, 1998) 475-96.
16. Jacob Neusner, *Messiah in Context, Israel's History and Destiny in Formative Judaism,* (Philadelphia, Fortress Press, 1984).
17. Handelman, *Fragments of Redemption,* especially 307-336 with reference to the work of Emmanuel Levinas.
18. Idel, *Messianic Mystics,* 58-100.
19. Isaac Deutscher *The Non-Jewish Jew and Other Essays,* (London: 1968) 26.
20. See Jürgen Moltmann, *The Coming of God: Christian Eschatology* (Minneapolis:

Fortress Press, 1997).

21. Theodore J. Adorno, *Minima Moralia. Reflections fom a Damaged Life,* (London: Verso, 1971), 247.

22. Franz Rosenzweig, 'The False and True Messiah' in Nahum N. Glatzer ed. *Franz Rosenzweig: His Life and Thought,* (New York: Schoken, 1961) 350.

16

THE BIBLE AND CHRISTIAN THEOLOGY: INSPIRATION, PROJECTION, CRITIQUE?

My title suggests that there is an ambivalence with regard to the issue of the role of the Bible in Christian Theology. The Bible may direct us to a correct understanding of the meaning of the Christian life (inspiration), it may be manipulated to legitimate our preconceived ideas (projection), or it may function as a challenge to all our values and attitudes, even our so-called Christian ones (critique). From this discussion it will emerge that the proper use of the Bible in Theology is not a simple issue in the present climate, given the complexities in our understanding of both the Bible and of Theology. Biblical scholars and Theologians have today very different training and background, adopt different methodologies in their work and can very easily pass each other by like ships in the night. I take it as my task to outline ways in which a more fruitful discussion can occur between the two, one that does justice to the respective disciplines and at the same time underlines their shared tasks and responsibilities.

Defining the Problem (Inspiration)

The obvious first step is to seek to define the problem more precisely: What is the Bible? What do we mean by Theology? And why is there a problem about their relationship at the present time?

The Bible ('*ho Biblos*', 'the Book') suggests that we are dealing with a single book, and hence the assumption must be that it has a single and coherent meaning or set of meanings. This understanding is expressed in the belief that the Bible is the inspired Word of God. The doctrine of the inspiration of Holy Scripture was developed over the centuries as an expression of the statement in the Nicene Creed; 'He has spoken through the Prophets'. It is probably one of the least understood and poorly developed doctrines in Christian Theology. Explanations range across a wide spectrum. At one pole there is the belief that the authors of the biblical books were actually dictated to in a special way by God, so that everything they wrote must be understood as the very words of God. On the other hand, a more modern, liberal understanding would claim that there is nothing special about the Bible, other than the fact that its writers, like all writers, enjoy certain gifts of expression or insight.

In Catholic Theology the former view was expressed by Pope Leo XIII in his encyclical *Providentissimus Deus* of 1893 as follows: 'The Holy Spirit so moved them (i.e. the writers) to write by a supernatural power, he so stood by them in their writing, that they correctly understood, willed to write down faithfully and expressed aptly and with infallible truth, all that and only that which he ordered them to write. Otherwise he would not be the author of Holy Scripture.' This can be said to be a maximalist view of what is meant by inspiration, and one that is shared by many of the more contemporary evangelistic Protestant groups also. It would be very hard to defend on either historical or theological grounds. Luke in his prologue (Lk 1, 1-4) does not regard himself so controlled or under the direct influence of the Holy Spirit in the task of writing his account of 'the things that from the beginning were said and done among us'. Indeed it is noteworthy that subsequent Papal (Pius XII, *Divino Afflante Spiritu*, 1942) and Conciliar (Vatican 2, 1965) statements retreated from this literalistic understanding to a more general one in which the autonomy and humanity of the writers is acknowledged, while affirming the special authority of their writings for the life of the Church. Similar views are today expressed by more theologically informed Protestant Theologians also.[1]

It is noteworthy that while the fact of biblical inspiration was accepted as a given from a very early stage in the Church's life (Cf. 2 Tm 3, 16 and 2 Peter 3, 16), it was only in the post-Reformation period that any serious consideration was given to the nature and effects of that claim, by both the Reformed and the Catholic traditions. The special reasons for this emphasis will emerge in the next part of this paper. What is more important in terms of the discussion about the true nature of the Bible is the recognition that in the early Church, the inspiration of the biblical authors was not an issue. What was important was the claim that the Spirit was at work in the whole Church, teachers and taught alike, in the understanding and living out of the meaning of the life of Jesus Christ in the world.

In coming to these articulations, the early Christians considered the Hebrew Scriptures to be the most appropriate source of understanding and reflection, since, it was believed, the claims about Jesus Christ were in continuity with, and the fulfilment of the hopes and aspirations of those writings. When in the second century the early Church felt the need to produce authoritative lists of its own writings, as an exercise in self-definition over against certain perceived extremes, there was no obvious agreement on all the books to be included. Consensus was gradual, with some surprising (to our eyes) doubts being expressed and some notable omissions. Similarly, with the Jewish canon, while it is generally recognised that the first two parts, the Law and the Prophets, were established relatively early in the Persian period (c. 400 b.c.e.), the third part, the Writings, developed piecemeal, with differences emerging between the native (i.e. Hebrew) and the Diaspora (i.e. Greek) collections, a distinction perpetuated today in the different collections of books in the Protestant and the Catholic Bibles.[2] Canonicity is, therefore, the privileging of certain books, not because they are deemed to be inspired, but rather because they came to be recognised as authoritative through a lengthy process of self-definition, in which the guidance of the Holy Spirit was believed to be involved in the whole life of the community. The doctrine of inspiration is thus the *a posteriori* way in which the special status of this collection is recognised and affirmed, and not the *a priori* cause of their canonisation.

Modern biblical criticism has reinforced the notion that the Bible is a collection or anthology of very diverse writings. As the norms of literary and historical criticism were applied to the biblical writings from the eighteenth century onwards, contradictions, inconsistencies and apparently irreconcilable differences of perspective began to emerge. The unity of the biblical point of view began to give way to the diversity of early Christian communities and their writings, with quite different Theologies (Johannine and Pauline, for example), different social and cultural locations (Corinth, Rome, Antioch, Alexandria, Jerusalem), and different lifestyles (Torah-free and Torah-observant, radical itineracy and house-Churches, for example). The picture of early Christianity that emerges from this study is one of difference, conflict and greater diversity than that which had obtained in earlier centuries.[3] Some scholars want to include early Christian writings that do not belong to the Canon, even prioritise them, in their accounts of early Christian development, writings like the Gospel of Thomas and the Gospel of Peter, or 1 Enoch.

Inevitably, the question arises as to the theological significance of all these developments. Is the Bible simply a collection of ancient texts, or can we discern a Theology or Theologies within it? Faced with the many questions that a critical study of the Bible has given rise to, it is quite common today to speak of the demise of Biblical Theology, meaning the refusal of biblical scholars either to engage in a theological reading of these texts, or to assist their erstwhile colleagues in Theology in such an enterprise. There are several reasons for this apparent impasse, not least the secularisation of Biblical Studies as a discipline, with a greater emphasis on the linguistic, social and cultural aspects of the texts rather than their theological significance. This latter focus is deemed too restrictive and distorting of the real impact and intention of the texts, a point of view forcefully expressed in a recent study of Mark's Gospel by Richard Horsley, *Hearing the Whole Story. The Politics of Plot in Mark's Gospel.* In the light of this turn to the social and the cultural, over the theological aspects of our texts, the question has to be posed: are the biblical authors Theologians at all, or at least in what sense can they be so described?

What is Theology?

Theology has been traditionally described as *'fides quaerens intellectum'*, 'faith seeking understanding'. Already such a definition suggests a distantiation between the present of the interpreter and the sources to be interpreted, particularly the Bible. One is talking about a Theology of the sources rather than a Theology in the sources. It is of course possible to speak of Theology, like philosophy, loosely to denote any serious thinking about God or life. But Theology in the strict sense is a separate discipline. It engages in a coherent, systemic and logical analysis, in which all aspects of our experience and thinking about God are examined, interpreted and arranged. The emphasis here is on systemic and logical, and this explains Theology's inherent relationship with philosophy: Augustine used neo-Platonism; Aquinas, Aristotelianism; nineteenth-century Liberal Protestants used Hegelian Idealism and many twentieth-century Theologians have employed Existentialism – all systems of thought that at different periods had imposed themselves on the prevailing ethos, and thus made it possible also to give a coherent and plausible account of Christian faith at different periods of history.

However comforting it may be to know that these different paradigms of Christian Theology were favourably received at different periods, problems inevitably arise with such syntheses when they are superimposed on the biblical data. To begin with, there is the ongoing danger of introducing an alien system of thought onto a collection of writings that at best do not easily allow themselves to be placed in a straitjacket. Worse still, is the approach that was often adopted by Theologians in the past of formulating a set of propositions dictated by reason or Conciliar definitions, and then randomly mining the Bible for suitable proof-texts, without any account being taken of the different contexts from which such proofs were being drawn. The problem becomes more acute still when, as in our own situation today, there is no longer any coherent system of thought that can persuasively impose itself on the culture as a whole. The very notion of a systematic Theology itself becomes problematical in these circumstances. The 'broken ontology' of which French philosopher, Paul Riceour speaks, has now had to give way to the post-modern deconstructivist mentality, which calls into question the very notion of meaning itself. Faced with this apparent collapse of confidence in western rationality on the one hand, and the increasing secularisation of Biblical Studies on the other, Christian Theologians seem to be caught on the horns of a dilemma, neither of which provides any comfort when it comes to attempting a synthesis of Christian faith that is both adequate in terms of the tradition and its claims, and critical in terms of our time. The temptation to revert to the secure orthodoxies of the distant or not-so-distant past, patristic, medieval or neo-orthodox, is very real indeed.

Attempts at solving the Dilemma (Projection)

Strange as it might seem, our problem of the Bible and Theology is not a new one. Before attempting some tentative suggestions for the current problem, it would be good to examine the ways in which our predecessors in the faith have dealt with the issues involved. In the Patristic period, and indeed down to the Middle Ages, 'all Theology was done in the margins of the sacred page.' By that is meant that Theology is largely a matter of commentary on the Scriptures. Admittedly, there were difficulties to be overcome. Jewish interpretation had developed the method of *midrash*, that is, a system of 'searching' the text for hidden or deeper meaning when the literal meaning no longer seemed appropriate or relevant. Consider, for example, how so much of the Hebrew Scriptures deals with the temple and its rituals in the books of

Deuteronomy, Numbers and Leviticus, all of which had ceased to be relevant after 70 c.e. Christian writers like Justin Martyr, Irenaeus, and Origen also developed various strategies, some borrowed from the Greek interpretation of Homer, and some from the Jewish Rabbis, in order to probe the deeper, or hidden meaning of the texts.[4] These texts were still regarded as 'holy', and therefore, possessing a deeper meaning that could be uncovered. The gulf between the interpreters and the biblical text, which we, with our modern historical consciousness, perceive, and which is the basis of so much modern enquiry of the Bible and its world, was easily bridged, insofar as it was perceived at all. In thinking their own thoughts about God, they believed they were thinking the thoughts of the Bible, something that is graphically illustrated in medieval art. There, both biblical and contemporary characters were portrayed side by side, all sharing current dress and settings. Thus the Bible, its characters and situations were deemed to be integral parts of medieval life.[5]

As is well known, the sixteenth-century Reformation changed this approach to the Bible, seeking to privilege it from the whole tradition that had grown up around it as part of the medieval synthesis. The *sola scriptura*, 'scripture alone', principle isolated the Bible as unique and separate from all other traditions. This had the inevitable effect of consigning the Bible to the past, so that we can say that historical consciousness with regard to the Bible is the direct result of the Reformation. Thus the problem of Bible and Theology in its modern form had begun to surface. Inevitably, this problem was felt more keenly in Protestant than in Roman Catholic circles, where the notion of tradition as a separate source of revelation was enshrined in the promulgations of the Council of Trent, thereby seeking to maintain the medieval synthesis into the modern period. As already mentioned the Scholastics required the Bible merely as source of proof texts for their independently developed system.

Luther, Calvin and the other Reformers concentrated their Theology on the Bible alone, thinking the thoughts of the biblical writers rather than their own, before attempting to express its relevance for the contemporary Church. The bridge of tradition was jettisoned in the process as corrupt and distorting. One had to attend carefully to what the Bible was saying, its literal meaning, and ignore how the subsequent tradition had understood it. There was no room for a deeper or hidden meaning, which in their view was merely a vehicle for introducing extraneous ideas under the guise of a biblical dress. Thus the literal, once-and-for-all meaning of the text triumphed over the allegorical sense that had dominated Christian practice for centuries. This latter approach had testified to layers of meaning, not just in the Bible, but also in the world of nature that the Bible described. Paradoxically, therefore, in conspiring to free the Bible from traditional encrustations, Reformation concerns combined with Renaissance learning, allowed humans to explore the world in ways other than those in which it was described in the Bible. Galileo is the most outstanding example of this new-found freedom that could not be controlled despite the best efforts of the Inquisition. The 'sacramental' or symbolic understanding of nature that was central to the biblical understanding of the universe as God's creation, had to give way to a mathematical, and ultimately a scientific understanding as expressed in the seventeenth and eighteenth centuries with the scientific and Enlightenment revolutions. If the natural sciences were developed to describe the world as it really was rather than in terms of its symbolic meaning, then biblical scholars also had to develop a 'scientific' method in their study, one that was philological, textual and historical. The Bible, as the Book of God would be compared to the Book of Nature, which science could explore and in the process demystify.[6] Thus occurred what Theologian Hans Frei has described as 'the eclipse of biblical narrative', meaning the emergence of the 'story of time' that was very different from that which the Bible had described, and which up to that time had been taken as literally true.[7]

It is against this background, of both the recognition of the Bible as a historical collection from the past, and the emergence of a secular understanding of nature independently of the Bible, that the contribution to our discussion of one Johann Philip Gabler has to be judged. In a now famous lecture delivered in 1787, entitled 'Concerning the true distinction between Biblical and Dogmatic Theology, and the correct Definition of their Purposes,' he laid down a programme that was to play an important role in all subsequent discussion of the Bible and Theology.[8] Confronted with Lutheran orthodoxy on the one hand and Evangelical pietism on the other – both distortions of the true intentions of the Reformers – Gabler saw the need to establish the theological sciences on a proper footing. This could only be achieved by defining the different disciplines and the inter-relationships that should exist between them. His aim was to establish a systematic Theology that would be grounded and rooted in the Bible. To this end he proposed a science of Biblical Theology that would mediate the insights of biblical religion to the Systematic Theologian. Biblical religion is defined as 'the everyday, transparently clear knowledge that each Christian ought to know and believe in order to obtain happiness in this life and the next.' Systematic Theology, by contrast, is 'the subtle, learned knowledge, surrounded by many disciplines, derived not only from Scripture, but also from the domain of philosophy and history. It is a field elaborated by human discipline and ingenuity.' The mediating discipline of Biblical Theology is separate from each, but related to both. It should be accountable only to the biblical material which it sought to investigate, and not influenced by the outside concerns. It was only through such a discipline that Biblical Theology could claim to be scientific, and yet provide the necessary link between biblical religion and Dogmatic Theology, so that the latter could remain genuinely Christian, and not just follow every whim of contemporary thought. Biblical Theology as conceived by Gabler was alone capable of providing that stable basis for Dogmatic or Systematic Theology, whose task it was, not to question these findings, but rather to interpret them in a contemporary idiom.

In this view, Biblical Theology was essentially historical and its subject matter was a body of literature from the past. Yet Gabler recognised that even in this fixed corpus of writings one could distinguish between the contingent, or time-conditioned dimension, and the stable or permanent aspects. These two dimensions needed to be separated, and so he introduced a further distinction between true and pure Biblical Theology. In other words, two quite distinctive steps had to be taken. The first step, that of true Biblical Theology, was to gather and document all the conceptions and ideas that went with biblical religion, taking account of the various time periods, the different authors, and the different intentions of each – didactic, historical or poetic – and allowing for the differences between the two Testaments, and the different languages (Hebrew and Greek) in which they were written. In a word it was necessary to classify the ideas of each biblical writer separately, before comparing and contrasting these carefully, so that the distinctive ideas of each, and the importance that each gave to their various expressions might emerge clearly. The second step, that of pure Biblical Theology, is to examine each single opinion for its universal ideas, so that eventually it will emerge 'wherein the separate authors agree in a friendly fashion, or differ among themselves', so that eventually the pure Biblical Theology, 'unmixed with foreign things, can make its happy appearance.'

Gabler's thinking and formulations are quaint from our perspective, even though his objectives are clear enough. He wants to privilege the biblical categories in line with the Reformation thinking, in order to critique the prevalent chaos that obtained even in Lutheran Theology of his day with so many different and competing proposals. At the same time he is seeking a purified version of those categories, which he believes can be attained through the search for universal ideas in the midst of the contingencies of the various authors and their writings. This notion of universal ideas, i.e. ideas that are valid for all times and everywhere, which can be extracted from contingent utterances, is a reflection of the Idealist philosophy of his own time. He can, himself, therefore, be justly accused of introducing extraneous notions in order to construct his pure Biblical Theology, in much the same way as he is critical of the Dogmatic Theologians for following every whim of philosophy. Indeed, his method is not far removed from that of the allegorists who sought a deeper meaning behind the literal sense, which the Reformers had so emphatically rejected.

Some tentative lessons for the present impasse (Critique)

Gabler's project did not succeed in stabilising Christian Theology in the manner he had hoped. Yet his contribution in raising the issue clearly challenges us still today to develop a counter-proposal that will do justice to the centrality of the Bible for Christian Theology, while also recognising the importance of on-going rational enquiry for the vitality and renewal of Christian faith in every age. His true Biblical Theology, namely the investigation of the variety of authors, genres, situations and points of view, would seem to have triumphed as far as Biblical Studies have developed. This type of study is no longer described as Biblical Theology, but the whole programme of historical, anthropological and contextual studies of the biblical books, which was developed by the History of Religions School in the nineteenth and early twentieth centuries, can today draw on archaeology as well, in order to bring more precision to our understanding of life in early Israel, early Judaism and early Christianity and their literatures. This type of study is today so advanced that it is even customary to speak of Judaisms and Christianities in the plural, in order to underline the diversity and even the conflict that existed between various competing strands. In this respect, the Jesus-movement in its various manifestations can be seen as one more mutation within the diversity of what was Second Temple Judaism.

The spirit of the times would deal a deadly blow to the other aspect of his proposal, namely, the development of a pure Biblical Theology, which could provide a solid foundation for Systematic Theology. For one thing, the understanding of universal ideas has itself shifted considerably since the eighteenth century. Today, under the influence of philosophers of language such as Wittgenstein, it is usual to speak of 'family resemblances' as a way of describing the perception of the shared properties of things, rather than defining universals in terms of common identities. Moreover, developments in the field of semantics have challenged the notion of general terms providing univocal, universal names, since the meaning attached to common words and terms varies in different cultural contexts. This is something that Gabler also acknowledged in his article, attributing it to the contingent aspects of the biblical ideas, which in his view had to be discarded. The fact that even universal ideas must be expressed in language, with all the cultural variations involved, makes his call for a pure language seem unattainably idealistic and dangerously dualistic.

Despite this inherent problem with the proposal, efforts continued to be made to distil a Biblical Theology from the collection of writings. Rudolf Bultmann, the great twentieth-century German scholar, is a particularly interesting case in point. While his training was that of an Historian of Religions, and he was, therefore, interested in the diversity of backgrounds, sources etc, of the New Testament writings, as a devout Lutheran chaplain in the First World War, he recognised the need to articulate a coherent message of the Gospel for a despairing people. His call for demythologisation was a call to divest the biblical message of its mythological language and worldview, which belonged to the first century, and express its core meaning in terms that were accessible to modern Europeans. For him the philosophy of Existentialism provided the proper language in which to express that core: the message of the kerygma could properly be expressed as a call from inauthenticity to authenticity in terms of Existentialist categories, and this is the meaning of Paul's call to his converts to die and rise with Christ, or John's account of Jesus' ministry as a judgement on the world and a call for believers to walk in the light rather than in darkness. Thus, Bultmann's work embraces both aspects of Gabler's agenda, except that his New Testament Theology is a combination of the latter's pure Biblical Theology and Dogmatic Theology, since it reduces the message of the New Testament in its varied manifestations to a single universal idea about the nature of human existence. The only problem with this from a Gablerian point of view is that the discovery of that single universal stems, not from the New Testament itself, but from a contemporary philosophical system, namely Existentialism. In other words, Gabler would descibe Bultmann's project as Dogmatic, not Biblical Theology!

Canonical Criticism, especially as proposed by Professor Brevard Childs of Yale University, is another vestige of Gabler's programme.[9] Childs proposes to discover continuities and discontinuities between the two Testaments, as these constitute the Christian Bible. The common theme is that of God's redemptive will, which has been manifested in both the history of Israel and the life and death of Jesus of Nazareth. The various parts of the Bible (both Testaments) are read as independent witnesses to this central message of the Bible, each complementing one another in a harmonious whole. Childs displays an impressive array of scholarship and many helpful insights, and his proposal has the merit of adopting as its central theme one that is taken from the Bible itself and not imported from outside. Nevertheless, there is a tendency to find a harmony between various texts and traditions, which others would not so easily reconcile. Thus, Childs is forced to posit a greater unity to the collection of writings that constitutes the Canon of Scripture than appears to be the case when these writings are studied individually following the full rigour of the historical-critical method. In terms of Gabler's categories his work is an example of pure Biblical Theology, but without the idealistic and abstract approach that was characteristic of that original proposal. It is less convincing in terms of Gabler's true Biblical Theology, however.

On a less ambitious scale James G. Dunn's magisterial study of Paul attempts a synthesis of his Theology, but with the advantage of dealing with a corpus of writings that is intensely personal, covers a relatively short period of time and is engaged in dealing with (on the whole) clearly defined issues of practical Christian living. As Dunn himself, taking account of developments in New Testament studies since Gabler, describes the task, a Theology of Paul consists in 'a dialogue with Paul, and not merely a description of what he believed; a recognition that Paul's Theology embraced Christian living as well as Christian thinking; and a willingness to hear Paul's Theology as a sequence of occasional conversations.'[10] Dunn accepts as 'the template' for his study Paul's own most clearly articulated outline, the Epistle to the Romans, and this provides him with the overall outline and set of topics for his study: God and Humankind; Humankind under Indictment; The Gospel of Jesus Christ; the Beginning of Salvation; the Process of Salvation; the Church, and How Should Believers Live? It is interesting to note that in this outline the topic of eschatology as a future category is missing, subsumed under the process of salvation. One wonders whether this would be the case if Dunn had begun with a sequential reading of Paul's letters where the topic of eschatology in the sense of the *Parousia* or second coming, dominates in the earlier Thessalonian and Corinthian correspondence, only to be replaced by an emphasis on Christian existence in the present in the 'middle' letters of Galatians and Romans. In other words one's starting point will inevitably determine what one sees, even when dealing with a single author, whose persona is clearly visible, as in the case of Paul.

To be fair to Dunn, he operates with a more rounded view of what is involved in the theological enterprise as 'talk about God, *and all that is involved in and follows directly from such talk, including not least the interaction between belief and practice.*' (Italics added). This broader approach, which moves away from a conceptual understanding of Theology as a merely confessional or intellectual exercise, locates the discipline of Biblical Theology much closer to what in the past was described as a History of Religions approach, a topic to which we shall return later. Dunn also recognises in his *Postlegomena* that while his study has sustained the view that there is a stable foundation (and not the shifting sands of mere responses to different circumstances) to Paul's Theology, its fulcrum point, the Christ event, functions 'incarnationally', in that for the apostle, Christ is the definitive manifestation of what God is like, whether in dealing with God's self, or the place of Israel, or the role of Torah, or the nature of Christian living. Here Dunn's conclusion does not differ appreciably from the position of J. C. Becker, who describes the tension in Paul's thinking in his different letters as one of 'contingency and coherence' rather than a purely occasional response to different crises, lacking any inner coherence of thought.[11] Dunn's image of the fulcrum is helpful, but it still suggests a degree of stability that could be faulted in terms of Paul's own development, faced with the hermeneutical challenges which the development of his mission posed for him.[12]

Thus, even in dealing with a single biblical author, not to speak of a collection of writings as diverse as those of either or both Testaments, important issues arise with regard to the nature and practice of Biblical Theology, issues that are not easy to resolve, certainly not at the historical level only. It must be possible to evaluate theologically the significance of this diversity of content and emphasis in the different writings and our different ways of negotiating the dilemma that they pose in terms of a coherent sense of unity. As Ben Meyer so tellingly emphasises, the contrary of unity is not diversity but division, and the contrary of diversity is not unity but uniformity. Thus, there is no logical reason why Paul, or indeed the early Christian movement as a whole, might not at the same time have striven for both diversity and unity, since there is no contradiction between the two stances.[13]

Childs belongs to what has been described as the Yale School, whose general theological approach has been to view Christian texts in a special way, which demands a particular type of interpretation, differentiating them from all other texts, in faithfulness to the Reformation tradition.[14] Due to this process of special pleading, which avoids the rigorous demands of a general theory of understanding, such an approach is seen by others as being too inward looking and apologetic in its efforts to propose an adequate understanding of the Christian message for the modern world. Other scholars interested in the enterprise of constructing an adequate Biblical Theology have suggested an alternative hermeneutical model that would take account of the complexities of both Biblical and Theological Studies as these are practised today in the secular environment of the academy and the world. David Tracy's insight with regard to the Bible as a Religious Classic, especially as developed by his student, Werner Jeanrond, in terms of reading strategies, adopt a self-consciously literary approach.

Jeanrond proposes 'a conversational' model of interpretation, which allows not just for varieties of genres, forms, points of view and ideological biases of the texts to emerge, but it also involves the role of the reader and her situation in determining the meaning of the texts. The dialogue between reader and text, once it is critically conducted, that is, once it takes account of all the historical, cultural and social differences that separate the modern reader from these ancient texts – this dialogue dispenses with the need for an intermediate stage whereby an expert might try, a là Gabler, to distil a universal truth or set of truths from the variety of witnesses that go to make up the Bible, in order to pass these on to the Systematic Theologians for their reflection. The Theologian is already, or at least should be, a critical reader, or better still, in Tracy's and Jeanrond's view, should belong to a community of critical readers, within which dialogue and debate might occur with regard to the meaning of the text. Meaning embraces both the sense of the written words and the significance for living that the text discloses. Jeanrond in particular stresses the need for readers to be self-critical also, that is, to acknowledge explicitly their own interests as they engage in the interpretative reading process.[15] In this way, he believes, the danger of the reader introducing their own biases into the interpretation of the text can be obviated, whether those biases be personal, philosophical or ideological, and the proper ecclesial (not ecclesiastical) dimension of Biblical Theology is maintained.

In my opinion such an approach can do much to bridge the gulf that has emerged between Biblical and Theological Studies, since it does away with the spurious distinctions between Scripture Scholars/Exegetes and Theologians, the former being regarded as objective and the latter uncritically subjective in their approaches. It also means that those who have been trained in the biblical sciences must accept that while the collection of texts, which go to make up the Bible, can indeed be used for comparative, philological, social, religious and literary studies of the ancient world, they are above all theological writings, in the sense that they are all written from a theological standpoint in the first place, even if there was no consistent or fully worked out system in place, in the sense that this was developed later through the dialogue with philosophical systems. They have survived as a collection, and not by sheer chance, as in the case of the Dead Sea Scrolls, for example, because they have in one way or another been received by communities of believers as reflecting a shared theological point of view, which was deemed nourishing for Christian living and praxis. In Tracy's language, they constitute a classic, not a period piece, because they continue beyond their own particular time and place to engage people in serious reflection. One gets the distinct impression, especially in the academy, that when the word 'theological' is used, some colleagues immediately suspect an uncritical, or ecclesiastical bias, which is a constraint on the free enquiry of which academics pride themselves. This too can be a prejudice, the result, in all probability of the secularisation process in the west. However, as Jeanrond explains, all texts have a hierarchy of perspectives, and part of the interpretative enterprise is to critically discern which is the most important one and allow this to determine one's reading strategy, while, at the same time, not excluding the other perspectives, consideration of which will contribute to a more adequate interpretation of the work as a whole. Thus a social world approach to Mark need not, nor should not exclude a theological perspective that focuses on a proper understanding of the messianic claims of Jesus as the Christ. One can and must engage in this enterprise in order to be true to the demands of the texts themselves in the first instance, and not as a matter of loyalty to any particular confessional or ideological interests.

An immediate result of this approach is the recognition that one cannot easily reduce the Bible to a set of universal truths. Biblical Theologians are, therefore, rightly suspicious of all systems, insofar as they can be seen as an attempt to impose a Greek perspective on what essentially is a Semitic world-view. The one operates in abstract thought and the desire for formulaic expressions, while the other is perspectival and narratival in its approach.[16] Here Tracy's consideration of plurality and ambiguity is highly pertinent to our understanding of the theological significance of the Bible. What we encounter is a series of competing, and on occasion conflicting sets of witnesses. (Paul and John, contrary to Bultmann's existentialist harmonisation, for example). This does not exclude a family likeness between these texts, to draw on Wittgenstein's metaphor. Diversity does not entail uniformity as we have seen. Family quarrels, however, can be the most intense of all because there is so much else at stake! Consider the intensity of Paul's response to the Judaisers of Galatia, with their different appeals to the Restoration Theology of Judaism, or the animus of the Johannine community both towards the parent Judaism and the heretics from within as viewed through the lens of the Gospel and the epistles. A theological approach to the Bible that would take into account such differences and disputes, will not in the first instance seek to establish agreement between them in the name of a pure Biblical Theology. Ambiguity in these instances may be seen as a blessing rather than a curse. Questions need to be asked as to the theological significance of such diversity in terms of an understanding of God and of Jesus Christ, and what these different understandings might mean for Christian praxis in the community and in the world. The conflicting perspectives of the Hebrew Scriptures themselves, as reflected in myths, legends, historical narratives, prophetic oracles, various types of poetry and wisdom sayings and apocalyptic scenarios will also have to be evaluated theologically. Once one adopts the position that form and content are indivisible, it surely is neither appropriate nor possible to reduce all this material to a set of universal ideas. A true Biblical Theology will not confine itself merely to an approach which posits the Christian fulfilment to such a vast array of religious literature, ignoring their theological implications in the light of Israel's understanding of its God as the Unnameable One, who is yet very near.

There is one final step to be taken before this new approach could be described as adequate. Neither Tracy or Jeanrond address this issue explicitly, but both, I believe, would agree that it should find its place within a complete schema for an adequate Christian Theology rooted in the Bible. This step would involve exploring the larger world of the text, not simply as a way of providing a background, but rather as a theological necessity. A proper understanding of the theological import of the biblical texts of both Testaments demands that they must be read as witnesses to a way of life that was lived in the context of the Ancient

Near Eastern, Jewish and Greco-Roman religious beliefs and practices. These represent the competing voices that both the Israelites and the early Christians encountered in their search for an adequate understanding of the human condition, given their social and political situations. It is only when proper attention is given to this aspect of the texts, namely, the worlds of meaning that they created and fostered, that their distinctive perspectives can emerge and be properly evaluated. Archaeology in its various forms (ethno-, socio-, and gender), as well as cultural anthropology have an important role to play in such an enterprise, as I, and others, have tried to show with regard to the study of Galilee in the Roman period and the challenge posed by the Jesus movement within that milieu. Such a contextual approach helps to avoid modernising and individualistic readings, and clarifies the distinctive point of view and critical stance that the biblical writers adopted in terms of their own worlds and the value-systems that they encountered and challenged, thereby enhancing the possibilities for both feminist and liberationist readings of these texts in our own time.[17]

Conclusion

This paper is beginning to sound like an *apologia pro vita mea* and the approaches to the study of the Bible that I have been developing over the years! It is probably the delusion of ageing that causes one to see the various highways and byways that one has traversed as, in the end, providing some kind of complex yet coherent map. The Bible is a complex collection, but it is rich and diverse in its theological directions. Nothing should prevent those many and competing voices from being heard, even when they are only whispers from those works that did not get included, but that are on the margins of the Canon. When approached contextually and with an appreciation of their distinctive idioms and accents these many voices need not be regarded as a cacophony, but as a complex and intricate set of patterns that must await God's *eschaton* for their eventual harmonisation. In the interim we must be content to take it on faith that they are not a Babel, but a Pentecost, not confusion, but understanding in diversity. 'In many and varied ways God has spoken to our ancestors.' (Heb 1, 1-4). The fact that the early Christians also believed that he has spoken in a definitive way in the Son, did not preclude them from including those other older voices also in their and our Canon. As children of Abraham, we share with our Jewish and Muslim brothers and sisters those voices from the First Testament, even when we understand their message differently in the light of our own Christian claims. Familiarity can breed contempt and arrogance, however. To hear them occasionally as they have been received by those other traditions who do not share our understanding of their definitive meaning and have developed from them their own unique systems of salvation, can sensitise us to the fact that we too await the definitive disclosure of the God to which they bear witness, and that in the interim our texts and our readings are the product of both their and our contexts and cultures.

Notes

1. Sandra M. Schneiders' *The Revelatory Text. Interpreting the New Testament as Sacred Scripture* (New York: Harper SanFrancisco, 1991) is an excellent modern discussion of inspiration, especially 27-63. See also John Barton, *People of the Book? The Authority of the Bible in Christianity*, (London: SPCK, 1988).

2. Hans von Campenhausen, *The Formation of the Christian Bible* (English trans. Philadelphia: Fortress Press, 1972) is still the best account. See also Martin Jan Mulder, '*Mikra*. Text, Translation, Reading and Interpretation of the Hebrew Bible' in *Ancient Judaism and Early Christianity*, (*Compendia Rerum Judaicarum ad Novum Testamentum*, Assen and Philadelphia: Van Gorcum and Fortress Press, 1988).

3. Compare John Reumann, *Variety and Unity in New Testament Thought*, (London and New York: Oxford University Press, 1992) and Heikki Räisänen, *Beyond New Testament Theology*, (London and Philadelphia: SCM Press and Trinity Press International, 1990) for two very different proposals, based on contemporary scholarly discussions.

4. See Rik van Nieuwenhove, 'Diversity and Unity in the Scriptures: the Patristic Perspective,' in Sean Freyne and Ellen van Wolde eds. *The Many Voices of the Bible*, Concilium, 2002/1, 93-101; also David C. Steinmetz, 'The Superiority of Pre-Critical Exegesis' in Stephen E. Faul ed. *The Interpretation of Scripture. Classic and Contemporary Readings*, (Oxford: Blackwells, 1997) 26-38.

5. See Robert M. Grant and David Tracy, *A Short History of the Interpretation of the Bible*, (London: SCM Press, 1984), especially 83-92. For a brief, but lucid tratment of the history of New Testament Theology see Hendrikus Boers, *What is New Testament Theology?* (Philadelphia: Fortress Press, 1979), especially 16f on medieval interpretation.

6. For a highly illuminating account see Peter Harrison, 'Fixing the Meaning of Scripture: the Renaissance Bible and the Origins of Modernity,' in *The Many Voices of the Bible*, 102-111.

7. Hans W. Frei, *The Eclipse of Biblical Narrative. A Study in Eighteenth and Nineteenth Century Hermeneutics*, (New Haven: Yale University Press, 1974).

8. See John Sandys-Wunch and Laurence Eldredge, 'J.P. Gabler and the Distinction between Biblical and Dogmatic Theology: Translation, Commentary and Discussion of his Originality,' *Scottish Journal of Theology*

33(1992) 132-158. For further discussion see Ben C. Ollenburger, 'Biblical Theology: Situating the Discipline,' in James T. Butler, Edgar W. Conrad and Ben C. Ollenburger eds. *Understanding the Word. Essays in Honor of Bernhard W. Anderson*, (Sheffield: JSOT Press, 1985), 37-62.

9. Brevard S. Childs, *Biblical Theology of the Old and New Testaments. Theological Reflection on the Christian Bible*, (Minneapolis: Fortress Press, 1992).

10. James D. G. Dunn, *The Theology of Paul the Apostle*, (Edinburgh: T. and T. Clark, 1998) 12.

11. Dunn, *The Theology of Paul the Apostle*, 716-29; J. C. Becker, *Paul the Apostle: the Triumph of God in Life and Thought*, (Philadelphia: Fortress Press: 1980) and 'Paul's Theology: Consistent or Inconsistent?' *New Testament Studies* 34(1988) 364-77.

12. A developmental approach based on Paul's emerging sense of mission has been argued in a very illuminating way by Ben F. Meyer, *The Early Christians, Their World Mission and Self-Discovery*, (Collegeville: Michael Glazier Books, 1986). See also Sean Freyne, 'Re-imaging Christian Origins. The Jesus-Paul Debate Revisited,' in K. O'Mahoney, ed. *Christian Origins*, (Sheffield: Sheffield Academic Press, forthcoming).

13. Ben F. Meyer, *Reality and Illusion in New Testament Scholarship. A Primer in Critical Realist Hermeneutics*, (Collegeville: Michael Glazier/Liturgical Press, 1994), especially 169-73.

14. For a discussion with particular attention to the role of the Bible in Theology see Hans W. Frei, *Types of Christian Theology*, (New Haven: Yale University Press, 1992), especially 56-69.

15. Werner Jeanrond. 'Criteria for a New Biblical Theology,' *Journal of Religion 76* (1996) 233-249; 'The Significance of Revelation for Biblical Theology,' *Biblical Interpretation 6* (1998) 243-257; 'Biblical and Theological Pluralism,' *The Many Voices of the Bible*, 111-121

16. For an interesting example of how pre-modern and modern approaches can coalesce in a highly significant theological way see George Limbeck, 'The Story-Shaped Church: Critical Exegesis and Theological Interpretation,' in Fowl, ed. *Theological Interpretation of Scripture*, 39-52.

17. See e.g. R.S. Sugitharajah, *Voices from the Margin. Interpreting the Bible in the Third World*, (London: SPCK, 1991).

Subject and Name Index

TEXTS, CONTEXTS AND CULTURES: ESSAYS ON BIBLICAL TOPICS